Emma Paterson, Trade Unionist and Feminist, In Her Own Words

Emma Paterson was a pioneer of trade unionism for women. In her short life, she set up a League dedicated to that cause, edited a newspaper to publicise it and travelled the UK working for it. Her spoken and written work addressed issues still with us today, from the gender pay gap to domestic labour, and those thankfully consigned to history, such as whether women should be able to vote or find clothes appropriate to industrial work.

Emma Paterson, Trade Unionist and Feminist, In Her Own Words brings together the major works that comprise Emma Paterson's written output, offering a unique insight into the struggles and concerns of women working in the workshops, factories, shops and homes of Britain's Industrial Revolution. This book includes a long biographical chapter from the editor, a preface from Frances O'Grady, first woman general secretary of the Trades Union Congress, and then an annotated selection of Emma Paterson's most important works, from her time as a young activist to her last days as an overworked editor and union leader.

This book will appeal to scholars and students of the history of Britain, of its women workers, of industrial, labour and publishing history. It addresses broader questions of class and gender, the interconnections that exist between them and the silences that often accompany them.

Steven Parfitt teaches in the UK. He publishes widely on British, American and global history, including *Knights Across the Atlantic: The Knights of Labor in Britain and Ireland* (2016), and in journals such as *Labor*, the *International Review of Social History* and the *Journal of Global History*.

Routledge Research in Gender and History

51 History and Legacy of the Suffragette Fellowship
   Calling All Women!
   Eileen Luscombe

52 Women's Amateur Theatre in Rural Britain, 1919–1945
   Bonnie White

53 Gender and German Colonialism
   Intimacies, Accountabilities, Intersections
   Edited by Elisabeth Krimmer and Chunjie Zhang

54 An Historiography of Twentieth-Century Women's Missionary Nursing Through the Lives of Two Sisters
   Doing the Lord's Work in Kenya and South India
   Sara Ashencaen Crabtree

55 Women and Family Property
   Edited by Beatrice Moring

56 Dr. Susan I. Moody's Travels to Iran, 1909–1934
   Courageous Odyssey
   Hoda Mahmoudi

57 Histories of Sex Work around the World
   Edited by Catherine Phipps

58 Emma Paterson, Trade Unionist and Feminist, In Her Own Words
   Edited by Steven Parfitt

For more information about this series, please visit: https://www.routledge.com/Routledge-Research-in-Gender-and-History/book-series/SE0422

Emma Paterson, Trade Unionist and Feminist, In Her Own Words

Edited by
Steven Parfitt
With a preface by Frances O'Grady,
General Secretary of the Trades Union Congress

NEW YORK AND LONDON

First published 2025
by Routledge
605 Third Avenue, New York, NY 10158

and by Routledge
4 Park Square, Milton Park, Abingdon, Oxon, OX14 4RN

Routledge is an imprint of the Taylor & Francis Group, an informa business

© 2025 selection and editorial matter, Steven Parfitt; individual chapters, the contributors

The right of Steven Parfitt to be identified as the author of the editorial material, and of the authors for their individual chapters, has been asserted in accordance with sections 77 and 78 of the Copyright, Designs and Patents Act 1988.

All rights reserved. No part of this book may be reprinted or reproduced or utilised in any form or by any electronic, mechanical, or other means, now known or hereafter invented, including photocopying and recording, or in any information storage or retrieval system, without permission in writing from the publishers.

Trademark notice: Product or corporate names may be trademarks or registered trademarks, and are used only for identification and explanation without intent to infringe.

ISBN: 978-1-032-54738-1 (hbk)
ISBN: 978-1-032-54739-8 (pbk)
ISBN: 978-1-003-42727-8 (ebk)

DOI: 10.4324/9781003427278

Typeset in Sabon
by codeMantra

Contents

Preface		*vii*
FRANCES O'GRADY, PAST GENERAL SECRETARY OF THE TRADES UNION CONGRESS		
Acknowledgements		*ix*
	Introduction: The Life of Emma Paterson	1
1	Building a Movement, 1874–April 1879	18
2	Societies and Struggles: May 1879–1884	71
3	Final Years: 1885–1886	143
4	Obituaries – 1886–1921	200
	Index	*217*

Preface

Frances O'Grady, Past General Secretary of the Trades Union Congress

Emma Paterson was a trade union pioneer who changed history. A writer, feminist and organiser, she helped advance the lives of some of Victorian Britain's poorest, most exploited working women. She challenged the domination of men in the trade union movement and beyond. And though the Women's Protective and Provident League – which offered companionship, support and solidarity – she showed that collectivism gave women agency.

This wonderful book does an important service, giving Emma the historical recognition she deserves, as a major figure in the labour movement. A vibrant collection of her speeches, articles and contributions to debates, it is a tremendous resource for both students of labour history and contemporary activists and campaigners. While the need for trade union organisation and the struggle for equal pay and rights dominate the pages, there are also reminders of Emma's broader commitment to women's equality – on subjects as diverse as leisure, holidays and clothing. And throughout, this book makes a crucial point: that labour history is about the collective struggles of women as much as men.

Along with Edith Simcox, in 1875, Emma was of course the first woman delegate to the TUC Congress. Determined, clever and consistent in her arguments, she faced down male derision and made an impact on the broader trade union stage. A compelling and persuasive speaker, she used wit to puncture both arguments and overblown egos, winning support and respect in the process. Her bravery and raw talent paved the way for other trade union women, laying the foundations for the more representative movement we take for granted today.

Emma lived for just 38 years, but her short life bequeathed decades of positive change for women. After travelling to New York to investigate societies of working women, she put into practice the lessons of what she saw. Emma toured the country to speak to women, propagated her ideas through the *Women's Union Journal* and campaigned for universal suffrage, seeking to give working-class women greater voice within the burgeoning feminist movement. At every turn, Emma sought to show that women would always be stronger together – in a union.

Throughout her life, Emma challenged the norm of men as breadwinners and women as homemakers, exposing the stifling social mores of so-called Victorian values. Her single-minded courage not only gave impetus to the suffrage and feminist movements but also inspired the collective confidence of generations of women workers. From the chainmakers of Cradley Heath and the matchwomen of east London to the sewing machinists at Ford in Dagenham, Emma's legacy is profound.

And so many of the lessons from Emma's life remain relevant today. Almost a century and a half on from her first appearance at Congress, women are still paid, promoted and trained less than men; still struggle to balance work and childcare; and still face discrimination and harassment in the workplace. And that's why we need a new generation of female activists, organisers and leaders to lead the fight back against modern-day injustice. For inspiration, they should look no further than Emma Paterson.

In 1913, Frederick Rogers, a union friend and the first chair of the Labour Representation Committee, said Emma 'exercised an influence on the labour movement which no other woman has equaled since her day, and its secret lay in her entire sincerity and absence of pose. She never cared for the limelight, and never thought herself great; but she was great in the truest sense of the word.'

Emma Paterson was just that: a quiet, modest colossus of our movement. One of our greatest educators, agitators and organisers, she took on the political establishment – and the trade union establishment – and won change for ordinary working women. So much of the progress we take for granted today – from equal pay legislation to greater women's representation in trade unions – can trace its lineage back to Emma's groundbreaking work.

Recent and current leaders of the TUC, Scottish TUC, Wales TUC, Irish Congress of Trade Unions and International TUC have all been women. Some of our unions, both big and small, now have women general secretaries. Unthinkable just a generation ago, these advances would not have been possible without the hard graft of visionary pioneers like Emma.

This rich collection gives historical context and meaning to that work. It rightly depicts Emma Paterson as a champion of all working people. And it gives voice to someone who deserves to be remembered as a true hero of our movement.

Acknowledgements

This book was written in difficult times, and therefore the debt to others is even greater than usual. I want to acknowledge my parents, Julia and Graham, and brother David for their indispensable love and support, and for Ghazal, despite everything. Then to my former colleagues at Loughborough University, especially Rakesh, Pete, Marcus and many others.

I want to thank friends in the UK, New Zealand and around the world, too numerous to thank all individually here, and to those I met as I retrained as a history teacher at secondary school – to Nick, Yasmin and Aidan at Hobsonville Point Secondary School, Nigel and Luke at Glenfield College, and Chiara, Luke, Kazu and other student teachers on my programme at AUT University. Education is in good hands! I want to also thank my old supervisors, Chris Wrigley and Nick Baron, for their continued support long after their formal responsibilities to me ended. Many thanks must also go to the British Library and the TUC Library Collections at London Metropolitan University for allowing me to reproduce work stored in their important collections.

Finally, I want to thank all the women trade unionists I have been privileged to know in my years as a trade union member and delegate. Thanks in large part to your work, the movement still survives, and carries with it the continued hope of success in the future.

Introduction
The Life of Emma Paterson

Emma Paterson devoted her life to the struggles of working women. As a young secretary to the Women's Suffrage Association, she argued for their right to vote. As founder of the Women's Protective and Provident League, she worked from morning to night for women to form unions of their own. As editor of the *Women's Union Journal*, she threw her passion and wit into the public square and pushed the gospel of women's unions to the widest possible audience. As first equal woman delegate to the Trades Union Congress (TUC), she made the men of the trade union movement take note that the women of the working class had interests and demands the men must hear. She fought not just for women to have an increase in wages, but to have the time away from work to enjoy life. Yet, she spurned leisure for herself. After a decade of seven-day weeks and fourteen-hour days writing and organising and agitating, she succumbed to overwork and diabetes in 1886, at the age of only thirty-eight.

Emma Paterson's life and work forms part of the great struggle of working-class people in Britain and beyond to achieve basic rights: the right to have their views reflected in political life, the right to end by their own efforts their exploitation at work, the right to enjoy humanity's common heritage, from music and literature to education itself. Emma understood that working women, as the doubly oppressed half of an oppressed class, had the most to gain from the general fight for freedom. But she also knew that women would only get their share of emancipation if they organised themselves alongside the men. The TUC, which Emma first attended as a delegate in 1876, was one venue where the interests of men and women seemed to collide. Some of the male delegates, out of conviction or self-interest, or both, proved sympathetic to Emma's assertion of a greater place for women in the trade union movement. Other followed Henry Broadhurst, the stonemasons' leader, Liberal MP and Parliamentary Secretary of the TUC, in openly wishing that women would leave paid work, and the work of making progress, to the men. 'It was their duty as men and husbands,' he said,

> to use their utmost efforts to bring about a condition of things where their wives should be in their proper sphere at home, seeing after their house and family, instead of being dragged into the competition for livelihood against the great and strong men of the world.[1]

How far we have moved since Broadhurst's time! When Emma Paterson attended the 1875 Congress she was one of two women in a sea of men. In 2024, a clear majority of British trade union members are women, as was the TUC's previous General Secretary, Frances O'Grady, and a growing number of leaders and officials across the individual unions. Their participation in the movement has blunted, if not transcended, the unique problems of working women that Emma identified and agitated against. Only cranks still imagine that women can be removed from paid work, so long as paid work still exists. No one now would dare get up at a Trades Union Congress and suggest that the women there return to the kitchen. Trade unionists must struggle to make up the influence and millions of members lost since the 1970s, but at least their movement has opened itself to the gendered fullness of the human race.

Emma Paterson's contribution to these processes of emancipation was great. But it was not always recognised by those who came afterwards. As we will see in this book, when she died in 1886 she was acclaimed in the press and in the TUC as the leading champion of working women in Britain. Her comrades in the women's unions wondered what would become of their struggles without her. Yet, the memory of her deeds and achievements faded with time. She and her husband Thomas lay in an unmarked grave, uncommemorated by the trade union movement she served. In 1968, a union official named Harold Goldman was taken to the grave by a friend, obsessed with labour history arcana, who had found it. As Goldman wondered who this Emma Paterson was his friend summed it up. She was, he remarked, 'labour's forgotten woman.'[2]

Goldman went on to write the only book-length biography of Emma Paterson. In the same year as his visit, the TUC put a plaque at the grave. In the 1960s, 1970s and 1980s, a new wave of feminists fighting for equal pay and equal rights went looking for their ancestors and found Emma amongst them. At the same time, historians of the labour movement began to unearth the rich achievements of women within the wider story, even if they didn't always acknowledge or emphasise them.[3] This long neglect of women workers has an obvious cause. As Mary Davis writes, 'labour history has always been a male preserve,' and 'women write women's history and men write about the labour movement.'[4] Working women have often fallen in the gap between these two branches of history. Yet, thanks to female and some male historians of labour, we know a great deal more about the women workers of the past than was known in 1968, and of Emma Paterson's contribution to that past. She is no longer labour's forgotten woman.

So why this book? Memory of Emma Paterson may have been saved for posterity, but she still remains an obscure figure in the history of women and workers both. Where she does appear it is largely in the words of others: this book is dedicated to telling the story of her life as far as possible in hers. Those words tell us much about the suffering and struggles and ideas and conditions of her time. They also have much to tell us of ours. The Victorian slums have been cleared, the London smog has (to some extent) lifted, and the wages of working women are not quite as low or their conditions as dire as they once were. But the gender pay gap, though narrowed, remains. The uncertainty of casual workers is again endemic. Working-class women still exist suspended between the demands of work and the home. So long as the great struggle for emancipation remains unfinished, and women must still fight to claim their share of it, Emma Paterson's words and works will still be relevant. Before we turn to them, I want first to give you a greater sense of her life and ideas, and what exactly this book contains.

Her Life and Ideas

Emma Paterson was born in 1848, the year revolution swept Europe. Governments toppled. Kings fled their capitals. The whole political order created after the Napoleonic Wars went to pieces. Two obscure German radicals, Karl Marx and Friedrich Engels, wrote a manifesto predicting that the European social order would soon go the same way. Britain's first great working-class movement, the Chartists, demanded manhood suffrage and a social Charter and swelled to such numbers that the authorities feared revolution at home. But if Emma Paterson was born in a year of revolutions, she came to adulthood in the afterglow of their failures. The kings returned to their capitals. The French traded their monarch for the Emperor Napoleon III. The Chartist agitation fizzled after a great demonstration on Kennington Common in April 1848.[5]

Emma Paterson grew to maturity as the British labour movement went through a period of transition. After the Chartist disappointment, British trade unionists built a new constellation of local and national trade unions, worker co-operatives and trade councils. The first Trades Union Congress (TUC) convened in 1868. British trade unionists provided much of the money and muscle for the International Workingmen's Association, or First International, which from 1864 proclaimed and acted towards working-class solidarity across national borders. And the word 'transition' is used to describe the time of Emma's life for a reason. In terms of British labour history, she agitated in a period of retreat and consolidation between one radical phase, Chartism, and another, the years of the 'new unionism' and the slow birth of the Labour Party from the late 1880s onwards. Born too late for the first, she died before the second.

The movement for women's emancipation also gathered steam in Emma's time.[6] Over the course of the nineteenth century, campaigns by determined women, along with some men, began to break down the legal disabilities all women faced. The Married Women's Property Acts narrowed the gap between the property and inheritance rights of men and women. Changes to the Contagious Diseases Acts limited the policing of the bodies of women in the sex trade. The temperance movement became an international cause. Educational opportunities widened for some women. Yet that vital political right, the vote, lay out of woman's reach as it still did for most working-class men. And the millions of women who went out to work as domestic servants, in grimy factories and unsanitary workshops, found themselves ignored or treated as objects of charity or condescension. The Factory Acts of the 1870s even placed working women on the same legal plane as children. Unlike the men, both had their working hours restricted by law. Emma Paterson would spend many hours at the TUC rejecting the paternal embrace, and urging the men to drop it. The gap between the trade union and women's movements of Emma's time began as Grand Canyonesque.

Emma Paterson grew up in this strange and contradictory time without the advantages that usually allowed women to take on a public role. This meant inheriting wealth and titles, or marrying them. She did neither. But she did have parents who thought that daughters deserved the same education as sons. Her father Henry, a teacher, was ideally equipped to do this. The young Emma learned German and Italian and became so thrilled with the written word that friends and family alike nicknamed her 'the bookworm.' Henry's guidance set Emma on her future path as a writer and publisher. Yet he died of typhoid fever when she was only sixteen. Emma and her mother (also Emma) had to not only mourn his loss but also assume his debts. With no savings to fall back on, mother and daughter twice tried their hand at running a school. Both failed. Having been for some time apprenticed as a bookbinder – another tie to her later publishing career and agitation among working people – she then found work as a governess. Glorified babysitting wasn't to her taste, and in 1866 she found a job that set the rest of her life in motion. A secretary for London's Working Men's Club and Institute Union needed help, and Emma began work as her assistant.

We now consider workingmen's clubs such a defining part of working-class life and culture in Britain that we forget they were initially created in part from outside by the great and good.[7] The rationale was simple. Working men must be reformed, kept away from the pub and trained to adopt the high morals of their betters. The Club and Institute Union in London (now the Bishopsgate Institute) set the standard.[8] Workers would be tempted away from earthly pleasures by a library and reading room, stocked with non-alcoholic refreshments. This may sound like a poor bargain. But the zest for self-improvement – or in this case, the desire by the high for the self-improvement of the low – fit neatly with the desire of many workers to make up for the education they never had. One of these workers was Thomas Paterson, a Scottish-born cabinetmaker and probably the first bona fide working-class man to sit on the governing council of the Club and Institute Union. His path crossed with Emma's soon after she took on a full-time position at the Club and Institute Union's library in 1867. They married on July 24, 1873.

Thomas Paterson belonged to a type once common, now rare: the self-taught working-class intellectual. Like Emma he was a tireless reader, intellectually curious and politically active. He wrote but never finished a manuscript which aimed to connect psychology with political economy, which Emma brought to completion after his death, and when he was not scribbling away in the reading room of the British Museum he filled his time with debate and conversation. 'My husband's evenings,' she later wrote, 'were frequently engrossed by meetings of the Council of the Workmen's Peace Association, the Labour Representation League, the Free Libraries' Association, and the Land Tenure Reform Association.'[9] Their shared trips to street debates in London, covering every conceivable political and scientific subject, give a flavour of their early married life:

> When some ardent exponent of Secularism had apparently silenced, if not convinced, all his hearers, my husband, who usually joined the first named group, would by means of a few well-put scientific questions, completely rivet the attention of all, and evidently lead many of the listeners to reconsider their hasty conclusions. [...] Frequently, upon breaking up a discussion prolonged until nearly midnight, two or three of the more eager enquirers walked with us, far on our way home, still debating, with intense interest the views put forward by my husband.[10]

And Thomas, just like her father, placed no obstacles in her path and helped create the conditions that allowed her to pursue a public life. 'Not only did he afford me invaluable advice and aid in the formation of the Women's Protective and Provident League in 1874, and in its subsequent work,'

Emma wrote, 'but he also most generously sanctioned the absorption of much of my own time in the movement.'[11]

Before she hit on the idea of the League, and even before she married Thomas, Emma also threw herself into the campaign to give women the vote. Harold Goldman wrote that Emma's time at the Club and Institute Union 'began an association with working people which continued to the end of her life.' In 1872, she left the Club and Institute Union to build the same association with politically active women, as secretary to the Women's Suffrage Association. Her time there was short. According to one friend, the women heading that Association let Emma go with one of the greatest misjudgements by an employer of an employee in recorded history. 'The ladies having complimented me on my zeal, but they say my bodily presence is weak, and my speech contemptible,' Emma told the friend. 'So I must make room for someone who can represent them better.'[12] It seemed that the conventional women's movement held no place for Emma Paterson.

She decided instead to create her own. What became the Women's Protective and Provident League was firstly the product of her own experience. After she married Thomas in 1873, they exhausted what savings they had and went on a kind of working honeymoon to New York. Thomas met with trade union activists. Emma met their equivalents among the women. The exploitation she saw there, among women in the so-called sweated trades who worked long hours for low pay in what can only be described as inhuman conditions, left a deep impression. But she was equally impressed by the work of some of those women to shave the sharpest edges from exploitation by building and maintaining societies of their own. Those societies provided money in case of sickness, unemployment or death to their members, and Emma spent much of her post-nuptial holiday with representatives from one of them, the Female Umbrella Makers of New York. Their success in keeping the organisation together, despite the low pay of their members, proved to her that women workers could organise together if given the chance.

Emma's League also grew out of a wider and startling development in the British labour movement of the 1870s. Trade unionists in the cities had long written off agricultural labourers as almost beyond the reach of their movement: remote, isolated, easily replaceable and still touched by the old deference of peasant to lord from feudal times. In 1872, seemingly out of nowhere, agricultural labourers proved them wrong. Huge meetings sprang up and down the British countryside, local unions formed and within several months the National Agricultural Labourers' Union brought them together. By 1874, the union represented more than 80,000 members and had won numerous local struggles for higher wages and a shorter working day.[13] For Emma, this group of highly exploited workers – written off, condescended to – was not so different from women workers. They suffered similar condescension from the labour movement and outside a small number of industries, especially textiles, were not even represented within it. Her experiences in New York proved that women could and had organised, if on a small scale. She reasoned that if the agricultural labourers could organise on a large scale, then perhaps women could as well.

Here was the inspiration for her first major article, the first of her work in this book, and a document that gave birth to a movement: 'The Position of Working Women, and How to Improve It.' In it, she framed the problem in clear terms:

> At three successive annual congresses of leaders and delegates of trades unions, the need of women's unions has been brought before them, and each time someone present has asserted that women *cannot* form unions. The only ground for this assertion appears to be that women *have not* yet formed unions. Probably they have not done so, because they have not quite seen how to set about it.[14]

Emma proposed to remedy that situation. What women needed, she thought, was a wide general union which all could join. Individual trade unions would come out of this general structure once enough women in a specific trade or industry had organised in sufficient numbers to stand on their own. She even proposed a precise system of membership fees, benefits and a blank membership form, all based explicitly on the model of the National Union of Agricultural Labourers. Referring to the dramatic growth of that union, she reasoned that 'if men whose circumstances were so unfavourable to combination as those of most agricultural labourers have been successful in this effort, there is every reason to hope for the success of unions of women.'[15]

Emma did not promote women-only unions as rivals to their male counterparts. She saw them as necessary given the uniquely high levels of exploitation women faced at work, and especially what we now call the gender pay gap. In her time, as she wrote, 'not only are women frequently paid half, or less than half, for doing work as well and as quickly as men,' but even skilled women workers could expect to receive less pay than the average unskilled man. Given those discrepancies, many male trade unionists who should otherwise have been their fiercest allies instead preferred two other remedies: limiting the hours of women through legislation and attempting somehow to remove women from the labour market altogether.[16] Emma saw the first as condescending and done without input from the women concerned and the second as not only unfair but also impractical.

I say many men, and not all, because one group missing from her opening article included the tens of thousands of women already enrolled in unions of men and women combined, especially in the textile industries of northern England. Yet it remained a fact that women remained on the margins of the labour movement. If they were to occupy the central place they deserved they would have to do it themselves. In Emma's view, collective action by women would breed what we now call empowerment, and what she described as 'the feeling of strength and mutual sympathy and helpfulness afforded by close association with others in the same position and labouring under the same difficulties as ourselves.'[17] Spreading that feeling would open the way to further advances, from female-led co-operative enterprises to reading rooms and educational programmes aimed at women. To Emma, female emancipation led directly through trade unions of their own.

To build their movement women would need help from sympathetic men, and Emma always insisted that the growth of women's unions would benefit male and female alike. 'So long as women are unprotected by any kind of combination, and are consequently wholly at the mercy of employers for the rate of their wages and the length of their working hours,' she argued, 'working men not unnaturally look with suspicion on their employment in trade in some branches of which men are engaged.'[18] Only unions of women, in other words, could prevent men from being undersold by their female co-workers. By these arguments, she hoped to win the benevolent neutrality, if not outright support, of union members and leaders for her work. Nor did she spurn offers of advice and assistance from sympathetic male trade unionists, or indeed from men or women outside the labour movement. George Shipton, George Odger and other leading figures on London's trade union scene became influential early supporters. So did clergyman such as Charles Kingsley and high-society ladies like Emilia Pattinson, later to become the wife of the Liberal MP Sir Charles Dilke and herself a future leader of the women's union movement.[19]

They were among those who attended the conference that arose from Emma's article. At the Quebec Institute in London, on 8 July 1874, she addressed women and men on the subject of her work, with Hodgson Pratt, her husband Thomas's friend from the Club and Institute Union, in the chair. The result of the meeting was the Women's Protective and Provident League. The choice of name was not exactly what Emma wanted. She had in mind a League more obviously designed to promote trade unions among women. Yet she was constrained in these early years by wealthy supporters who took fright at the association with trade unions and conflict between workers and bosses, and she herself set out with an essentially liberal view of industrial relations, in which she hoped that women's unions could promote what Gerry Holloway terms an 'entente cordiale between worker, employer and consumer.'[20] In 'The Position of Working Women,' Emma certainly maintained that the low wages women received was due less to a social system that discriminated against women at work, and more to specific unscrupulous employers who not only underpaid women in their employ but also forced good-hearted employers to underpay their women or else go out of business.

This sense, of the League as a society of well-to-do ladies with good intentions but no real base (or place) in the labour movement, persisted throughout its history. Some hostile men used it as grounds to try to deny the League representation at the TUC or support among the unions for its work. Yet it was never more than partly true, and only a small part at that. Emma attracted a number of influential working women beside her, including the shirtmaker Edith Simcox, the printer Emily Faithfull, the Huddersfield weaver Hannah Ellis, the bookbinder Eleanor Whyte and the young upholsteress Jeanette Wilkinson.[21] Collectively, they decided to build the League on more modest lines than the ones Emma suggested in her article. Rather than serving as a general union of all working women, it would promote the creation and development of individual unions across a range of industries. The League would supervise and nurture each new union until it could operate on its own and serve as a centre where women from across the movement could meet, exchange experiences and drive their struggles forward.

The body of this book is testament to the scale of Emma's work on behalf of the League. From 1874 until her death, she addressed meetings across England, Wales, Scotland and Ireland to encourage women to create unions or grow them. She managed the League's correspondence, its finances, and organised large and small ventures for its members: holiday excursions, a reading room at the League's headquarters, a swimming club, even a small savings bank so that working women could pay the rent between jobs or starting a new one. As if that wasn't enough, she then took on a massive undertaking to spread the gospel of women's unions further. She founded, edited and wrote much of the *Women's Union Journal*, a monthly magazine that first appeared in February 1874 and carried on uninterrupted for the rest of her life.[22] The *Journal* reported on the struggles of working women, on reports from the rest of the press on those struggles, discussion of working women at the TUC and the labour movement in general, and on many of the wider issues that women faced, from the struggle for the vote to the need for decent holidays.

Sheila Lewenhak writes that 'Emma Paterson's first achievement in 1874–75 was simply the establishment of the League,' but her 'second and greater success' came as a delegate at the TUC.[23] To get there, she first had to overcome the strong suspicion of many leading trade union men to the representation of women at their meetings. We have already met Henry Broadhurst, who wanted union men to keep their wives at home, but at the Congress of January 1875, it was FJ Whetstone of the Amalgamated Society of Engineers who sounded the alarm at what might result from the presence of women among them. In the future, Whetstone warned, men might represent one society while their wife sat on the other side of the Congress representing another – an invitation to anarchy and disorder![24] Emma had indeed wanted to send a female delegate to the January 1875 Congress on behalf of the National Union of Working Women, an organisation of 300 members in Bristol which was related to Emma's new League. They decided to send a man, HM Hunt, to represent them, over the objections and warnings of the Whetstones of the Congress that a woman would be next. At the next Congress, in October 1875, Emma and her close colleague, Edith Simcox, decided to test the matter further. They appeared themselves as the two first women delegates to a Trades Union Congress.

For me, the transcripts of Emma's appearances at successive TUCs are the most striking part of her canon. They testify to her determination, and her intellectual and rhetorical gifts. Time and again she held her own against the leading men of the labour movement, with all their credentials, parliamentary seats and experience – Broadhurst, soon to be a junior minister in Gladstone's brief 1885/1886 Liberal government, was far from the only MP at the Congresses – and won over to her point of view men who were at first condescending, if not openly hostile. She did so with evidence, logic, wit and the well-timed interjection. She clashed with Broadhurst at her very first Congress over the Factory Acts, and their legal restrictions on the working hours of adult women and children. As he lectured the delegates on the importance of shortening the working day for women, Emma broke in. 'By union,' she said. 'Certainly by union if possible,' he replied, 'but if not possible by union, then by some other means.' He then went on to insist, as quoted earlier, that union men save their wives and daughters from the indignities of working outside the home. Regardless, Emma had made the nature and the scale of their disagreement clear for all their later clashes at the Congresses.

Her position never wavered. She wanted trade union men to speak up against solving the problems of working women by legislation such as the Factory Acts and instead support women to form unions and solve those problems themselves. If they would not do that, and the Factory Acts remained in force, then she wanted TUC delegates to have working women and working men appointed as factory inspectors. At each Congress from 1875 onwards, whenever the question of lobbying Parliament to appoint trade unionists as inspectors came up for debate and the resolution called for the appointment of 'working men,' she proposed an amendment adding 'and working women.' To her surprise at first, successive Congresses approved her amendment and put the unions on record as supporting women factory inspectors. She almost certainly wasn't surprised when, after each victory, someone would come forward at the next Congress with a resolution that mentioned working men and left women out. As you will see, Emma's many interventions at meetings of the TUC revolved around this question, and more broadly on Emma's distaste for paternalism, for any notion or legislation based on the idea that women needed special protection from politicians or priests or the public at large.

Her contempt for paternalism sometimes put her at odds with her colleagues in the League. They included Edith Simcox, whose address to the TUC in 1875 accepted that women would need special protection from the law against long working hours until they had the power to shorten them by their own efforts. It was all well and good, she and many others thought, to insist that the only true path to a shorter workweek came through trade union work. But working women needed relief from long hours now! The middle-class composition of many of the League's leaders, and their distance from the working-class membership, further magnified these political disagreements. Gerry Holloway argues that this distance 'probably discouraged more women than it attracted to becoming activists,' and further led to Emma's 'status as a working woman being ignored or discounted [...] by many male trade unionists eager not to address women's real grievances if they clashed with their own interests.'[25] We might say in passing that these dilemmas exposed the lack of real democracy within the Women's Protective and Provident League. Real power to make decisions within it always lay with Emma and her closest colleagues. We can say, at least, that Emma never pretended to speak at the TUC as if she represented the specific views of all working women or even all members of the League. She was an excellent advocate, if not a pure democrat.

And so, between 1874 and 1876, Emma's work laid the pattern for the rest of her life. The introductions to each chapter of this book list many of the individual struggles and strikes, organising work, connections with women workers in other countries and debates within and without her own ranks that make up her published work. I leave those until then. From 1876 until the end, she continued to agitate for the League, edit and write the *Journal* and advocate the interests of women workers at the TUC. She was able to do all this because of the help and loyalty of her family. Her father educated her. Her husband Thomas never stood in her way, as other Victorian men might have done. And her mother made it possible for Emma to work long hours day after day by keeping the Paterson household. We rightly ask of historical figures who did their washing up. In the first years of her League, Emma's was done by others.

That all changed when her mother died sometime at the end of the 1870s. Emma had only barely recovered from the shock of her death when she was also made a widow. Thomas Paterson died on October 14, 1882, at the age of 47. He left behind great sheaves of manuscript, which Emma was to turn into a published book as a gesture of love to her late husband. He also left debts and no savings. Emma adopted a strict austerity regime, sending letters on scraps of paper and generally scrimping where possible; she also kept up the same taxing regime of speaking, writing, editing and running an organisation at all hours. To make matters worse, the League never quite lived up to her early hopes. It assisted the birth of many women's unions, but most died within the first year. The total membership of affiliated unions never reached above 3,000 in Emma's lifetime. Compare that with the tens of thousands of women enrolled in mixed unions in northern England, and with one of Emma's models for the League, the National Agricultural Labourers' Union, which at one point in the 1870s boasted upwards of 80,000 members. At various points in the early 1880s – and reprinted in this volume – Emma was forced to make public calls for money to keep the League going and call conferences to discuss the League's future and whether it should even continue at all.

Still, she kept her punishing work schedule and her determination to convince working women that their best hope lay in the growth of women's unions. Men in the labour movement had a habit of replenishing that determination by their attitudes to the women. In 1884, for example, a metalworker from the Black Country, Richard Juggins, called on the TUC to demand an end to the employment of girls to make chain, nails and other small metal goods, which he described as 'a calling which was a disgrace to their sex.'[26] In this, Juggins had the support of a wide constituency of people in Britain who were fed countless horror stories in the 1880s and 1890s about the suffering of the women and children of the Black Country.[27] Not so Emma. At the Congress, she courted controversy by claiming that 'she had seen women employed at the class of work referred to, and found them merrily singing hymns. She saw nothing objectionable.' Most of the delegates, including some of the other women, agreed with a Scottish speaker who replied that 'although Mrs Paterson had found the children singing hymns, if she had gone a little farther she might have found them saying prayers to their Maker to be delivered from such a state of bondage.'[28]

Yet she did not end the matter there, and took it up in her *Journal*. 'We advise Mr Juggins,' she wrote, 'to invite the women to join his trade union, instead of trying to "ameliorate their condition" by the harsh and undeviating operation of a law forbidding them to work.'[29] That refusal to compromise on what she considered uncompromisable was already well recognised at the Congress. In 1880, Henry Broadhurst almost certainly had Emma in mind when he was moved to say this to the Congress in a debate over women factory inspectors:

> Why would not ladies be reasonable for once in their lives (oh) – and agree that the first matter was to get more men appointed, and afterwards

consider whether the word "women" should or should not be introduced into the Act of Parliament. But they all knew how unreasonable ladies were – (oh, oh) when a practical question was under discussion. They would have all or none of whatever they went in for. Half measures never satisfied them.[30]

This was not the first or the last occasion when Emma drew a self-pitying sigh from the men of the TUC.

But Emma did a pay a price for her failure to tolerate half measures, at least when it came to her own work. Not long after Thomas's death she learned that she had diabetes. Now a manageable disease, diabetes was then untreatable. Combined with overwork, it proved deadly. Emma's eyesight began to fail. She continued to speak at meetings across Britain, including a long paper at an Industrial Remuneration Conference in 1885, along with regular articles in the *Journal*, but in the middle of 1885 her health sharply worsened. Her friends urged her to see a doctor. Unsurprisingly for an advocate for women workers, Emma chose Elizabeth Garrett Anderson, one of only two female doctors then practicing in Britain.[31] Anderson prescribed her a special diet and suggested she take time off in a milder climate. Emma agreed and spent several weeks at the start of 1886 in the Channel Islands. But when she returned to London, and to work, her health worsened again.

She never recovered. Her last days were spent, as so many previous ones were, agitating and organising and writing. On November 29, 1886, she returned to her home in Westminster from speaking at Tunbridge Wells. She had a fever. Yet she worked on correspondence well into the next morning. On November 30, she found it hard to breathe. Still, she insisted that she correct the proofs of the November issue of her *Journal*. She then lost consciousness. On the night of December 1, she died. Five days later, she was buried at Paddington cemetery in that unmarked grave, next to Thomas. The mourners included friends and colleagues from her League, from the labour and women's movement, and as a representative from the TUC itself, her old antagonist Henry Broadhurst. No one, perhaps, would have been surprised if she had reared out of her coffin for one last swipe about the need for women factory inspectors.

Her death sent the League into crisis. In January 1887, the first issue of the *Women's Union Journal* without Emma in charge began in this way:

> It is probable that after heading the sad news of Mrs Paterson's death, the second or third thought of many of our readers has been: "What will become of the League?" "How will it go on without her?"[32]

Emma had put so much of herself into the work of the League and taken on so many responsibilities within it that there was no clear successor, or group of successors, ready to keep the work going in her absence. It took time for the League as a whole to recover, and we might even say that Emma worked too hard on behalf of the League, and her unwillingness to delegate the mundane tasks of organisation to others left a hole not easily filled. Yet the movement carried on, renamed as the Women's Trade Union and Provident League in 1889 and the Women's Trade Union League in 1891. Under the leadership of women including Clementina Black, Gertrude Tuckwell and Mary Macarthur, and thanks to the renewed upsurge of trade union action in the late 1880s, especially among the least organised sections of the working class – the 'new unionism' – its fortunes improved.[33] The League ended in 1921, when it became the Women's Department of the TUC and its remaining members joined the union relevant to their industry. By that time, it better approximated Emma's early idea of a general union for women workers, and its membership – which reached nearly a hundred thousand in the early twentieth century – better reflected her early hopes.

To measure Emma Paterson's contribution to the British labour movement, and women's place within it, we should start there, with a long-term perspective. In her lifetime, the WPPL survived but never prospered. The *Women's Union Journal* kept the cause of women's unions in print but never broke through to a mass audience. Her interventions at the TUC forced the men to discuss the concerns of women – but even here, it was only after her death that the cause of so much debate on the floor of one Congress after another, women factory inspectors, was achieved in practice. In her lifetime, she never succeeded by any of the measures she must have had in mind when she first conceived of a League of women workers.

Her success lay in clearing a path for women to come. She entrenched the connection between women and unions, provided examples for future women of what and what not to follow in the labour movement and forced a wider conversation about the problems of women workers. Those problems remain with us. We still await their solution. Emma Paterson was one of the women who first made us consider them, and she remains an indispensable link in the chain that connects the man-first mantra of Henry Broadhurst's TUC with the female-majority TUC of the 2020s. That is the historical debt we all owe her. Now that she is no longer labour's forgotten woman, she also deserves to be heard in her own voice. We now turn to how that work is structured in this book.

Her Works

Those who write history know the anguish of leaving out a detail, a source or an apt quotation in the interests of space. Emma Paterson's body of work is so large that selecting the best from the rest felt like an amputation of the historical record. What remains after this sawing away of sources is, I hope, a fair reflection of her range as a writer and speaker. There are long pieces on the rationale for women's unions, the causes and scale of the gender pay gap, and numerous reports on meetings, strikes, conferences and organising work she conducted from the start of the League to her death. Two consistent threads are worth noting here. The first concerns debates at the TUC over women factory inspectors, and the second a long-running struggle by women working at the army clothing depot at Pimlico, which began in 1879 and only ended after Emma died. Next to these are her thoughts on subjects some might think frilly and inconsequential but she considered essential: holidays for working women, swimming lessons, practical women's fashion, free libraries, and access to all the culture that would make the life of working women more than a succession of work and family duties. I have also included, at the end, obituaries and reminiscences after her death from those who knew her, so you may get an impression of the esteem and significance with which her contemporaries viewed her life and work.

I have tried to maintain the same diversity of types of sources as I have of the range of subjects covered. The bulk of the individual pieces come from the *Women's Union Journal*, of which Emma edited more than 100 issues. These articles acquaint the reader with Emma's reactions to news of the day, to struggles of the moment, and to the wider political and cultural issues facing working women. Then, there are her longer essays, beginning with 'The Position of Working Women, and How to Improve It,' and including long papers presented to the Social Science Association in 1875 and an Industrial Remuneration Conference in 1885. These are the best sources to understand Emma's arguments for women's unions, her description and diagnosis of the gender pay gap, and what she hoped to achieve by organising women together. Alongside these written sources are a number of letters Emma wrote to major newspapers, especially the *Times*, to rebut some accusation or other or draw attention to the work of the League and other women workers. The final and perhaps most unusual kind of source in this book are the transcripts of her contributions at the TUC. Here we see Emma in the midst of battle, pushing trade union men to accept trade union women and drop the paternal routine. Where possible I have included the words of those arguing with (and sometimes for) her to keep her remarks in context.

I have arranged these sources in chronological order, rather than by topic or theme. Many of her works, especially the longer essays, covered a wide variety of themes and so defied easy categorisation. Presenting her work by source would have led to repetition, especially with her debates at the TUC, and would prevent the reader from seeing the progression of her views and work and the various issues and struggles that informed her work on other subjects. Her work is presented in the order it occurred because that is how she lived it. Readers can still follow the thread of a recurring struggle, as with the workers at Pimlico, or debate, as with factory inspection at the TUC. They do so having read about Emma's other preoccupations at the same time. Chapter 1 runs from 1874 to 1878, Chapter 2 from 1879 to 1884 and Chapter 3 covers 1885 and 1886. Chapter 4 provides a selection of obituaries and reminiscences about Emma after her death.

Each chapter has an introduction that sets up the major topics and events mentioned within it and adds further context to that provided here. Reading on, you will see how much she deserves the honourable titles of trade unionist, feminist and radical. You will grasp how far we still have to go to right the wrongs to which she devoted her life. And you should come away with the message that Emma preached, and which can be summed up by paraphrasing the Irish socialist James Connolly, himself a noted writer on the emancipation of women: the cause of women is the cause of labour and the cause of labour is the cause of women.

Notes

1 Trades Union Congress, *Report of the Proceedings of the Trades Union Congress* (London, 1877), p. 18.
2 Harold Goldman, *Emma Paterson: She led Women into a Man's World* (London, 1974), p. 14.
3 J. Bellamy and J. Schmiechen, "Emma Anne Paterson (1848–1886), Trade Unionist and Feminist," in *Dictionary of Labour Biography*, Vol. IV (London, 1977), pp. 167–70.
4 Mary Davis, "The Making of the English Working Class Revisited: Labour History and Marxist Theory," in Mary Davis (ed.), *Class and Gender in British Labour History: Renewing the Debate (Or Starting It?)* (Pontypool, 2011), pp. 16, 17.
5 For the Chartists see Malcolm Chase, *Chartism: A New History* (Manchester, 2007), or a new collection of older work by Dorothy Thompson which emphasises the contributions of women to the movement: Stephen Roberts (ed.), *The Dignity of Chartism* (London, 2015).
6 For an overview of the movement and some of its key figures, see, for instance, Barbara Caine, *Victorian Feminists* (Oxford, 1993).
7 Richard N. Price, "The Working Men's Club Movement and Victorian Social Reform Ideology," *Victorian Studies*, 15:2 (1971), 117–41.
8 George Tremlett, *Clubmen: The History of the Working Men's Club and Institute Union* (London, 1987).
9 Emma Paterson, "Preface," in Thomas Paterson (ed.), *A New Method of Mental Science, With Applications to Political Economy* (London, 1886), p. iv.
10 Emma Paterson, "Preface," p. iv.
11 Emma Paterson, "Preface," p. iv.
12 Quoted in Goldman, *Emma Paterson*, p. 28.
13 Reg Groves, *Sharpen the Sickle: The History of the Farm Workers' Union* (London, 1981).

14 Emma Paterson, "The Position of Working Women, and How to Improve It," *Labour News*, April 1874.
15 Paterson, "Position of Working Women."
16 Sonya O. Rose, "Gender Antagonism and Class Conflict; Exclusionary Strategies of Male Trade Unionists in Nineteenth-Century Britain," *Social History*, 13:2 (1988), 191–208.
17 Paterson, "Position of Working Women."
18 Paterson, "Position of Working Women."
19 Betty Askwith, *Lady Dilke: A Biography* (London, 1968).
20 Gerry Holloway, "United We Stand": Class Issues in the Early British Women's Trade Union Movement," in Davis (ed.), *Class and Gender in British Labour History*, p. 138.
21 For Emily Faithfull, see James S. Stone, *Emily Faithfull: Victorian Champion of Women's Rights* (Toronto, 1994). For Jeanette Wilkinson, see June Hannam, "Wilkinson, Jeanette Gaury, 1841–1886," in *Oxford Dictionary of National Biography* (Oxford, 2004). She also has an obituary in the *Women's Union Journal* later in this volume.
22 For an extended treatment of the *Journal*, see Melissa Walker, "On the Move: Biography, Self-Help, and Feminism in the Women's Union Journal," *Victorian Periodicals Review*, 50:3 (2017), pp. 585–618.
23 Sheila Lewenhak, *Women and Trade Unions: An Outline History of Women in the British Trade Union Movement* (London, 1977), p. 21.
24 Goldman, *Emma Paterson*, p. 60.
25 Holloway, "United We Stand", pp. 136, 140.
26 For more on Richard Juggins and his organisation, see Eric Taylor, "The Midland Counties Trades Federation, 1886–1914," *Midland History*, 1:3 (1972), pp. 26–40.
27 For some background on the Black Country metalworkers and "sweating," see Sheila Blackburn, "Working-Class Attitudes to Social Reform: Black Country Chainmakers and Anti-Sweating Legislation, 1880–1930," *International Review of Social History*, 33 (1988), 42–69.
28 Trades Union Congress, *Reports of the Proceedings of the Trades Union Congress* (London, 1884), p. 41.
29 "Women as Nail Makers," *Women's Union Journal*, November 1884.
30 "Trades Union Congress," *Women's Union Journal*, October 1880.
31 Jo Manton, *Elizabeth Garrett Anderson: England's First Woman Physician* (London, 1965).
32 "The Work of the League," *Women's Union Journal*, January 1887.
33 For the development of the League see, amongst others, Norbert Soldon, *Women in British Trade Unions: 1874–1976* (London, 1977); Barbara Drake, *Women in Trade Unions* (London, 1984); Lewenhak, *Women and Trade Unions*. For a comparative perspective, see Robin Miller Jacoby, *The British and American Women's Trade Union Leagues, 1890–1925: A Case Study of Feminism and Class* (New York, 1994).

1 Building a Movement, 1874–April 1879

Between 1874 and 1878, Emma Paterson went from an unknown secretary to the foremost advocate for women's unions in Britain. This chapter is a guide to that transformation. We begin with the two essays that made her name and brought together the sum total of her thinking and experience to that point, 'The Position of Working Women, and How to Improve It,' and 'The Position of Women Engaged in Handicrafts and Other Industrial Pursuits.' As she wrote in the first of them, men at successive Trades Union Congresses had 'asserted that women cannot form unions. The ground for this assertion appears to be that women have not yet formed unions. Probably they have not done so, because they have not quite seen how to set about it.' For Emma, that assumption was about to change.

The rest of the chapter records her agitation for women's unions around the country. There are reports of meetings in industrial centres from Leicester to Sheffield where Emma hammered home her arguments for women's unions and sought to grow her new League beyond its London base. Here you can see her style in person as well as on the page. Then there are her first clashes with the men of the Trades Union Congress. Her arguments with Henry Broadhurst and other leading men of the Congress are reproduced here: they include the long-running debate on the appointment of women as factory inspectors, the proper place of women in the labour market and the best means by which women could have their interests protected.

Emma, naturally, gave an unambiguous answer to that last question – women's unions – while Broadhurst and most of the other delegates thought that protective legislation remained the best and most effective option. What emerges from these exchanges is not just her refusal to waver in the face of powerful opposition. You can also see her use of wit and the one-liner to defuse opposition and win the respect of the male delegates. When pressing her amendment for women factory inspectors in 1878 she added that 'she would be sorry to have it seem to the public that he working men wanted to keep all the loaves and fishes to themselves,' to the general laughter of the Congress; so too when replying to Broadhurst's suggestion that pushing for working women as factory inspectors would imperil the appointment of working men. He did so, she said, 'so dolefully that one could almost see the trembling in his eye.' Cue more laughter from the delegates.

The events of the period provided extra ammunition for her insistence on women's unions. Emma used a strike by non-unionised cotton workers at Bristol in 1878, a strike that ended after five weeks in defeat for the women, as a source of useful lessons. Having a union behind them, she argued, would have made victory in the strike more certain, would have given them access to a strike fund and so prevented the misery attending it and even made the strike itself unnecessary, as a union might have won their demands without the need for action. And she contrasted the potential power of unions to give women independence with the with the powerlessness imposed on them by charity. Philanthropy, she argued before an audience of concerned clergy, had the tendency to entrench the misery of working women rather than remove it; here, to use the modern term, Emma makes the case for unions as key to the empowerment of working women.

The very experiences that led Emma to consider a federation of women's unions always had an international dimension. That women umbrella makers in New York had managed to build a union in the most degraded sweatshop conditions had convinced her that similar organisations could and should emerge in Britain. That international dimension recurs throughout this chapter. She reported with great interest in 1877 on attempts by Parisian working women to create a League modelled in some respects on Emma's own. There seemed every prospect that working women might link arms across the English Channel as well as across the industrial centres of Britain. Those early hopes were dashed, but Emma always saw the cause of women's unions in international relief.

Even her arguments for women factory inspectors acquired an international flavour. In 1878, she explained that in France, women were only governed by their equivalents of the Factory Acts until the age of 21 and that the municipal government of Paris hired women as well as men as factory inspectors. Pulling at the patriotic heartstrings of her readers, she hoped that these innovations 'will soon be followed in this country; so that we may not have to repeat the old saying 'they manage these things better in France."

The chapter ends, appropriately enough, with Emma's own assessment of the League's first four years. 'The Organisation of Women's Industry' rehearses the arguments for women's unions, their necessity and practicality, and points in an oblique way to internal arguments within the League. Some, she suggests, wanted to emphasise the 'provident' aspects of the

League at the expense of its 'protective' one: that is, to stress the benefit features of the League over its trade union features. 'Working women,' she said in response, 'have well shown how provident they can be [...] they need to be encouraged to protect themselves by Union and to strengthen themselves by it.'

She didn't hesitate to list the achievements of her League in terms of members gained and unions formed, and the many fringe benefits, from a lending library to a small money-lending service, that the League now provided to its members. She also didn't exaggerate those achievements. 'Only about 1000 workwomen in London have yet been directly reached by the Unions formed,' she wrote, and 'the vast size of London and the variety of trades make the work of organization especially difficult here.' That, of course, would come as no surprise to the Emma Paterson of 1874 when she penned her first statement on women's unions, to which we now turn.

'The Position of Working Women, and How to Improve it,' *Labour News*, April 1874

It is seldom disputed that the rate of wages paid to women is, in many occupations, disgracefully low. This may not be so glaringly the case in the great mills and factories of the North, but, in addition to cases which privately come to the knowledge of everyone, disclosures are not unfrequently made in the newspapers, showing how sadly many working women need some improvement in their position.

Not long ago a case appeared in the London papers which must have horrified all who read it. A woman had been working in a white-lead factory near London; the factory was 3 or 4 miles from her lodging; she had to walk to and from morning and night. She could not pay the smallest amount for riding, nor provide herself with proper food, for her wages were but 9s per week for work occupying 12 hours each day. She bravely battled with her difficulties for some time and managed to keep alive herself and three children, but, at last, nature could hold out no longer; she died, and her death, leaving the children unprotected, brought to light the fearful tale. Had she supported herself only, the facts might never have been known.

Not only are women frequently paid half, or less than half, for doing work as well as quickly as men. The following statement, made by a large manufacturer on the occasion of a recent deputation to the Home Secretary, shows that they are sometimes paid much lower wages for superior work: 'Skilled women, whose labour required delicacy of touch, the result of long training as well as thoughtfulness, received from 11s to 16s, and 17s a week, whilst the roughest unskilled labour of a man was worth at least 18s' (*Times*, March 27).

Employers alone are not to blame for the evils of underpayment. There are many just and right-minded employers who would gladly pay their workwomen a fair rate of wages: but however willing they may be to do this, they are almost powerless so long as the women themselves make no stir in the matter. If they were to pay higher wages whilst other less scrupulous employers could, without difficulty, obtain the serves of women at about a third or fourth of the fair payment, they would simply be unable to carry on business, because the unscrupulous employers would be able, by paying less for labour, to undersell them in the market. Employers have been known to express their regret that they could not pay their workers better wages because those workers made no efforts in that direction.

The present isolated position of working women reacts injuriously on their prospects in many indirect, as well as direct, ways. The object of this paper is to endeavour to point out some of these evils, and to urge on the earnest attention of all concerned in the question that which the writer believes to be the only true remedy for them.

So long as women are unprotected by any kind of combination, and are consequently wholly at the mercy of employers for the rate of their wages and the length of their working hours, working men not unnaturally look with suspicion on their employment in trades in some branches of which men are engaged. The fear that the employment of women will lower their wages has led the men to pass rules in many of their trade societies positively forbidding their members to work with women.

They have also carried on, and are still continuing, an agitation, in which they are aided by many benevolent persons who desire to improve the position of women, in support of a Bill now before Parliament, to limit the hours of women's work in factories and workshops. This Bill is intended to apply also to children, with whom working women are classed, thus conveying and endeavouring to perpetuate, the idea that women are entirely unable to protect themselves, a position, to a certain extent, degraded and injurious.

Women, more than ever, urgently need the protection afforded by combination, as it is possible that, if these suggested restrictions become law, further legislation in the same direction may be proposed, and at present the women affected by it have no means of making known their collective opinion on the subject.

There can be no doubt that it is desirable, in many cases, to shorten the hours during which women work, but if this is done by legislative enactments instead of by the combined action of the workers themselves, the result may merely be the reduction of wages, already often insufficient, and sometimes complete exclusion from work, thus becoming, in place of protection, a real and grievous oppression. Where there is combined action among the workers, as in the case of men, it has been clearly seen, of late years, that no such legislation is necessary.

It is true that working men, who are joining in these well-meant but mistaken endeavours to improve the position of working women, might offer the same kind of protection which they themselves adopt. They might invite women to join their trade unions, or to assist them to form similar societies. But they do not seem to be inclined to do this. At three successive annual congresses of leaders and delegates of trades unions, the need of women's unions has been brought before them, and each time someone present has asserted that women *cannot* form unions. The only ground for this assertion appears to be that women *have not* yet formed unions. Probably they have not done so, because they have not quite seen how to set about it.

The following is an outline of a plan, in some respects similar to that of the 'National Agricultural Labourers' Union,' for a general organisation of working women. This organisation might ultimately be divided up into societies of different trades, but, at first, it appears desirable to make the basis of operations as general and the rules as simple as possible:

1 A central council or board, having branches composed of workers in any trade all over the country.
2 The name of the association to be the 'National Protective and Benefit Union of Working Women.'
3 A branch to consist of not less than 12 persons. Intimation of a wish to form a branch to be made to the central council, by whom the following form would be forwarded:
   We, the undersigned, agree to form a branch of the 'National Protective and Benefit Union of Working Women' in
   ....
   and we hereby appoint ....
   to   as   secretary,   and
   ....
   to act as treasurer to the branch.
   ....18............................

   Name.   Address.   Trade

4 On the return of the form, a supply of membership forms and cards, rules and subscription books, to be sent to the person named as secretary of the branch.
5 Subscriptions to be paid to a secretary of a branch each week, and payment acknowledged in the members' subscription books. In the first instance, until district boards could be formed, the secretary of each branch should be required to forward members' payments once every month to the central council, with a list of the names and addresses of

the members paying. A detailed receipt would be returned to the secretary, which she should be required to produce on application, for the satisfaction of the members.
6 The subscription to be 1½d per week, and the entrance fee 4½d.
7 The entrance fees to be devoted to the working expenses of the society, including cost of printing the rules, subscription cards and forms, with which the branch members and secretaries would be supplied. Any surplus at the end of each year to be paid over to the benefit fund.
8 The subscription fees to be deposited in a bank in the name of the society, at interest, as a fund for benefit and trade purposes, by trustees appointed by the central council, who names and position would be sufficient guarantee against fraud. The subscriptions not to be drawn upon for any working expenses. The entrance fees to be deposited in a separate fund, and to be drawn upon by the treasurer, by written order of the central council only.
9 No member to be entitled to receive sick or out-of-work benefits until she has paid subscriptions for six months; the sum then granted to depend on the amount of funds accumulated.
10 Strict investigation to be made into applications for benefit payments.

It must be borne in mind that the main object in view is to accustom women to the idea of union. If this object is once gained more elaborate plans may before long be found necessary, and, as a knowledge of the strength of each trade in certain localities is arrived at, classified unions of women will be more practicable. To give an idea of the strength of working women as regard numbers, four trades may be mentioned which it may be hoped could ultimately support separate unions:

Tailoresses (number in England and Wales shown by Census Returns of 1871)	38,021
Earthenware manufacture	15,953
Straw plait manufacture	45,270
Bookbinders	7,557

A general union, as a commencement, would afford excellent facilities for the formation of separate unions. By the classification of the different trades of the members by the central council, it would readily be seen when a sufficient number of members of one trade were enrolled to make a union of that trade strong enough to stand alone. There are now in New York some very successful unions consisting of, and managed entirely by, working women. Two of the largest are the 'Parasol and Umbrella-makers' Union,' and the 'Women's Typographical Union.'

The advantage of a general union at the first onset are very considerable, as by its means those women who are tolerably well paid would help those who were very badly paid. If the well-paid and the ill-paid workers were to form separate unions, the ill-paid ones would be at a much greater disadvantage than if they belonged to a union having a far larger number of members than they could muster alone.

By way of encouragement, women may be reminded of what has been done by that, until recently, worst paid and most isolated class of men, the agricultural labourers. A movement, commenced amongst them only three years ago, has already developed into a powerful society, numbering about 150,000 members. Many labourers, who were earning wages only just above starvation rates, have now increased their earnings by one third or more. If men whose circumstances were so unfavourable to combination as those of most agricultural labourers have been successful in this effort, there is every reason to hope for the success of unions of women.

There is one point with regard to the low wages of women which may here be referred to. Any remarks on this subject are often met by a reply involving a common fallacy, viz., that 'all cheap production is a benefit to the producers.' Does it, however, benefit women, or indeed men either, that cigars, for instance, should be made for 4d per 100, the price paid, according to the Beehive newspaper, to some female cigar makers; or that the production of cartridges, in which women are largely employed, should be cheapened; or that artificial flowers should be sold at so low a price that they are wasted and thrown away as of no value; or that jewel cases can be procured at very small cost? Even in the case of articles of direct use to working women, cheap production is of but little more benefit. Wages of from 6s to 12s per week leave a very small margin for any purchases beyond those of the bare necessaries of life – food and fuel – and are often insufficient for a proper supply of these. Cheap production, which involves, for the producers, want, degradation and even, occasionally, starvation; or which, when starvation is avoided, throws them upon the poor rates for maintenance, can surely not be beneficial to them or to the community.

At present, only two advantages of union have been enlarged upon in this paper: the means of raising wages and of shortening hours of labour.

But were the position of working women all that could be desired with respect to both wages and hours of work, there are of benefits of union of the greatest importance. One of these is the means afforded for help in times of sickness or of temporary depression of trade. Women have suffered deeply from the want of such assistance.

At a time of great slackness of trade among the bookbinders, in 1871, caused by a delay in passing through the House of Commons the revised Prayer book, it was stated that during 16 months two of the men's unions had paid £2,500 in relieving their unemployed members, but that the women in the trade, having no union to fall back upon, had suffered the greatest distress.

The 'Female Umbrella-makers Union of New York' has paid for sick benefits alone, during the three years of its existence, over 1,000 dollars (£200). One member, a widow, was supported entirely by the union, during an illness lasting two years.

The union might also afford valuable aid to its members by instituting inquiries by means of the central council, into any cases of imposition or fraud which might be brought to the notice of the council. There are many gentlemen who would probably be willing to assist such an association by giving legal advice in these cases. The Working Women's Protective Union of New York has taken up this work, and frequently with great success. In the case of machine workers, employers have sometimes refused to pay for the work, under the presence of its being badly done, and have even required the forfeiture of the workers' deposit as compensation for pretended damage to the material. The union has investigated such cases and, where expostulation with the employer has failed, has undertaken his prosecution at law. Such frauds are now becoming every day more rate in New York, because it is now known that a powerful society is ready to protect women in this way. So long as women do not combine they are powerless under dishonest treatment, because they are well known to be too poor to follow up the defrauders.

Another service the union might render is suggested by the mention of deposits required on work. Workwomen often find it very difficult to make these advances, and the union might assist its members either by lending the deposit money, or by becoming responsible for the return of the material.

Another important advantage is the feeling of strength and mutual sympathy and helpfulness afforded by close association with others in the same position and labouring under the same difficulties as ourselves. Out of such union, too, might grow many movements for still further improving the position of women, such as some kind of co-operative workrooms, in which women when temporarily out of employment might find means of subsistence until they obtained permanent work; educational efforts, emigration clubs, reading rooms, etc.

The writer earnestly begs all persons interested in improving the social condition of women to communicate with her with a view to action in this matter and especially invites information and suggestions from women engaged in trades.

Emma A Paterson, April 1874.

The Position of Women Engaged in Handicrafts and Other Industrial Pursuits, *The Englishwoman's Review*, XXI, January 1875

The women of England have reason to be deeply grateful to the Social Science Association for the readiness which it has always displayed to consider questions respecting their welfare and their advancement, and for the indirect impetus thus given to many of the excellent movements now at work for the benefit of women.

Among the numerous subjects affecting the position of women, which have from time to time been discussed at the Social Science Congress, the employment of girls and women in handicrafts and other industrial pursuits, has not been overlooked and has always met with considerable attention. Difference of opinion has often been expressed as to the good or evil results of such employment, and probably some members of the Association may still consider that the exclusion of women from factories and workshops, and indeed from any kind of competition with men's labour, would be beneficial to society. The great fact, however, remains and must be dealt with, that every year the class of wage-earning girls and women is becoming larger. Each census has shown an increase in the number, until now it has reached upwards of three millions. Without entering into the question of whether well-regulated work does not exercise a good influence over women as well as over men, it is evident that the removal of women from the labour market grows more and more remote, and in proportion, as the number of female workers increases, the importance of their position in relation to society in general is increased. If it is found that we have a rapidly growing class of the community who are sober and industrious, working with the greatest energy and application, and yet – with all their exertion – unable to support themselves by the payment for their labour, and consequently obliged to depend partially on outside aid, the question will be seen to be a very serious one. That this is the position of a large proportion of working women, a consideration of the wages paid to them is sufficient to convince us.

In some of the best paid employments, in which both women and men are engaged, women may manage to obtain nearly a third of the wages of men, but in other trades they earn considerably less than this. When the worker is a girl who lodges at home and takes some meals there, she does not, of course, feel so acutely the want of higher payment, and the aid she has from her relatives enables her to subsist. But when a woman is obliged to depend entirely on her earnings, and perhaps also to support or assist others depending on her, the difficulty is felt and the poor rates have to be drawn upon, or some local charities to be appealed to, to make up the deficiency. How often recourse is had to immoral means of raising money, no one can say, but sad histories of such cases are not altogether unheard of. Women of independent spirit are occasionally to be found who will go through much suffering, and even die in their attempts to support themselves, rather than have recourse to charity. When these women are beaten in the struggle, and death gains the victory, a newspaper report of the case appears, and considerable sympathy is for a time expressed; the sympathisers more often, however, blaming the victims for not seeking charity, than denouncing the vicious system of underpayment for their work. It must not be forgotten too, that the aid from parents or other relatives by which many women are enabled to subsist, is a form of charity, though it does not fall upon the rich, but upon persons who can often ill-afford to give it. If a workman has two or three daughters, or even one only, he should no more be expected to contribute to their support, when they are able and willing to work for themselves, than his sons to that of the similarly circumstanced. No consideration as to subsidiary assistance should be allowed to enter into questions of payments for work. It is said that men are PAID HIGHER WAGES than women because they have FAMILIES TO SUPPORT, but no one ever proposes to pay single men lower wages than married men. WOMEN ARE OFTEN LEFT the sole protectors of, and providers for themselves and their CHILDREN, OR THEIR ARGED OR INFIRM PARENTS; yet their earnings are insufficient not only for the support of a family, but also, in many cases, for the bare subsistence of one person. Of the 879, 173 widows enumerated in the last census, it may fairly be assumed that two thirds are of the poorer class. Not long ago an account appeared in the London papers which excited some attention at the time of its publication. A woman had been working in a white lead factory near London, three or four miles from her lodging. She was obliged to walk to and from morning and night. She could not spare the smallest amount for riding nor provide herself with proper food, for her wages were but 9s per week for twelve hours work per day. She struggled on for some time to keep herself and her three children alive, but at last nature could hold out no longer, and her death brought to light the fearful tale.

Another case reported in the London newspapers so recently as September 5th deserves notice here. A woman who worked for an army clothing contractor, summoned the foreman of the shop for an assault which had arisen out of a dispute as to her claim for payment. She claimed 14s 9d for machining soldiers' trousers and stated, in court, that she was paid seven farthings per pair, the work on each pair occupying three quarters of an hour. By working 12 hours per day, she could thus earn 2s 2¼ d, or 13s per week if her work were passed by the foreman. The foreman's approval, however, is far from certain. In the case referred to, a deduction of 7s 2d was insisted on, on the plea of a large portion of the work being badly done. The woman maintained that it was properly done, and hence arose the dispute. Six other women were at the same time subjected to similar deductions, and disputed the justice of them. It appears extraordinary that the fear of such serious deductions from their scanty earnings should not keep the work of the women up to a passable standard, and that so many as seven women in one day and at the same shop should have been fined. Without further evidence than that given in the newspaper report, the merits of this particular case cannot be entered into, but there is too much reason to fear that employers, or their foremen, sometimes take advantage of the unprotected and miserably low position of the women, to reduce, by various pretexts, wages already barely sufficient to support life. This has been so frequently the case in New York, that the working women's Protective Union of that city has found it necessary to prosecute as many as 160 employers in one year for illegal stoppages of wages.

The low rate of women's wages has long been a subject of remark. Various causes have been assigned for it, those most frequently urged being, the absence of skilled work among women, their inability to do as much work in a day as men can perform and the superabundant supply of labour in employments open to them.

The following evidence will, however, show that these reasons are not entirely satisfactory. In regard to skilled work done by women, a large manufacturer, who went on a Deputation to the Home Secretary in favour of the Factory Acts, stated that 'Skilled women whose labour required delicacy to touch, the result of long training, as well as thoughtfulness, received from 11s to 16s and 17s per week, whilst the roughest unskilled labour of a man was worth at least 18s' (Times, March 27th 1874). This was in answer to the argument that legislative restriction of the hours of women's labour would tend to make it more difficult for women to obtain employment.

The 'Beehive,' the organ of men's Trade Unions, a paper not over favourable to the employment of women, says 'The men employed in the cigar trade make nothing but the best goods, yet it is not all left to them, their numbers being too small to supply the wants of the trade with that class of goods. Therefore the best female makers are employed to make what the men are short, and although they may not be able to make them quite so well as the men, yet the difference is so slight that it is almost impossible to perceive it even by the most experienced judges and is quite compensated for by the females being able to produce them quicker" (Beehive, 25 January 1874). Yet the wages of the best female cigar makers are 40 per cent lower than those of the male workers. They are usually apprenticed seven years to the trade. The following testimony as to the energy and skill of women in work is given in the Report of Dr Bridges and Mr Holmes on the employment of women in textile manufactures.

> It would seem to us to be as easy to goad women as it would be difficult to goad men into doing the greatest amount of piece work in a given time. The admiration of their companions and the approbation of the overlooker appear to be at least as powerful inducements as the increase of their wages. A woman who can mind four looms

without an assistant has attained a certain position, and is an object of attention.

With regard to the charge of inferiority of work amongst women, it may also be added that where this is well founded, underpayment is the most likely means of producing such a result. How can women, who must work incessantly for 12, 15 or even 18 hours per day to earn the merest pittance, be expected to take a pride in their work, or to aim at perfection in it? As to the oversupply of labour in women's occupation, a glance on any day at the columns of that important advertising medium, The London Daily Chronicle, shows that even in some of the worst paid trades there is a constant demand for the work of women and girls. Artificial florists, bead makers, bonnet makers, book folders, boot closers and many other trades, the mention of which would occupy too much space, are advertised for. In the work parts of London, too, bills may often be seen posted up, inviting applications for work in such trades.

The employments open to women of the middle class, or rather those which they are able or willing to enter into, being very limited in number, are undoubtedly overstocked – that of governesses being especially so. But for women of the working class the occupations are far more numerous. In theone case, the leading employments amount to about half a dozen; in the other, according to the census, they number at least seventy.

Sufficient has now been said to show that other causes than those usually assigned must be sought for to explain the low rate of women's wages. Of these, the most obvious appears to be the fact that women have made no permanent united efforts to increase their wages by means of representations and appeals made to their employers through trade combinations.

A proposal that women should protect themselves by union, as men have done, will probably be met first by an objection that be taking such a step, women would be involved in strikes and their attendant evils.

Setting aside for the present, the question of the attitude of well-regulated trade unions regarding strikes, it may be well now to point out that women, although they have no trade unions, have yet not unfrequently originated or taken part in strikes. They have shared largely, in what is considered by many person, to be the most objectionable feature of unionism, without participating in other advantages of it, the benefits of which are seldom disputed. The men's unions have usually been very ready to help women 'on strike,' and in trade in which persons of both sexes are employed, when the men strike, the women frequently back them up by striking at the same time. In these cases, the women either depend on donations, hastily collected in other shops or in districts where no strike exists, or on a weekly allowance from the funds of the men's societies to which they have contributed nothing. They are thus placed in a position of complete dependence on the aid of others, so long as the strike lasts, and when it is over they return to their former state of disorganisation and isolation, until some new difficulty arises. Some of the more important strikes of women have been that of the female bookbinders, employed by a contractor for the British and Foreign Bible Society, in 1849, the great strike of tailors in 1867 and more recently that of the mill workers in Belfast, when several thousands of women struck with the men, to resist a proposed reduction of wages. In the last named instance, the men, by the aid of their union, succeeded in abating the proposed reduction for themselves by one-half – whilst the women, who had no union, were obliged to submit to the reduction in full.

As to the effect of unions on strikes, the following extract from the Report of the Committee of the Social Science Association, on Trade Societies, presented in 1860, may be quoted:

> A great many strikes originate in trades which have no then existing organization, but if a strike assumes any considerable proportions, a governing body is appointed at the time to carry it on. The committee are disposed to believe that leaders of a strike, where there is no regularly organized society, are likely to prove more unreasonable and more violent than where there is.... The Committee have not found that the constant assertion, that strikes are scarcely ever successful, is at all borne out by facts. They are further disposed to believe that in some cases, the existence of a regularly organized trade society, has prevented the frequent occurrence of strikes.

In all the generally recognised advantages of Trade Unions, women have not shared; the assistance when from depression of trade, or other causes, they are thrown out of work; the encouragement given to good work by the maintenance of a certain standard of efficiency; the facilities afforded for gaining information as to demands for labour in different localities, a valuable safeguard against an oversupply of labour in any one place; the travelling allowances to members in search of work; the regulation of hours of labour; the allowances in sickness; and above all, the encouragement and feeling of strength afforded by close union with those who are subject to similar conditions of employment, and to similar difficulties and drawbacks. The distress occasioned amongst the bookbinders in 1871 and 1872, by a delay in passing through the House of Commons this revised Table of Lessons, and the consequent delay in the issue of a new edition of the Prayer Book, is a striking instance of how greatly women have suffered from a want of the first of the benefits. At that time, during sixteen months, two of the men's unions paid £2,500 in relieving their unemployed members, but the women in the trade not having the aid of a union, were in the greatest difficulties.

Working men have often been blamed for showing a disposition to exclude women from competition with themselves in the labour market, and the attitude assumed on this point by some of their unions, and in their Trades Congress and newspapers, is no doubt much to be regretted. Considered impartially however, it cannot be regarded as remarkable. Owing to their disorganised position, women are obliged to take any wages offered to them, and the introduction of women into a trade is invariably followed by a marked fall in wages, both for time work and piece work. Employers, too, are sometimes censured for paying their workers so badly, and the public are censured for allowing such a state of things to continue. But neither employers nor the public voluntarily remedy the evil. Combined action of the part of the workers can alone do this. So long as women are not united, one unscrupulous employer who should obtain their labour at the present rate, could, by underselling, force every other employer to do the same, or to become bankrupt. A large employer of women's labour, a very benevolent man, on being appealed to on this subject not long ago, said, that he would gladly pay the women better wages, but that he could not afford to incur the loss which would arise from the underselling of his goods by other employers less considerate as to proper payment for work. He acknowledged that combinations of the workers could alone bring about the desired change and said that he should gladly see efforts made in this direction.

In addition to the low wages and long hours of work, prevailing in many of the industrial occupations of women, there are injustice and hardships which union would do much to suppress. The system in the clothing trade of demanding money security for work given out, for instance, often entails great deprivation which might be alleviated by a trade union. Women cannot find this security out of their scanty wages and are frequently obliged to pawn furniture and other articles to obtain it. At a conference held in Bristol, last month, it was stated that one employer was known to have obtained the use of £3,000, by demanding heavy security from each of his workpeople.

The truck system which has received so much attention as affecting men and has been to so large an extent weakened by the opposition of their unions, is still in operation in some employments of women. One notable instance of it is afforded by some large drapery establishments, where the female assistants are required to dress fashionably and even richly, so that they may be able to show off to advantage, on their own figures, mantles and other outdoor garments. One of these houses, at the West End, deducts so much from the wages of the women for costly black silk dresses, that they seldom receive more than a small balance in money. People who are inclined to censure shop women for their extravagant dress need to be informed of this fact.

It has been said, and may be again repeated, that women have not the qualifications requisite to enable them to form and keep up unions. This is a mere assertion, easily made, but facts to the contrary are not wanting.

American working women have made some successful efforts to protect their labour, and to otherwise assist themselves by combination. In 1871, the proposed reduction of the already small wages of women, employed in New York in umbrella and parasol making, led to the formation of a women's union in that trade; 900 women joined, about nine-tenths of the whole number in the trade in New York, and the reduction was successfully resisted. The union has prospered up to this time, and the President of it – a woman formerly in the trade – who has devoted much attention to the society, is now gratefully acknowledged by her fellow workers as having accomplished for them a lasting benefit. No strike has been engaged in since the first struggle in 1871, but the wages of the women generally have been raised. A considerable portion of the society's funds has been expended in aiding members temporarily out of work, or in sickness. The 'Women's Typographical Union' of New York is also flourishing, and several unions exist in other States.

Before closing this paper, the recent extension of the Factory Acts as affecting the position of working women, should be commented on. As to the benefit of the great limitation of the hours of labour there can be no dispute. But it is difficult to see how legislative enactments can ever be so effective, as measures initiated and watched over by the workers themselves. In the largest factories, where government supervision and inspection can readily be adopted, such acts may be rigidly carried out, but the numerous small workshops, can easily and do frequently evade them. Often the workers are glad, owing to their small payment, to connive at such evasions and to make a trifling addition to their scanty earnings, by working overtime work. Others are afraid, that to give information against their employers, might lead to their dismissal. Union of the workers, whereby they would exercise a check over each other, is the only true remedy for long working hours, if accompanied, as it certainly would be, by increased wages for ordinary hours which would make overtime less attractive. Besides the long hours of work, the condition of some underground places and lofts, used as workrooms, is a source of many evils.

English working women are now commencing efforts to obtain the benefits to be derived from combination. A simultaneous movement, in this direction has been made during the last few months in London, Bristol and other parts of the country. A conference held in London, in July, on the 'need of union among working women' resulted in the formation of a 'Women's Protective And Provident Committee,' a kind of consultative and advising body, whose object is to assist women desirous of forming unions and to collect and diffuse information likely to be useful to them. Amongst the members of the Committee, are ladies and gentlemen well known for their various earnest and disinterested efforts to improve the position of the working classes. By the aid of the Committee, a Society has already been established by the women employed in folding, sewing and other branches of bookbinding, which promises to be very successful.

As soon as the formation of a few Societies in the more remunerative trades has clearly shown the practicability of women's unions. The efforts of the Committee, will be directed to the lowest and worst paid class of workers. In this, the most difficult part of their work, scope will be afforded for much of that devoted and self-sacrificing work, which educated and enlightened English women have shown a readiness to give into these movements for the social advancement of women. Working women need such aid, far more than working men have needed the aid of the higher classes. Working men have long been accustomed to meet together and to organise various associations, building societies, land societies and others. The women of the same class have no business experience whatever. The necessity they are under of working incessantly to obtain a bare subsistence, makes it the more difficult, too, for them to give the time and thought required in forming association for their mutual help and protection. Working men have nevertheless, long had the friendly advice, counsel and co-operation of many leading men of the professional and richer classes of society. In the discussion on the Report on Trade Societies above referred to, at the Social Science Congress held in Glasgow, in 1860, these gentlemen took part and spoke in the highest terms of the men's union and of friendly intercourse with their leaders. No alliance at present exists between women of different classes, such as that by which so much good has been accomplished among men. Working women are eagerly looking for it. They are ever ready to speak in terms of the warmest gratitude, of any one who shows an interest in their condition. Those of them who would most quickly resent any offers of charity in the sense of almsgiving, are the readiest to welcome kind sympathising intercourse and efforts to help them help themselves. Many charitable societies are maintained principally by ladies; many refuges and penitentiaries for fallen women; but comparatively little has yet been done by women of education and leisure, to encourage their poorer sisters to arouse themselves to a nobler and more independent existence, to prevent them from falling into crime or shame, rather than to wait, until, often from poverty, they fall, before offering sympathy and aid.

Might it not be possible to enlist helpers, who shall so guide this new movement of women, as to place it on a sound basis, avoiding alike the errors arising from excessive timidity, on one hand, or from passion and prejudice, on the other.

With an earnest appeal for such sympathy and co-operation, this paper must now be brought to a close.

'Factory Women,' *The Times*, 2 April 1875

Sir – will you kindly allow me space for a few words regarding the work of the Royal Commission whose appointment is announced this morning, so far as it relates to the laws affecting women?

One question to be considered by the Commission is, whether the operations of the existing Factories' and Workshops' Acts may properly be extended.

Without expressing any opinion as to the necessity or desirability of any such legislation for women, I am anxious to urge the extreme importance of obtaining the evidence of some of the women whose work is at present regulated by the Acts.

In the Report of Messrs Bridges and Holmes on Textile factories, published in 1873, it was stated that those gentlemen held five conferences with associations of employers and ten with associations of workmen, but it does not appear that they made any systematic efforts to ascertain the views of the women, although they stated that they had 'reason to believe the among the women there was in some cases positive opposition to the proposed legislative changes.'

Possibly at that time some difficulty existed in ascertaining the opinion of the women owing to the absence of associations among them. Now, however, that the women in several trades have successfully formed Unions, this difficulty no longer exists. The facilities for making known the views and wishes of large numbers have afforded one of the most important advantages of men's unions and women's unions may be similarly useful.

In the intelligence and energy displayed in the formation of their societies and also in the recent strike and successful negotiations with the employers at Dewsbury, working women have given proof of their power of organising and of putting forward their wishes in a sensible and moderate manner.

I trust that these considerations will not be overlooked by the Royal Commission now appointed and that a due proportion of the witnesses examined will be women employed in trades regulated by the Factories' and Workshops' Acts.

I am, sir, your obedient servant, Emma A Paterson, Hon. Sec. Women's Protective and Provident League, 31 Little Queen-Street, Holborn, 31 March.

Report of the Trades Union Congress, 1875, pp. 24–25

On the motion of Mr Shipton (of London) and seconded by Mr Kane (of Darlington), the following motion, coupled with a vote of thanks to Miss Simcox, was adopted:

> The members regard with much satisfaction the developments the first helping and self-relying trades-union movement among women

employed in the various industries, and pledge themselves to assist in promoting it in their respective localities.

Before the resolution was passed, Mrs Paterson gave a brief account of the progress of the women's trade union formed in London and urged all members of the Congress in whose trade women are employed to forward the movement by assisting in convening meetings of women to consider the subject. She pointed out that whilst many women either did not marry and remained at their trades for many years, or returned to their trades after the death of their husbands, others who did not marry would be the better fitted to support the trade union principle of their husbands from having themselves had practical experiences of the benefits of union before their marriage.

'Introduction,' *Women's Union Journal*, February 1876, p. 1

The work of establishing Protective and Benefit Societies among women employed in various industries, commenced by the Women's Protective and Provident League in July 1874, has met with considerable response from the women on whose behalf it was undertaken and may therefore be considered to have justified its initiation and continuance.

The Societies already formed under the auspices of the League are making good progress and others are about to be established.

As the movement extends, the want is increasingly felt of some means of periodically recording its progress, of facilitating intercommunication between persons interested in it and especially of collecting and diffusing information about the condition of the different trades engaged in by women.

It is hoped that this want may be met by the monthly publication of a journal mainly devoted to the purposes indicated, although admitting, when practicable, information relating to other interests of working women.

The commencement here made is a very humble one, but it is confidently believed that the numerous friends of the League will readily assist in developing both the dimensions and circulation of the Journal.

Any suggestions with this view, also letters, articles or reports, for publication in future numbers would be gratefully received by the Editor, at the Office of the League, 31, Little Queen-Street, Holborn.

'Every Trade…,' *Women's Union Journal*, March 1876, p. 7

EVERY TRADE in which WOMEN are Engaged should have its PROTECTIVE AND BENEFIT UNION.

The objects of such societies are:

1. To protect the trade interests of the members by endeavouring, where necessary, to prevent the undue depression of wages and to equalise the house of work.
2. To provide a fund from which members may obtain allowance weekly in sickness or when out of employment.
3. To arrange for the registration of employment notice, so that trouble in searching for work may be avoided, and to collect useful trade information.
4. To promote arbitration in cases of dispute between Employers and Employed.

The members of each Union arrange the rates of payment and other Rules at their general meetings. In some of the Societies, the subscription is 2d or 3d per week, the entrance fee 1s or 2s and the allowance in sickness or non-employment 5s per week, for from one to eight weeks during the year.

The business of each society is conducted by a Committee of the members, subject to approval of quarterly meetings of members.

THE WOMEN'S PROTECTIVE AND PROVIDENT LEAGUE affords advice and information as to the formation of unions, provides places for holding Trade Meetings and Conferences, the temporary use of the Office and the personal assistance of Provisional Honorary Secretaries and assists in defraying the preliminary expenses of organisation.

A list of the Societies now Established in London is given ay page 8. Enquiries may be address to the Hon. Sec. of the League, MRS PATERSON, at the Office, 31, Little Queen-Street, Holborn.

'Women's Union Movement in the North,' *Women's Union Journal*, May 1876, pp. 17–18

The meetings held on 1st and 2nd May are reported as fully as space will permit in this number of the Journal, but as they are of much interest in showing the progress of the Union movement among women, a few remarks about them may not be considered superfluous. The facts that the Meeting at Sheffield was under the auspices of so important a body as the Sheffield Trades' Council and that the President and several Members of the Council took part in it, are very encouraging. We have more than once heard a fear expressed that the women's unions might be supposed to be antagonistic to the unions of men. In proof that they are not so regarded by working men, it is satisfactory to be able to point to help such as that now alluded to; also to that of the Bookbinders, Upholsters and other men's societies in London, and to the cordial reception given to women's delegates at the Trades' Congress in Glasgow last year.

The meeting in Manchester was most enthusiastic and interesting. The unanimity of opinion among the large number of sewing machine workers present as to the need of a Protective Union, and the sympathy expressed when any statement of bad payment was given, showed that there must be good foundation for the complaints made in the correspondence reprinted in this Journal last month. It was sad to hear one of the workers, a young girl who spoke with much earnestness and good sense, relate that when she ventured to remonstrate with her employer about some fresh reduction of payment she was told that if she was not satisfied she had better take to an immoral course of life; and to learn from another, a widow, that in the busiest time her earnings were only 13s a week, out of which sum she was obliged to pay 4s 6d to have her children minded while she was away from home. One cannot but think that much of the deep degradation into which some women drift may be caused by inadequate wages and that the ladies who work in 'Woman's Mission to the fallen,' and other similar Societies would do well to consider this. Public sympathy and help were very readily given to the Agricultural Labourers, when the facts of their depressed condition became widely known, and surely women who determine to demand for their work payment on which, at least, they can decently support themselves, need not fear that their efforts will be disregarded and unaided.

'Combination of Sheffield Workwomen,' *Women's Union Journal*, May 1876, pp. 18–19

[...] The Chairman, after briefly stating the object of the meeting, introduced Mrs Paterson, who said she had felt for some years that union was strongly needed amongst women. Working men had been enabled by means of union to get their wages raised, and they had also obtained shorter hours of labour, as well as other advantages, by combination. The price of the necessaries of life had risen considerably within recent years, and working men had required, and got increased remuneration to meet that advance in prices, but she had not found any corresponding increase in the wages of working women; in fact, in many cases there had been a decrease in the rate paid to females, whose wages had been lowered rather than raised. She did not see any hope of permanent improvement without union, such as that adopted by working men. There were four principal objects to be gained by union amongst working women. The first related to higher wages. She did not urge the necessity of union with the smallest idea of promoting strikes, but it seemed to her that without union there was not a proper means of promoting a peaceful settlement of difficulties, such as by arbitration. (Hear, hear.) Frequent reductions had been made in the remuneration paid to females, and any one knowing anything at all about the question must be aware that in most cases the earnings of women were not sufficient to support them respectably. That such should be the case was a disgrace to society. (Hear, hear.)

Many of the workwomen of London were half-starved and half-clothed, looking like outcasts, who had committed some crime, rather than honest hard working people; but the fact was that women living by vice were far better off so far as material comfort went, than those who obtained their livelihood by industry. She did not see that it was any advantage to society for women to go on making these experiments as to how little they could live upon. (Laughter.) It was important that they should foster a spirit of independence amongst their own sex, who really ought not to be thankful for the smallest possible amount of wages. They did not wish to be antagonistic to the employers, but without union they could do very little, for if one master were willing to give a higher rate of wages he could not do so, because another employer, getting people to work for less wages, would be able to undersell him. It had been affirmed that women should be paid less wages than men because their wants were fewer than those of a man. (Laughter.) She had failed to make that discovery, for she found that she needed food, and clothes, and housing just as much as a man did. (Laughter.)

Women had not perhaps quite so many little extravagances as man – they did not go in for so much beer and tobacco – (laughter) – but they ought not to suffer on that account; they ought rather to be rewarded for their self-control (Hear, hear and laughter.) It was foolish of those who worked in tolerably well-paid trades to imagine that union was unnecessary, because even if those trades were paying good wages now, that was all the more reason why they should form a union, and endeavour to keep up the rate of wages. The speaker went on to show that union had caused a great saving in the rates, that it was the means of bringing about more equal and moderate hours of labour and that it also afforded an opportunity of getting information as to where work could be obtained. She then spoke of the success of several unions of working women in the metropolis.

'Projected Union of Manchester Sewing Machine Workers,'
***Women's Union Journal*, May 1876, pp. 19–21**

[...] Mrs Paterson, who began by expressing a hope that the energy displayed by the meeting would be directed to the formation of a union (applause), said she had read with the greatest interest some letters which had recently appeared in the Manchester Guardian touching the position of sewing machine workers. Such a union as she was now advocating, had been formed in London but if the London machinists complained of the low rates of payment, they were informed that the work could be done in Manchester for less money than they required. The letter signed 'A Sewing Machine Girl' ought to be read far and wide. They in London had reprinted it, and every rich and idle lady who thought that women were well cared for should read it to see what some of her sex had to contend with (applause). It was impossible for them to live upon 8s or 10s a week in the present day, and they ought not to be dependent on their fathers and brothers. Instead of so much money being given away in charity and poor rates to women, let the employers pay them fair wages. ('Hear, hear,' and applause.) She suggested that the meeting should appoint a committee to organise the union. (Hear, hear.) She was sure that the League of which she was the honorary secretary would be glad to pay for the use of some room in Manchester as an office once or twice weekly. (Applause.) Mrs Paterson then gave some information of the operations of the League which she represented, and of the advantages which had arisen in London from the Unions, which the League had formed among Women in the Bookbinding, Upholstery, Shirt and Collar Making and other trades.

The Chairman having asked for statements of personal experience, considerable excitement ensued. A deafening buzz of conversation arose, in the midst of which occasional peals of laughter could be heard; and several times the whole meeting rose like one woman to look at volunteer speakers. The Chairman (shouting): Ladies, do be quiet. I never presided over so many speakers before. – Several girls eventually stated what wages they obtained on the average, and it appeared that while a few could earn from 20s to 30s a week, others could only obtain 5s.

[...]

The above report is mainly taken from the 'Manchester Guardian' of May 3rd and the 'Manchester Examiner' of May 4th, but the reporters having left before the close of the meeting a few private notes may be added.

A great deal of excitement was caused by the presence of an employer or rather by his action in bringing with him four of his workwomen who, one after another, assured the meeting that they could earn from 25s to 30s per week. Most of the workers present seemed to regard these prices as fabulous and instead of there being no speakers from the body of the meeting as it was at first feared would be the case, the platform was soon crowded with women eager to relate their own widely different experience. Of course, we must put aside an insinuation made that the women who said they were so well off had been bribed to overstate their earnings, but in any case it was evident that the badly paid workers formed an overwhelming majority. A forewoman who had been many years in the trade said that she had been grieved to see the prices going lower and lower and had often wished that a Society such as that now proposed could be formed. Her own employer was a just, good man but there were many others who would take every advantage of the present defenceless position of the girls. Another lady stated that the average earnings in the busiest season now were 7s per week than they were two years ago. Another said that the system of fines and deductions had become most oppressive. Frequently work of the better class was given to girls who had not been long enough at the trade to do it properly and then heavy deductions were made from their wages for spoiling the work although, notwithstanding this, the bad work was often palmed off upon the public at the usual prices...

Several meetings of the Committee and a General Meeting of the Manchester Machine Workers Society have been held since May 1st. We are glad to learn that 230 names have already been enrolled. Further information regarding the progress of the Society will be given in our next number.

'Different Conditions of the Work of Men and Women,' *Women's Union Journal*, June 1876, p. 28

It has been suggested by a friend of the League, that in order to avoid all appearance of antagonism, the unions of women formed in trade in which men are also engaged should invite men to become members. We should be glad to receive any expressions of opinion about this suggestion, but since it is one of the most essential elements of effective organisation that there should be some kind of similarity between the rates of wages and other conditions of the work of the members, it seems scarcely likely that men would welcome the proposal. The wages of men are, as a rule, at least three times as much as those of women, and their power of working overtime when they wish to do so is not restrained by law. We doubt whether men would work as such a rate as that paid to women who scour files of which we give particulars; or whether they would like to have such close scrutiny about their work as an extract which we give from the latest Report of the Factory and Workshop Inspectors shows that women are subject to.

'Union in Holidays,' *Women's Union Journal*, August 1876, pp. 41–42

We have, this month, but little to record that is immediately connected with the work of the Women's Trade Unions. No meetings of any importance have been held since that in Manchester on July 18, of which we give a full report. The intensely hot weather of the past few weeks has aroused a general longing for the cool shade of country lanes and forests and the breezes of the sea. Those who have been able to indulge the longing have done so, and those who have been compelled to put it aside have probably limited their work as much as possible, to that of bare necessity.

We know that many of our friends belonging to the Women's Unions have sighed in vain for a little rest and change of air during the hot August days. Some of their fellow workers have been more fortunate, either in having 'country cousins' to go and stay with, or in having had constant work so as to have been able to save sufficient money for the expenses of an independent holiday. The dull time for business, when a holiday can be conveniently taken, comes of course to most working women at the close of the London season. Then, however, there is a general rush of all classes out of town, and the cost of a seaside lodging is much higher than it is earlier in the year. The expense of a short stay by the sea is consequently heavier than many women who support themselves by their work are able to incur. The excellent article in our last number by 'C.E.W.' urges women to consider the enormous advantages to be gained by co-operation of various kinds. The success of the Saturday afternoon excursions already organised by the Unions seems to us to indicate that co-operation in this direction might be very usefully extended to longer summer holidays. By putting together their small savings in a special fund for the purpose – a number of women might take a house in some seaside place, and the payments which they would now have to make for the rent of bedrooms would in a few weeks cover the year's rent of the whole house. There might be a general sitting room and arrangements for taking meals together. We have not space to go into details of the mode of working or to explain all the advantages of the plan, but we strongly advise our friends to consider whether they might not, next summer, make a small beginning. There is no reason why such a commencement should not grow until a Women's Co-operative Lodging House had been established in every popular resort. We should be glad to receive correspondence on the subject, or, if the suggestion seemed to be favourably received, to hold a meeting to discuss it.

'Trades Union Congress,' *Women's Union Journal*, October 1876, pp. 60–61

Mrs Paterson said that not only did she disagree with the resolution moved by Mr Allen but she thought that even the extension of the Factory Act as recommended by the Royal Commissioners would be a mistake so far as women were concerned. The new legislation proposed was spoken of in the Royal Commissioners Report as 'the general enforcing for the first time in 100,000 workshops of what is distinctly known as the factory system.' She believed that any attempt to enforce a hard and fast line, such as that work should be carried on only between certain hours 6 am and 6 pm, or 7 am and 7 pm – in all the widely differing trades carried on in the workshops throughout the country could not fail to lead to many objectionable and oppressive results to the women employed. Legislation which might be practicable in factories where large numbers of workers were employed and machinery was used was not equally applicable to smaller industries.

It was true that the Royal Commissioners proposed that several modifications should be granted, provided women in no cases worked away from home later than 9 pm but it seemed to be playing with the law to impose fresh restrictions with one hand and lay on modifications to meet them with the other hand. She was strongly in favour of the legal regulation of children's work and also of sanitary inspection for workplaces, but she thought that the time had come when no fresh legislation should be sought for in the work of women, even if the existing legislation were allowed to continue. Now that women were beginning to show a disposition to protect themselves against excessive hours of work and other evils by combination (the only effective protection) – as men had done, it would tend to discourage their efforts to impose their legal restrictions classing them with and treating them as children. It was well also to consider how the Royal Commissioners proposed to enforce this wide extension of the law if carried.

They seemed to see that an increase in the number of inspectors would not meet the enormous accession of work; as Mr Mundella had said to his evidence an army of inspectors should be assisted by local officers among others the Constabulary, or in plainer language the police. Before any Bill was brough forward in Parliament embodying such a recommendation would it not be well to consider whether it might not be highly distasteful to women that the police should have the power of entering a workshop and turning them out at a certain time whether they were working or not, for it was proposed that mere presence in workshops should be held as evidence of employment.

The Factory Inspectors showed by their own printed reports that the present system of inspection was most inquisitorial; for instance in the report of last October an inspector had related triumphantly as though he had done a most meritorious action how he had chased a work girl into a bed room which had entered *thinking it might be a workshop*. Surely if there must be such inspection as that the inspectors ought to be women not men. The Congress should be more certain than they now were whether women desire the extension of this legislation before pressing Government for it. They had just been discussing the Smoke Nuisance Act and the hardships it inflicted on journeyman bakers: when men continually called for this restriction on women's work one could not help wondering what they would think if women were to hold a Congress and pass a Resolution repaying that the Smoke Nuisance Act might be applied to all tobacco Smokers.

No doubt men had the kindest and most benevolent intention in thus desiring to shorten women's working hours by law and women might have the same kind of feeling in wishing to see the quantity of smoke emitted by some gentlemen limited for the good of their health (possibly, though not without some little desire for their comfort as well) but gentlemen might not approve of the means taken to carry out the benevolent intention. There were certain regulations in the Factory Acts as to the rooms in a factory where a woman might or might not eat her dinner but one was inclined to ask was it not more important to know that women had dinners to eat? Any one acquainted with the miserable payments in many women's trades must know that numbers had not a dinner at least a proper dinner to eat and probably they never would have until by uniting together they could command a better price for their work. The strongest objections of all however to this contemplated extension of legislation was that if it were carried out work would be driven more and more into the houses of the workers where it could be carried out without interference until midnight or later, frequently in a close room used for sleeping and living and consequently not so healthy as the workshop much of the evidence given before the Royal Commission proved that this had been the tendency of the present Workshop Acts.

Not only was the home work injurious to health but by it more than by anything else the rate of wages in a trade was reduced, since by it the workers were placed more completely at the mercy of employers. Instead of imposing new legislation on women it might perhaps be well to give men a turn now. The Factory Inspectors said in their reports that in the Black Country men were to be found lounging in public houses eating beef steaks and training dogs. Why should not such men's doings be inspected? An inspector might visit all the public houses taking with him a policeman and drive the men to work. She did say that she would think such action desirable, neither probably would the men – but it would be new and interesting experiment in legislation as to work of novelties in that line were wanted.

'The Church and Trades Unions,' *Women's Union Journal*, December 1876, pp. 74–76

Mrs Paterson, honorary secretary of the Women's Protective and Provident League, read a paper on 'The Organisation of Women's Labour,' which was very favourably received. In this, she stated that if the clergy were to decide that they could consistently with their duties as teachers of the Christian religion countenance and encourage trades unions, as the surest and soundest means of raising the social condition of the working classes, they would find ample scope for their labours among two sets of workers who are without political power and consequently comparatively neglected, and whose social position urgently demands improvement – namely, the agricultural labourer and working women. The condition of working women especially is most depressed, as the clergy must know from their visits. While the prices of food, fuel and clothing have risen considerably during the past few years, the wages of women have remained stationary, or gone lower, so that fifteen shilling a week is now considered high wages for a woman.

The physical and moral evils resulting cannot be overestimated. Women living at a long distance from their work, as they must often do in large cities, cannot afford to ride in bad weather, or to have boots and clothing strong enough to keep out the cold and wet, and when dinner-hour comes they have to content themselves with two-penny worth of wholesome pudding or a red herring. From such sources of weakness many of them suffer from diseases which weaken them for life, or kill them after a weeks' suffering in the hospital or workhouse. The burden, two, upon the poor rates caused by the low payment of women's work is also a serious evil, for it is notorious that a very large proportion of those in the receipt of outdoor relief are women. Because working women wore flowers, ribbons and lace, and other cheap finery, which could be had for the merest trifle, people thought their wages were good, but these little luxuries, which are in most cases the only solace of the poor women, were cheaper than the tobacco of which no one would like to deprive the poor man if it was a comfort to him.

The only practical and permanent remedy for these evils is to be found in trade combination. Charitable efforts are desultory, transient and ineffectual and are injurious as impairing self-reliance. Many employers wish to act justly, but others less conscientious take advantage of the defenceless and helpless condition of the women workers, undersell the better class of employers and bring down the trade to its lowest level. With organisation women workers could not only help themselves, but sympathising outsiders could help them as they helped the agricultural labourers, but without organisation they were perfectly powerless. The clergy could help women's trades' unions in various ways. They could appeal to the consciences of those women who take work at an unfairly low rate of remuneration merely to provide themselves with pocket money, while they are supported by their relatives, to the cruel wronging of poorer women, who live only by labour, and whose very bread is thus taken out of their mouths. The teachers of the religion of Christ should wage war against all selfishness, and especially such selfishness as this.

Almsgiving and charitable gifts, as a rule, are not real helps, but rather hindrances to the poor. Women workers want outside help in the organisation of their unions. It is sometimes said that they can act as men acted, and dispense with such outside help but we must take into account certain important differences in the two cases. First, we must remember that the employment of women in trade to the extent it now exists is of comparatively modern growth. From various causes the number of wage-earning women has rapidly increased and is still increasing, as the Census returns show. Modern invention has to a great extent transferred needlework from the isolated worker in her garret to the worker of a sewing machine in a large workshop, or even in a factory where the machines are driven by steam. Men when they commenced their unions had had their trade handed down to them from time immemorial; they had their traditions about it; women are in quite a different position; brought together, comparatively new to the changed condition of things and bewildered by it. Their inadequate payment, too, obliges them to strain every nerve to their work, so that little time is left them to think of anything beyond. Then, again, they have not had the opportunity of meeting together out of the workshop that men have had. They have not frequented public houses, and one cannot wish them to do so. Men have had the public house as a meeting place, and frequently the landlord has given no inconsiderable help in the work of their unions by taking charge of the out-of-work book. He has not been a disinterested friend, of course, but has undoubtedly been very useful. The clergy could further help in giving the use of the schoolroom for women's trades' meetings, and other outsiders might teach women a little of business methods of which they are deplorably ignorant, and from their ignorance of which they have to suffer so much.

Many well-meaning people tell the poor workers to be provident and to save, but refuse to have anything to do with any combination respecting wages for work. This is to mock the poor by telling them to save out of wages which will not keep them, and not to countenance them in securing a fair price for their labour and a fair price for their labour and a fair share of the profits of their employer. It is the old heartless story to say to the poor,

> Only save, and be provident, even take alms to enable you to do it, but don't ask a fair price for your labour – don't inquire whether too large a share of the profits of your work goes into the employer's pocket, or whether the public pay a fair price for what you produce.

It is simply mockery to tell people with 5s or 7s a week that they should save. Many people of the richer classes seem to think that the 'lower orders,' as they call the poor, are to be paid in any form but that which will give them a sense of dignity and responsibility and prevent their being degraded and humiliating by almsgiving. One objection frequently raised is, that women's unions can never stand, because women look upon their work as being only temporary; that they look forward to being married, and to being taken away from the necessity of earning money. There are even people who will tell you that it would not be well to make their work too comfortable, or they would not get married. One answer to this is, that numbers of women find that they are obliged to return to work after marriage, or when they are left widows. Then, too, it should be impressed upon women that in becoming careless as to the condition of their trades because they hoped soon to get married and leave the work, they were wronging those sister workers who might be obliged to work for a livelihood during the whole of their lives. At the close of her paper, Mrs Paterson read some extracts from correspondence respecting the Honiton lace workers, which bore strong evidence of the said condition in which they were placed from lowness of wages.

'The Seamers and Stitchers Society and Menders Society, Leicester,' *Women's Union Journal*, February 1877, pp. 3–4

Mrs Paterson after speaking of the advantages of Trades Unions generally and of the great improvement brought about by Union in the position of agricultural labourers gave an account of the establishment and progress of the Women's Trade Unions in London; she also referred to the benefits already derived from the Seamers' and Stitchers Union and congratulated the members on the admirable course adopted for obtaining an advance of payment. The Union having been organised, a Board of Arbitration was formed and the advance was agreed to and brough about quite peaceably. Probably many of the employers did not grudge the advance at all: they knew it to be just but could not have given it had not the general demand been made through the Unions. It appeared from handbills issued by the Committee to the members that a further advance would be sought at some future and more prosperous time, since the payment was still far from adequate.

The leaders of the Union showed wisdom and moderation in waiting until trade became better before seeking a further advance. They could not be accused of rashness or of a desire to extort pieces which the trade would not bear. And here one most important use of a Union showed itself. Its leaders could watch the trade and could collect and use information about it which no individuals could very well gain or could use if they did gain it – so as to know whether the members would be justified in asking for an advance. Until within the past three or four years working women had not, except in very few cases, united to improve their position and, of course, people were justified in supposing that 8s or 10s was quite sufficient for women to live comfortably upon so long as they themselves said nothing to the contrary. They had been far too ready to accept things as they were, without considering what they could do towards improvement and they had also been too much inclined to look to others to bring about changes which could alone be accomplished by themselves.

With regard to the trade in which they were engaged, the women of Leicester might be thankful that it could not be so much affected by fashion as some other women's trades were. At present, efforts to form Women's Unions in trade where there were frequent changes of fashion had been less successful than in other cases. The workers were less settled and consequently not so ready to attempt organisation. One would suppose there could not be many changes in the hosiery trade, at all events in stockings. It was true that a short time age a rage for broad stripes or narrow stripes, horizontal or perpendicular stripes upon stockings seemed to have broken out among fashionable ladies; that would alter the patterns for weaving but the shape at least could not be altered, so that the seaming and stitching and mending need not be interrupted. Rich women had yet to learn how seriously the position of their working sisters was often affected by sudden changes of fashion; perhaps if they thoroughly realised this they would become less fickle about their dress. Mrs Paterson expressed a hope that as the Annual Trades Congress was this year (in September) to be held in Leicester, two or three members of the Seamers Society and of the Menders' Society would be appointed as delegates to the Congress. In 1875, two women appeared as Delegates; in 1876, there were three and it was to be hoped that in 1877 the number would still be further increased.

'Proposed Union of French Workwomen,' *Women's Union Journal*, August 1877, pp. 49–50

A member of the League Committee, Miss CE Williams, has kindly sent us the following very interesting account of her recent visits in Paris, to promoters of the French workwomen's League. Mdlle. Raoult is one of the women who took part in the Labour Congress held in Paris last October. Her speeches were the most able descriptions of the wants and difficulties of French workwomen and those who remember reading the reports in the English papers will be especially glad to hear of her again. Mrs Heatherley (another member of our League Committee) who visited Mdlle. Raoult four months ago, gives a similar account to that which we now publish – respecting the proposed League. She also explains that to be legally constituted, in France, the League must be a commercial society, and that 30 shareholders are required to form it. The shares being fifty francs (£2) each, a sum which few working women can afford, one difficulty is to find shareholders. Three or four English friends have already taken shares but the necessary number is not yet made up. It is proposed that the Commercial element of the League, when the latter is formed, should be the sale of articles (artificial flowers, underlinen, etc.) made in Co-operative workrooms.

Readers of the Journal may be interested to hear of the visits paid lately by a member of the League to two representatives of the French League which is to be. Unluckily it does not yet exist. The lady who is doing all she can to help on every movement for the benefit of women, and the eloquent working woman, Mddle. Raoult, who is so able and willing to promote the interests of her working sisters are both discouraged by the difficulties in their way in France, at present. Government is jealous of any attempt to get up meetings. While Political feeling runs so high it is very natural that what is uppermost in men's minds creeps even into their plans for social reforms. Thus the elaborate rules that have been framed for the French League might be intended as the Constitution of a small republic.

In England, the few men and women of different classes of society who tried to form the Women's Protective and Provident League regarded themselves, as they still do, as merely useful still the importance of Unions had been established among working women. Their object was to collect together women working in various trades in London in order to lay before them the advantages of uniting for protective and provident purposes and after giving them some assistance in forming their societies to encourage them to take their affairs in their own hands, as they have successfully done. In France, the meetings to promote the League have been attended with the greatest difficulty. No women of leisure and wealth have been induced to give their countenance to the movement. On the contrary, ladies ready enough to aid charitable efforts have been so suspicious of this attempt to rouse women to help themselves that they have actually taken away their custom from the noble Sempstress, Miss Raoult, who has helped so much by her eloquent speeches and disinterested efforts. The working men, on the other hand, who have taken an interest in the movement have done it at their peril. Government has been alarmed by the somewhat ambitious programme set forth by the League, of the Social revolution to be expected from 'Ameliorating the condition of Women.'

The police have been sent to the meetings and the working men who were present at the last of these, are actually at this time under sentence to pay fines which they cannot afford, or to go to prison. Meanwhile the sempstress is also an object of suspicion to the authorities and the police are set upon her track to discover if possible something treasonable or wicked in her conduct. What would members of the English League say to receiving a visit from a detective who under the pretence of a desire to join the new Society wished to unravel the supposed conspiracy? Yet this had happened to the lady above referred to and her husband. None of these discouragements quench the hopes of Mdlle. Raoult, who looks forward to better times for the completion of the list of shareholders in the League and to its further development. In her little room at the top of one of the high houses near the Seine, let to the working classes, her bright looking old mother and herself are busily working for their livelihood, ready when any opportunity offers to lend a helping hand to the good cause. Mdlle. Raoult is cheered by visits from those who wish well to it and expressed herself very sensible of the freemasonry that exists between people having the same objects in view however, widely 'Continents or seas may separate them.'

The advantages which are to be expected from the 'amelioration of the condition of working-women' are not overstated in the elaborate programme of the French League. It *will* be a great social revolution when a fair share of education is extended to them, when they are instructed in all that concerns their health, when they are made acquainted with their rights and duties, and above all when Union for protective and provident purposes has made them stronger and more independent. But as things are now at Paris there is a painful contrast between this brilliant future and the gloomy present. It would seem necessary to begin the movement from its more practical side as we have done in England, by the gradual establishment of Unions, leaving these great results to follow as they inevitably will. We can do little for those two noble women except by freely communicating our experiences to them, and by showing our sympathy in every possible manner.

'Trades Union Congress,' *Women's Union Journal*, October 1877, p. 65

At the Tenth Annual Trades' Union Congress held in Leicester from the 17th to the 22nd of September, one hundred and twelve trade societies and Trades Councils were represented by one hundred and forty delegates. Amongst these, the 'Society of Seamers and Stitchers' (women) in the hosiery trade of Leicester and Leicestershire, was represented by Mrs Mason; The 'Society of Women Employed in Bookbinding' and the 'Society of Upholsteresses' London, by Mrs Paterson; the 'Society of Shirt, Collar and Underlinen Makers' London, by Mrs Brown. We now give a full report of a Conference held during the Congress week, on the subject of Women's Trade Unions, at which Mr Thos. Brassey MP presided; also of the long discussion which took place in the Congress on Factory and Workshop Legislation. These reports occupy so much space that all account of the other proceedings of the Congress must stand over until next month. The views expressed by the women delegates on the question of workshop legislation have received considerable attention from the Press this year – leading articles upon them having appeared in the Daily News, Pall Mall Gazette, Echo, Dispatch, Queen and Figaro. The members of the Congress listened very patiently to views quite opposed to those of the majority present; only three gentlemen spoke in support of the views referred to, but all the speakers were at least so good as to argue the question, instead of making silly puns or howling down the subject as gentlemen in 'another place' sometimes do when the interests of women are being discussed.

'Trades Union Congress,' *Women's Union Journal*, October 1877, pp. 70–71

Mrs Paterson (London) resumed the discussion on this question. She said that Factory and Workshop legislation was assuming a different aspect to that which it formerly bore. It was becoming more and more exceptional legislation for women, whereas the first Factory acts applied to men and women alike. They might perhaps now leave children to the care of School Boards and dispense with the legal regulation of working hours altogether, but even if continued for children, women did protest against legislation for them. She was somewhat startled the preceding day to hear three delegates declare that when they got this bill passed, they would next try to get a bill to remove women from certain branches of work (agriculture and chain making) altogether. When Mr and Mrs Fawcett some time again had said that Trade Union men wished to turn women out of work, great indignation had been expressed and a strict denial given to the charge.

She (Mrs Paterson) had been glad to fully accept the denial and she hoped the charge was not going to turn out to be true after all. She asked them to help women by combination to increase their wages, and not to attempt to drive them from work altogether. There was not sufficient domestic work to employ all women, especially as that work was being continually decreased by the aid of domestic machinery. No doubt some women were engaged in unsuitable occupations, but let them remove them from these objectionable sphere of labour by persuasion and by the force of public opinion, as had already been done to a large extent. As to chain making, she felt bound to say that having visited several of the workshops where it was carried on, it had appeared to her that the heat of the fires was not greater than that of many kitchen fires prepared for roasting, near which cooks had to stand. As to government inspection to prevent over work she had no faith in it, and members of the Societies she represented had often stated at their meetings, how ineffectual such inspection was. She considered that the Reports of the Factory inspectors recently published, were calculated to mislead people as to the position of working women. It had there been stated that since the application of the Factory and Workshops Act to London industries 'a substantial addition has been made to the rates of wages and especially so the wages to those classes who come under the protection of those Acts, namely women, young persons and children".

The Report went on to say that this is a point which is within the experience and can be confirmed *by almost every employer in London*. Of course, employers liked to prove that they paid high wages; probably they had shown the inspectors their wages books but had not said how many hours work each entry represented. Such entries not uncommonly represented work taken home and done up to a late hour at night as well as that done in the workshop. Why did the inspectors not go to the workers sometimes for their information? They would hear a very different tale then. When the statement just quoted was read out at a meeting of London workwomen there was an indignant outcry from all present that it was not true. In all the different shops they had worked in they heard of no 'substantial addition' such as the inspectors had discovered. It was as injurious to the interests of women to have it represented to the public that there has been a 'large increase in the remuneration which women as a class have received,' as it was degrading that they should be hunted about by Factory inspectors. She would not move any amendment but would again ask the Congress to try to look at this question of legislation from the women's point of view.

Report of the Trades Union Congress, 1877, pp. 17–18

Mrs Paterson (London) said that the societies of women which she represented felt that further legislation [The Factory and Workshops Acts] was necessary on this subject. They could not allow the exceptional legislation for women to be passed over without a protest against it. As regarded chain making, the fires used for the purposes of the work were not hotter than ordinary fires, and the work she considered was not too hard for the females employed at it in the Black Country. Women should be allowed to earn their own living without undue restrictions. To remedy many of the evils now existing in connection with female labour, persuasion instead of legislation might be used with good results. It was a degrading thing for a woman to be hunted about by a factory inspector. (Hear, hear.)

Miss Brown (London) followed in the same line. She contended that exceptional legislation for women was bad and degrading in its effects. She thought that on the principles laid down by trade unionists and acted on by them, legislation affecting wages or hours – which indirectly affected wages – was inexpedient. They felt that women must know what was best, as they must feel where the shoe pinches. At the same time, she did not think that trade unionists meant to be unjust; they acted as they did with the best intentions, and thinking, no doubt, that the plan of exceptional legislation which they advocated was the simplest way to remedy the evil. They should remember, however, that –

Evil is wrought by ward of thought
As well as want of heart.
(...)

Mr Broadhurst (London) was astonished to hear Mrs Paterson question, and even deny, the accuracy of the reports of Her Majesty's Inspectors, than whom he did not know a more able, accurate and conscientious set of gentlemen. For himself, he placed the most implicit confidence in their reports and knew from personal experience that they were correct. They knew it was very natural for ladies to be impatient of restraint at any time (laughter) – and therefore they might imagine the uneasiness which would be created when the law of the nation prescribed rules and regulations. It was a well-known fact that women had been employed in occupations totally unfitted for them, and they were unable to do anything to help themselves unless someone stretched out a helping hand to them.

No doubt they might form unions, but their wages and their ever-changing positions in life rendered them unable to do any effective work towards the emancipation of their class from degrading labour. Much good had been done by Mrs Paterson, and other ladies, in forming and maintaining unions, but they would never be able to lift woman to her proper sphere unless they had some restrictions put upon the greed of those who would work their mothers or sisters like dogs or slaves for the sake of gain. (Applause.) There was another phase of it: they had the future of their country and children to consider, and it was their duty as men and husbands to use their utmost efforts to bring about a condition of things where their wives should be in their proper sphere at home, seeing after their house and family, instead of being dragged into the competition for livelihood against the great and strong men of the world.

'French Workwomen's League,' *Women's Union Journal*, December 1877, p. 83

We have several times referred to the difficulties by which working women in France are met, in efforts to improve their industrial position. A further account of these difficulties, as experienced not only by the working women but also by the men who have been trying to help them to form trade Unions – is given in a report by Mr Hodgson Pratt contained in the following letter. We are glad to announce that in response to the appeal for the fund for paying the fines so arbitrarily inflicted, Mr Hodgson Pratt has received the following contributions:

	£	s	d
GM Hicks, Esq.	2	2	0
Miss C Williams	1	1	0
FAA Rowland, Esq.	1	1	0
Miss Julia Macfarren	3	0	0
Miss Muller	3	0	0
Mrs SW Browne	1	1	0
Miss Browne	1	1	0
Hodgson Pratt, Esq.	1	1	0
Mrs Heatherley		5	0

The above amounts have been remitted to Paris by Mr Pratt and have been gratefully acknowledged by a French newspaper, Le Bien Public, in a paragraph giving a short account of the objects and work of the Women's Unions in England. Other contributions are promised and will be acknowledged in this Journal.

Emma Paterson, 'Working Women's Unions,' *The Times*, 3 December 1877

Miss Emma Paterson, Hon. Secretary of the Women's Protective and Provident League, writes to us from the offices of the League, 31, Little Queen-Street, Holborn –At a meeting of the Committee of the Women's Protective and Provident League, held last week, Mr Hodgson Pratt gave a very interesting report of an effort recently made to establish a similar association in the French capital. The miserable pittances earned by women in various trades in Paris, and the consequent moral and physical evils, has attracted the attention of several persons, and they accordingly put themselves in communication with the London Society, which occupies itself with the organisation of women's union. Those who took up this question in Paris represented not only the middle class of society, but the workers also. It was accordingly determined to hold a meeting for the organisation of a league on precisely the same footing as the one established in London.

It being impossible, however, to obtain authority for a public meeting in our sense of the word, it was decided to hold what is termed in France a 'private' meeting – i.e., one to which admission could be obtained only by special invitation. Just as this moment the visit of members of the Municipal Council, with M Bonnet-Duverdier, their President, was made to London, and their visit and the report made on their return seem to have given umbrage to the French Government. Finding that M Bonnet-Duverdier had been asked to preside at the proposed women's meeting and to describe what we had done in London, it was determined to stop the proceedings. A police officer called upon the lady who was issuing the invitations for the meeting, asked to see one of the letters, and, after a little conversation, requested the favour of a glass of water. The lady having left the room to fetch it, the officer at once searched for the rest of the invitations, found them and carried them off. These letters were printed forms with blanks left for the names of the persons to be invited; but the officer reported that they were being issued wholesale without any names.

This was made the ground of proceedings before a magistrate against the president, two vice-presidents and the secretary of the new society, and a fine of £56 was imposed. If this fine is not wholly paid up within a few weeks from this time, imprisonment will follow. None of these gentlemen are persons of independent means, and Mr Pratt reports that they are unable to meet the fines. Indeed, the President of the Women's League is already liable for £120 for fines incurred in his connexion with meetings of the same character. He is a well-known worker in the cause of social reform and is an engraver by profession. Of the others, one is a medical student, the second a bookseller, and the third a journalist. The workwomen themselves have raised £2 towards the payment of the first instalment, and efforts are being made by one or two ladies to raise a further sum.

It appears to the Committee of the English League that such an opportunity should not be lost of manifesting international sympathy and goodwill. This is especially a case where a very small amount of aid rendered on this side of the Channel to the working women of Paris and their courageous friends would do much good. It would strengthen the hands of those who are working in the excellent cause and show the authorities that attention has been called to the matter in England. The Liberals in France always hail the sympathy and example of 'monarchical' England in every effort they make on behalf of social and political progress, and they find that such reference to what we are doing always strengthens them in their daily struggles with the Government. Mr Hodgson Pratt authorises me to say that he will be glad to receive any contributions towards the payment of the fines. Communications should be addressed to him at 5, Redcliffe-square, South Kensington, W.

'Holidays,' *Women's Union Journal*, April 1878, pp. 17–18

The Committee of the League have several times had under consideration a plan suggested in this Journal some months ago for obtaining by co-operation the use of a house at the seaside. They have also twice brought the subject forward at Meetings of the Women's Unions, when entire approval of the plan was elicited, several of the members stating that the difficulty of finding a comfortable lodging at a moderate cost had often deterred them from seeking the much wished for enjoyment of a few days at the seaside.

Whether they desire it or not, most London workwomen are obliged to take two or three weeks' holidays in the summer or autumn season, when trade is slack, but it must not be forgotten that they are obliged to pay for their holidays themselves. Governesses, school teachers, clerks, some shop assistants; any persons engaged by the quarter or by the year, usually have holidays allowed them, and they have an advantage in this respect over the work who is paid by the day or by the week. The latter, when it suits the employer's convenience, is told that he or she may 'take a holiday' for two, three or more weeks, but no wages are then forthcoming. Sometimes it is to be feared, that this pleasant form of expression is but a grim satire on the way the time is spent. With those women – who may be numbered by thousands – whose work is so badly paid that they can gain only a bare subsistence, 'taking a holiday' may mean bitter privation. It is well for them if those holidays are given only in summer time. Frequently owing to fluctuations of trade, they are given in winter also, and then miserable indeed is the lot of those who have been unable to provide for such times. Yet we hear constantly hear it said that labour has no risks; that only the capitalist incurs risk.

This appears like a long digression from the subject, but it is intended to show how especially important it is that working women, even those of them who are best paid, should find economical means of obtaining in their summer holidays that change of air and of scene which is surely so much needed by those who spend the greater part of their lives in close and crowded workrooms, as by any other class. No doubt co-operation is the true solution for this as for many other more important questions. To take a house, however, and furnish it, being at the same time, somewhat in the dark as to the number who would use it, has hitherto appeared to be rather too formidable an undertaking for the League or for the Unions. The League Committee are exceedingly glad, therefore, to have been able to make a beginning in the direction indicated, which, whilst placing on them only a small share of the pecuniary responsibility will enable them to judge as to the probable success of a larger enterprise. Nine ladies who believe in the power of co-operation have, under the able leadership of Miss Orme, joined together in taking a house at Southend. Each shareholder is to pay £5 5s 0d per annum for the first three years, to cover rent and purchase of furniture; for this sum she will have at her disposal the whole house, accommodating five persons, for five weeks in the year. Ten shareholders were originally proposed and the League has been permitted to be the tenth of these. The Committee are therefore in a aposition to offer twenty-five members of the Unions very comfortable lodging accommodation for one week each. The terms and the dates offered are given on page 19.

'Employment of Women in Factories,' *The Times*, 11 April 1878

Sir – Lord Shaftesbury's burst of admiration in the debate last night at the 'close investigation' made by the Home Secretary in the preparation of the Factories and Workshops Bill, might have been somewhat modified had he known that the only adults whose work is interfered with by the Act had been refused a hearing. Mr Cross has patiently listened this Session to several deputations of employers and from Men's Trade Unions; but when requested to receive a deputation of representatives of Women's Trades' Unions he refused to do so. On a former occasion, when some factory women requested permission to wait upon him to state their views regarding the Factories (Health of Women) Bill of 1874 he returned a similar answer. The effect of factory legislation for children is probably highly beneficial – whether it is equally beneficial for women, who, having often to bear all the responsibilities of heads of families, might at least be allowed some voice regarding the regulation of their work – may be doubted, especially since it seems to produce, as shown by Mr Cross's action, an impression that the wishes of women, even on their own affairs, are not worthy of notice.

The question of the wisdom of continuing to include women in this legislation has been more than once raised in the House of Commons. Before the Bill passes into law surely some notice will be given in the House of Lords to so important a point. They might usefully consider a suggestion made by you a short time ago, 'That the dependence and weakness of women hand can only be cured by throwing upon them the responsibility of their own actions.'

I am, Sir, your obedient servant, Emma A Paterson, Hon. Sec. Women's Protective and Provident League, April 10.

'Women as Factory Inspectors,' *Women's Union Journal*, September 1878, pp. 57–58

Le France of July 8th contains the important intelligence, that in the department of the Seine it has been decided to appoint women as Factory Inspectors and to appoint them not merely to subordinate offices, but on an equal footing with men. The means of inspection hitherto existing are said to have been inadequate. In the department of the Seine (including Paris) there are, it appears, 145,000 workshops and factories, in more than 20,000 of which apprentices are employed, and there has been a staff of only fifteen general Inspectors for all France. The departmental authorities have the power of supplementing the state inspection, by the help of local inspectors paid from local funds, but hitherto this power has been seldom used.

The new staff about to be appointed by the Council General of the department of the Seine, will consist of two chief inspectors, one of whom will be a woman, and of twelve inspectors of the second class, of whom six will be women.

The French factory law differs from the English in one important particular; it deals only with children and with girls under age. At twenty-one years of age, women in France become free from Factory legislation. In England, on the contrary, women of whatever age, whilst employed in Factories and Workshops, are under legal inspection. There is therefore an even stronger case in this country, than in France, for the appointment of women as Factory Inspectors. Factory legislation has now been in force in Great Britain for over thirty years; by far the largest number of persons whose work hours, meal hours and other conditions of employment are under inspection, are women and girls; yet not one woman has ever been appointed to the office of Inspector. The great desirability of appointing women as Inspectors, was represented to the Royal Commission in 1875 by the evidence of some working women, but in the Report of the Commission the subject was not even mentioned. When the Factory Acts Consolidation Bill was before Parliament last Session, Sir Harcourt Johnstone asked whether provision would be made for appointing women as Inspectors, and the Home Secretary replied, that he had not thought of the suggestion, but that he would consider it. Shortly afterwards, the Home Secretary was asked to receive a deputation of representatives of Women's Trade Unions on this subject, but he declined to do so, and in the Act since passed there is no trace of any result of his consideration of the matter.

Most persons, even those who doubt the expediency and value of Factory legislation, will agree that while such legislation exists, the work of inspection attending it should at least be *shared* by women, especially when the supervision of sanitary and other conditions regarding the work of women and girls, is the principal object of the legislation.

We hope that the good example reported in the following extract translated from La France, will soon be followed in this country; so that we may not have to repeat the old saying 'they manage these things better in France.'

'Five Shillings and Sixpence per Week,' *Women's Union Journal*, November 1878, pp. 75–76

The strike at the Cotton works in Bristol was brought to a close on September 13th. In recording the fact, several newspapers calculated the sum lost by the 1,600 workers during their five weeks' strike and administered the rebuke and warning usually given to those who presume to have a word to say about the price at which they will sell their labour. Probably, however, the difficulty is not so easily to be solved, although the workers are for the time conquered. Mr John Morley in his address to the Trade Congress said that regarding proposed reductions of wages 'the workman is bidden to be dumb as a sheep before the shearers.' That bidding has not always been obeyed by work*men*, but it has in most cases, by work*women*. They have indeed been 'dumb before the shearers.' Even an eminent political economist has been obliged to point to prejudice rather than to economic laws for an explanation of their low wages. When therefore women begin to protest, and when, unaided by Trade Unions or by outsiders, they for five weeks hold out against a threatened reduction of only five per cent, we cannot doubt that real necessity and a keen sense of wrong, impel them to the action.

When these women at last yielded, they did so by the advice of Trade Unionists, of those very leaders who are supposed to spend their lives in fostering strikes. It may be that the latter advised it, because they saw the helpless condition of the women, without any organisation and employed in an isolated Cotton factory far from the district in which they could gain the knowledge of current prices of labour and the strength given by the concentration of an industry in one locality. But, in advising them to return to work, one of the men of long experience among the North of England Cotton workers, clearly indicated the need for some enquiry into the cause of the small earning and pointed to some defect in the machinery as being against the operatives. Is not this then a case calling for careful consideration and investigation by the employers? If it is the fact that they choose to use defective machinery rather than go to the trouble and expense of replacing it by improved machinery, are the workers to suffer by constant reductions in their small earnings?

There are rich men concerned in the proprietorship of these Bristol Cotton Works; some of them are, we believe, connected with the noble Society of Friends, noted for Christian feeling and action. There is a Christian work and duty close to them if they will do it. Why do they not, at such a time as that of the strike, meeting their workers either in a body or by deputation, instead of leaving all negotiations in the hands of a paid manager? Many employers complain, as Mr Samuel Morley has done, that Trade Unions tend to keep masters and men apart, but no Trade Union was intervening here. We venture to think that had the employers been present at that last meeting of which we give an account on another page, the strike might have been concluded in a very different spirit. Now, the women have returned to work smarting under a feeling of injustice and the trouble may crop up again.

Until employers appear to be more alive to their duty towards their 'hands' until they realise that the hands have also heads requiring reasonable explanation, hearts requiring conciliation and sympathy and insides and outsides requiring food and clothing not to be obtained for 5s 6d or even, properly, for 12s 6d per week, can they wonder that the old method of strikes should be resorted to, even where, as in this case, a Trade Union does not exist.

We trust that the Bristol women will not neglect the lesson given them by this five week's experience. Had they been united in an organisation their position at such a time would have been far stronger. A subscription of 2d per week from only three fourths of the 16,000 workers would realise £5 per week and a fund could thus be gradually accumulated which, even if not required for trade purposes would be valuable for other benefits; and when organised, other organisations could assist them in a manner in which individuals cannot as well be assisted.

'Trade Union Meeting at Colston Hall, Bristol,' *Women's Union Journal*, November 1878, pp. 78

[...] Mrs Paterson supported the resolution,[1] and said one of the strongest proofs of the need of combination for self-defence and mutual benefit was the position of working women throughout the country. The fact that until recently they had never had any kind of organisation was the reason of their very miserable condition. They had often to live on the poorest pittance, so that it was impossible for them to save even the smallest amount towards the time when they might be out of work or be ill. They were supposed to be well paid if they had 12s or 15s a week, and as many had to support sick mothers and fathers and young sisters and brothers, of course the amount was very inadequate for their support. The London unions of women, which she had the privilege of taking some part in the formation of, were at present only few in number. There were now Unions of women formed in six of the London trades; these had been formed during the past four years; She hoped there would soon be more. The society she represented at the Congress was the Society of Women employed in bookbinding; it numbered 300 members and had an accumulated fund of over £200 (Applause).

Compared with men's unions this was perhaps a small amount, but when it was considered that it had entirely accumulated from the women's weekly contributions of twopence and that they had paid all the working expenses, as well as expended money in benefits, the balance in hand was a very fair one. She urged the desirability of forming unions of working women in the city of Bristol and hoped that ere long some determined stand would be made with regard to the hours of work. She considered the legal hours very much too long, ten and a half hours was too long a time for women to work when nine hours was considered long enough for men. (Applause.) She thought that of all the charges brought against trade unionists, that of selfishness was the most unjust one. The unionist pledged himself to defend and aid his brethren. In many cases, he might have to forego individual advantage for the sake of the whole body of the members. Not long ago the London Times in an article on the cotton strike had said

> There are happily hundreds of instances in which working men, by capacity, industry, diligence, have raised themselves to become masters or even great capitalist; but there is no instance, so far as we are aware, in which such prosperity has fallen to the lot of a workman who was ready to engage in strikes, or to abandon the honest pursuit of his calling in order to live upon doles or upon credit for the realization of some impracticable idea.

It appeared to be just the type of a selfish man that the *Times* had praised, the man who was ready to advance himself without regard to others. The principle of trade unionism was opposed to such action.

Report of the Trades Union Congress, 1878, pp. 81–82

Mrs Paterson (London) suggested that the resolution should be amended so as to recommend the appointment of a number of practical working men and women. (Hear, hear.)

Mr Cocking (Blackburn) seconded the resolution.

Miss Merrick and Mr Harry supported the suggestion of Mrs Paterson.

Mr Cook (London) said it was evident either that the inspectors now engaged did not do their [last line illegible – find again] frequently evaded, and he was sorry to say the evasion was in some cases assisted by the workmen; which would be prevented if the proposal contained in the resolution were carried out.

Mr Birthistle consented to amend his resolution so as to include working women where necessary.

Mrs Paterson did not think the addition of the words 'where necessary' would meet the case and moved as an amendment the insertion of the words 'and women' after 'practical working men.' Efforts had frequently been made to secure the appointment of women inspectors, but the question had been shirked from time to time, and she hoped the Congress would adopt the amendment, which would assist them in attaining the object in view.

Miss Simcox (London) seconded the amendment and urged that it was desirable to have as inspectors persons who understood the working of the particular trades.

Miss Brown supported the amendment, remarking that what she wanted was to get the necessity of appointing women inspectors recognised by the Congress.

Mr Broadhurst pointed out that the Congress in their fight to obtain the passage of the Factory and Workshops Act encountered great opposition from the female organisations, and it seemed most extraordinary that, having opposed the Factory Acts, the lady delegates should now ask to be placed in a position to see that the Acts were not administered, for he thought that would be the result. He mentioned this in order that the Congress might not place itself in the ridiculous position of asking Parliament to appoint as inspectors those who had been the most determined opponents of the Act.

Miss Simcox was afraid Mr Broadhurst had fallen into the popular error of thinking that all women were of one opinion. She denied that the appointment of women would tend to the evasion of the Acts, but contended that it would lead to their being more efficiently carried out.

Mr Yorston (Edinburgh) was opposed to the appointment of women, on the ground that in many instances the office of inspector would be one which women would not be fitted to fulfil. He was of the opinion that the Consolidated Bill, if properly put into force, with an adequate number of inspectors, would be a great improvement, and if ladies were not appointed he trusted the male inspectors would feel it their duty to defend the interests of females under all circumstances.

Mr G Potter suggested that instead of the resolution reading 'practical working men and working women where necessary,' they should substitute 'practical persons.'

Mr Michael (London) suggested the substitution of the words 'practical workers in trades coming under the provisions of the Act.' He hoped the lady delegates would accept this.

Mr Johnstone (Glasgow) had no sympathy with the jealousy against women inspectors.

Mr Fox (Bristol) saw no reason why women should be shut out from being inspectors in places where women and children were chiefly employed.

Mrs Paterson said she felt sorry that she must press the amendment. She would be sorry to have it seem to the public that the working men wanted to keep all the loaves and fishes to themselves. (Laughter)

'The Organisation of Women's Industry,' *Women's Union Journal*, April 1879, p. 25

By special request we publish in full the papers read, and the discussion which took place, at the Conference held in St Paul's Chapter House on Saturday, March 15th. The Conference was widely noticed by the Press and was reported at considerable length by some of the London daily papers, but even the partial condensation of the reports has led to misunderstandings on one or two points and it is hoped that these may be set right by the publication of a complete account. For instance, an article appeared in the Evening Standard of March 17th, regretting that anything should have been said or done at the Conference 'to encourage women in the belief that by banding themselves into Trade Unions and organising strikes they could better their position.' It will be seen however from our report that not one of the speakers recommended women to organise strikes, but that on the contrary it was shown that Unions would tend to prevent strikes. The remarks concerning domestic service, also, have been deepened in colour by the editorial ink of the Pall Mall Gazette, Figaro, Hornet and Manchester Examiner. The words 'domestic service is a kind of slavery' have been especially enlarged upon. Amid attempts to disprove these words much has been said against the idea that a domestic servant should be able to consider her work as finished at any one hour of the day or should, after that hour, be permitted to employ her leisure in her own way. Such criticisms only tend to confirm the view that domestic service presents, under existing arrangements, some of the aspects of slavery. Another partial confirmation of this view was given at the Conference on 'Arbitration' held on March 29th. A letter was read from Mr Davis, a member of a Board of Arbitration in the Midland Counties, which contained a passage representing as quite unreasonable and ridiculous a proposal that arbitration should be adopted between domestic servants and their employers.

If any of our readers wish to continue the discussion of the question we shall be glad to insert their letters.

'The Organization of Women's Industry,' *Women's Union Journal*, April 1879, pp. 26–30

One of the more important discoveries of recent years is that women have certain necessities identical with those of men, other than those of food, clothing and shelter. It is now recognised that women have mental as well as bodily necessities. From this discovery has proceeded the better education of women. That movement has been advocated mainly on two grounds; first, that of the advantage which men would derive from intellectual companionship and, secondly, the advantages, both moral and material, to women themselves. The movement for trade organisation among women may be advocated in a similar manner. By the organisation of women's work, men will be defended from the danger that has been found to be not an imaginary one – namely, that women, whilst ignorant, from the want of union, of the proper rewards of labour, may bring down the wages of men by working for a much lower rate of payment. Men will also receive more sympathy and support from their wives and daughters in efforts to maintain their industrial position if those wives and daughters have themselves learned by experience the benefits of organisation.

The advantages to workwomen themselves, since many women who work at trades have no male relatives to consider, are however still more important to be borne in mind. Professor Leone Levi in his recent statistics of the earnings of the working classes, placed the number of wage-earning women at 3,800,000 and gave the average weekly earnings of every woman of full age, at 13s 8d. This average was obtained by throwing in the very large class of domestic servants – 1,300,000 at the last census. Leaving out this class and reckoning only women who work at trades, an average of 12s per week is about correct, though rather above than below the mark, for at most trades at which women work there are at least two months of slackness in every year, when they are either discharged or kept on at about half work. In the Upholstery trade of the West end of London, the average is as high as 15s per week, but that is a small trade, and against it must be set the large number of East end workers of various trades earning but 6s, 7s or 8s. Taking the average however, at 12s, it is difficult to see how a woman on that income can properly feed, clothe, and house herself in London. Professor Leone Levi lately gave the budget of a working man earning 30s per week; but he has not yet given the 12s budget, and it would puzzle him to do so (hear). It is obvious that any surplus for intellectual enjoyment is impossible.

We cannot suppose that such a rate of payment is always in due proportion to the price at which the articles produced by the work of women are sold to the public. We do not find that as a rule, such work is sold at an especially low rate. Dressmakers' charges for instance, are high enough, though the workers are but poorly paid. There are, it is true, some articles from the price of which we know that the workers cannot be properly paid and for which most purchasers would gladly pay a penny or two more, in order to have better work, but I have facts at hand, which I could quote if necessary, to prove that frequently the employer alone is the gainer by the cheapening of women's work. Mr Mill said in his 'Political Economy' that 'custom grounded on prejudice' has much to do with the lowness of the wages of women. The supposition that women have only themselves to provide for, has, no doubt, a good deal to do with the custom. It is not realised that many women are obliged to support, or to help to support, relatives. A member of one of the London Women's Unions found herself left not long ago, with the responsibility of providing for eight little brothers and sisters. Even when women have to support themselves only, it should be borne in mind that one person cannot live so economically as, in proportion, a family can; also that the very fact of their being alone in the world makes it the more necessary that they should have some margin of wages – beyond the amount required for present maintenance, out of which to provide for old age or sickness. Aged or sick parents are in many cases helped by their sons and daughters, but if a woman is alone in the world she is scarcely likely to find any help but that of the workhouse, when she is unable to work at her trade. There is a special danger from the inadequate payment of women, in the temptation to gain money by immoral means. The majority do struggle on honestly, soberly and creditably, although the privations and miseries through which they fight their way are almost inevitable.

The attempt to organise the trades of women is so new that we may expect some years to elapse before any strongly marked improvement is brought about; but the attempt has not been made a day too soon. The industrial position of women has been rapidly becoming worse, not only in consequence of the action of their employers, but also because of their entire ignorance of the condition of their trades. Through trade organisation women will be able to learn, with a view to a more uniform price, the rates paid in different establishments; without organisation it is almost impossible to get this general trade information. Not only ago, instances were found of women who had been working at the East End in tailoring, offering in sheer ignorance, at shops at the West end, to make waistcoats at 2s or 3s, under the rate usually paid at the West end.

The time of slack work is another difficulty to women's trades which can only be met by organisation. The uncertainty of regular work in trades is not sufficiently realised by the richer classes or by those who in Government or other offices draw their salaries regularly, whether their work has been required or not. It is often repeated that the capitalist has all the risk, but surely this uncertainty is an element of risk of equal importance to the labourers. Women have in their work, more than men have in theirs, to meet the uncertainty arising from changes of fashion, but there are other fluctuations of trade arising from causes seldom or never known to the public. An account given in the Women's Union Journal this month, of the Leicester Cigar making trade, shows clearly the need of provision for times of non-employment. The cigar trade in Leicester is usually slack from Christmas time to the beginning of April and it has been more than usually so this season. The manufacturers await with anxiety the annual Budget of the Chancellor of Exchequer, and fearing that fresh duties may be levied on tobacco they restrict production in order to show a bad quarter's trade just before Budget time, as an argument for lightening their duties. The additional duty of 4d in the pound, put on last year, was very obnoxious to the manufacturers, who have been consequently making special efforts to get it removed this year. In this case, they, not the workers, have been limiting production. The women working in the trade finding that some of their number have been offering to work at less than the ordinary rates, in consequence of having no Society to fall back upon when out of work, determined to form a Union to prevent this. They saw that it was to their interest to unite to pay a weekly allowance to members out of work: they know that the employers who refuse to give work at the full rate of payment manage to find it if any one offers to work for less and that when once a few women have taken the lower price, their action is quoted against the other workers and the reduced is soon further extended.

In connection with the out-of-work benefits of trade organisation, must be mentioned the advantage of having a common centre, the Society's Office, where work may be heard of. The great economy of time and strength thus effected, in the avoidance of journeys from shop to shop in search of work is so obvious that it need not be enlarged upon.

Another advantage will be in the recognition of the work of women as being worthy the dignity of trade organisation. There is too much a tendency to look upon it as insignificant (partly perhaps because of its paltry payment) and as only worthy to be considered unskilled labour, incapable of classification.

One of the objections made to the Women's Protective and Provident League when it started was that it would encourage women to strike and that women being more impulsive than men would be even more ready to take that step. We have not found it so in London: even in clear cases of oppression and injustice we find a strong desire to avoid strikes. No doubt in the factory districts the women are less cautious: we not unfrequently hear of them entering upon strikes, although they have no Unions behind them. Probably if the factory women *had* Union their strikes would be less frequent. When people have a common fund they take time to think before risking their money in a trade dispute; women in the factory districts often rush into strikes because they have little to lose by doing so; when the men strike at the same time the women usually receive an allowance from the men's Union through they pay no contributions to those organisations. The assembling together in large masses in factories gives a kind of rough organisation, and it may be argued that, as shown by their not fearing strikes, the women are well able to take care of themselves without Unions. May it not however be argued, on the other hand, that such women greatly need the *moderating* influence of trade organisation? With the large class of workwomen of miscellaneous trades in towns, the *strength* of Union appears to be most needed.

The League Committee have been sometimes urged to drop the Protective portion of the scheme and to limit their advocacy and aid to the Provident side. It seems, however, that working women have well shown how provident they can be; some of their richer neighbours might learn from them with advantage, reasons of thrift. 10s or 12s cannot admit of much extravagance in living; they need to be encouraged to protect themselves by Union and to strengthen themselves by it, so that whenever they become convinced that the 10s or 12 ought, in fair proportion to the employers' profits, to be 12s or 20s, they may endeavour to bring their wages up to that point and thus give themselves a chance of being more provident, of saving more, than is now possible.

Another objection sometimes brought against our work is, that although organisation may be very well for the most poorly paid class of workwomen, it is quite unnecessary for those who are highly paid. We are told of sewing machinists who earn 25s and 30s per week; of others who earn less but are yet not badly off, as they have fathers or husbands to help to provide for them and to enable them to work for pastime or pocket money rather than for maintenance. This view is I think a narrow and selfish one; it will certainly not bear the light of the Christ precept that we should love our neighbours as ourselves. With some, with most persons, let us hope, the selfishness of the argument has only to be clearly shown as a reply to it. The few whose human sympathies are not to be touched, who reason selfishly with their eyes open and admiring themselves for their worldly wisdom, must be met upon their own ground. It must be proved to them that they cannot long hope to keep this prosperity to themselves; that unless they share the burdens of others, unless they with their strength try to help the weak, their own position will assuredly be weakened. Union is needed quite as much to keep up good wages as to raise low wages. The danger is all around the well-paid workers; women who have nothing to fall back upon are waiting ready to offer their work at a lower rate. By union only can this danger be met.

Again, those women who have husbands or fathers to help them cannot tell how soon they may be thrown upon their own resources. In consenting as they often do, or in offering, to take work below the ordinary rate – below a rate at which a woman can support herself – they do not know how much grievous trouble they may be bringing upon themselves when in after years, they may require work not as pastime or for pocket money, but for all the necessaries of life. Women who work for wages have one common interest, whether they are well paid or ill paid. Many sewing machinists and other workwomen know now that the well-paid trade of today may become the ill-paid trade of tomorrow, if not organised. It is said also that women work at trades only temporarily, leaving before long to get married, and that it is therefore not worth their while to pay much attention to trade organisation. Sir Henry James, the other day urged a similar objection against the Women's Suffrage Bill but he also gave, I suppose unintentionally, one of the best answers to it. He said that he believed the proper profession of women to be marriage, but added in almost the same breath that there are 900,000 more women than men in this country. The preponderance is rapidly increasing, and out of the number of surplus, or as some people perhaps think them, superfluous women, many large Unions may be formed.

But as I have before said, the support of husband or father is an uncertainty; after their marriage women are often obliged to return to their trade undesirable as this may be; or when their work is such that it can be done at home they take it there and if not protected by Union are then more than ever at the mercy of the manufacturers or 'sweaters' as regards wages. Even if they never return to their work, however, they are not worse wives and mothers for having taken some thought about keeping up the position of their trade, and the women who remain in the trade are all the better.

Another objection raised is that girls should go into domestic service and not enter trades so much as they now do. There are many reasons for the great disinclination which girls have for domestic service, but it would take too long to go fully into these. In all but large, rich households, where there is much idleness and waste, domestic service is incessant hard work at all hours of the day and sometimes of the night also. It is all the best but a kind of slavery, and when a girl has a home it is only a human feeling, and one that we should respect, if she prefers to undertake work in trades, because she can return at night and on Sundays to the home circle. At a meeting last year of factory women at Bristol who were earning only 5s or 6s per week, I urged upon them the advisability of going out to service rather than submit to such low wages, but without an exception the advice was rejected by all. The idea of servants combining together under present conditions was spoken of by all the newspapers as utterly ridiculous when a few years ago the Dundee servants held meetings with a view to bettering their position.

One feasible suggestion of an improvement is a system of superior charwomen, under which servants could go home at night. They would then know when their work for the day was over, and their industry could be organised and thus placed more on a footing with other trades. Heads of households might then have to wait upon themselves a little more than they do now but much of the service now regarded as necessary is really only to gratify pride and to keep up appearances. At any rate, girls of the working class and their parents are just as much entitled to freedom of choice as any other persons are and we must try to avoid the constant danger there is of indulging, like Mr Honeythunder in Dickens' 'Edwin Drood,' the tendency to 'bump' people, especially women, into what we think are their places. If the choice falls upon trades instead of upon service, this is no reasonable excuse for neglecting our sisters and leaving them to endure the bad conditions of the work they have selected.

Since the movement for organising Women's trades began four years ago, six women's unions have been formed in London – (1) Women employed in Bookbinding, (2) Upholsteresses, (3) Shirt and Collar Makers, (4) Sewing Machinists, (5) Dressmakers, Milliners and Mantle Makers, (6) Tailoresses. The first four are at present located at the offices of the League, 36, Great Queen-Street, WC, the rooms of which, by arranging their business meetings for different nights, suffice for the whole. An economy in rent is thus effected. The payments are 1s entrance fee, and 2d per week, and in four years the amount contributed by the members of the three first named Unions was £680, out of which £150 has been paid for out-of-work and sick benefits, and the balances in hand amount to £363. All that the League does is to show the women the way of making a beginning and to help them to help themselves. To many of them, self-help and independence are new sensations and it is hoped by the means of these Unions to root out the idea of reliance on charitable help. That idea is one of the greatest difficulties with regard to attempts to organise the most poorly paid class of workwomen. Bad wages have often been made a reason by charitably disposed persons for giving money to the poor. The money is given with the kindest and best intentions but something more than almsgiving is needed. When any of the clergy or district visitors are brought into contact with such cases, it is much to be wished that they should enquire into them. They may feel bound to give money to relieve immediate necessities but they should not stop there. They could do much towards improving the position of working women by learning the particulars of the work so badly remunerated and by communicating the same to the Committee of the Women's Protective and Provident League, who would always gladly consider such communications and if possible take action upon them. The workers, too, should be counselled not merely to get along as well as they can, but to strive for better payment, if their work appears to be worth it.

Only about 1,000 workwomen in London have yet been directly reached by the Unions formed; the vast size of London and the variety of trades make the work of organisation especially difficult here. The idea of union is however rapidly spreading and is also taking root in some provincial towns. In Leicester, there are now three Unions. The first of these is the Seamers' and Stitchers' Unions in the hosiery trade. A wonderful improvement has been effected by that Union for the women; one that shows how much may be done by organisation eve as regards homework, which is usually supposed to be least open to such influences. The seaming and stitching work is all done by the women at their own homes and up to the Spring of 1875 it had been taken from the manufacturers and handed to the women by middlemen or 'sweaters.' At last, the oppression of this system became so great that the women determined to combine and to try to throw over the 'sweaters.' The women were earning no more than 4s and 5s per week whilst the middlemen at the same time were getting a comfortable living with very little labour. The Union through a Board of Arbitration sought an interview with the employers, who expressed great surprise at finding how large a proportion of what they paid was absorbed by the sweaters, and arrangements were made by which the middlemen were got rid of and the seamers received in most cases the full amount of their earnings.

Whilst continuing its chief work of organising Unions in the various trades in which women are employed, the League enters upon many other useful branches of work. At the League Officers, there is a reading room, open every morning, where papers which advertise vacancies for workers are taken; the League is also accumulating a library of interesting and amusing literature. Many employers send to the office when they want workwomen. Last March at the request of several women who are members of the Unions and with the valuable help of Miss Williams, a Bank was established, in which sums of one halfpenny upwards may be deposited. There are now nearly 200 depositors, who are invited to take a share in the management by attending general meetings. At the last meeting, they resolved to try the experiment of making small loans from the Bank funds, of interest of 5 and 10 per cent.

The League Committee wish to make their rooms as far as possible a centre of social life for the members of the Unions. Once a month, Social Meetings are held there, when there is singing, music and conversation; an opportunity us thus afforded for women of leisure and education to meet and to help to amuse, their working sisters. Such opportunities are much needed and it may be hoped that they will be multiplied by the establishment of Clubs for working women in different parts of London. The clubs could be used as branch offices for the Unions. It would be very undesirable that women should meet at public houses for their Union business and as the Unions become more numerous branch offices will be needed. Some few of the clergy are now taking up the important work of establishing women's clubs; the success of such institutions greatly depends on their being kept free from stiffness and from needlework classes.

Among the rules of a Women's Club recently started by some clergymen, is one providing for prayer and a hymn on the closing of the Club every evening, and another for the sale of work materials at 3d in the shilling under cost price: the first mentioned rule will probably tend to keep away the girls who most need to be brought under good influences, and the second introduces a charitable element which is not desirable in a club. When clergymen start a club for men they provide for recreation, not for work. Women, after they have been at work all day, equally require relaxation and all the freedom that can be afforded with due regard to respectability and the comfort of others. Wherever women go, it seems to be thought the right thing to thrust needlework into their hands; no one has yet held fathers' meetings at which work is carried on, useful as these might be. There seems to be also too much an impression that women require more exhortation to do well than men do; yet even the opponents of the theory of the *mental* equality of women and men, hold that women are *morally* equal and some even say morally superior. Women, at all events, do not seem to be so much more vicious than men as to require the extra amount of guidance and exhortation they receive. The emotional side of their nature, the praying and weeping, is perhaps too much developed. Women need to be turned to practical social work; they are ready enough to sit down and weep and think that they are too weak to do anything to improve the evils they see around them.

The clergy can greatly help the work of the League by making it known to working women in their parishes and by trying to interest women of the wealthy and educated classes in the difficulties of working women and in efforts to improve women's trades. The League has to thank the London Clergy for valuable help in lending school rooms for meetings. Only in two cases have applications for the use of rooms been refused; in many others they have been readily granted. The League Committee will at all times be glad to send papers for distribution or to give other information about their work; also to receive any suggestions as to openings for new Unions, from the clergy or from others interested in the movement.

Note

1 The resolution read: 'That this meeting, feeling satisfied that trade societies are powerful agencies as a means of securing to the workpeople of this kingdom a fair share in the product of their labours, earnestly urges all men and women engaged in trade to extend existing unions and form others in the various towns.'

2 Societies and Struggles
May 1879–1884

In 1879, imperial British red inked much of the landmass of the world. Soldiers of the British Army guarded the Khyber Pass, the African savannah, and far-flung outposts in the South Atlantic and South Pacific. Some of their uniforms were made in London, at the Royal Army Clothing Depot in Pimlico. They were cut and stitched and pressed by a small army of some 1,500 women, many of whom took the work home with them and fitted these symbols of imperial power together until the early hours of the morning. 'Homework' had a different meaning in London's age of sweatshops and domestic production.

As so often when public expenditure is involved, questions were asked in Parliament about the cost of these uniforms. As so often when those questions are asked, the Government promised to cut costs forthwith. On 26 March 1879, the 1,500 women who clothed the men of the imperial army were discharged, told to reapply at a lower rate of pay and denied the homework that gave some of them the chance at a reasonable standard of living. The women soon found how great the cut in their wages would be, and some 100 attended a meeting called by the Women's Protective and Provident League. Emma Paterson saw her chance to make a bright clear advertisement for the necessity of women's unions.

If the first chapter covered the years that launched Emma's name as chief advocate of working women, the second covers the period when she tried to parley that fame and the early promise of her League into a lasting movement. The struggle by the Pimlico women was the best known of these efforts, because the dispute involved government ministers, questions in Parliament, a patriotic imperative – and because the dispute would rumble on for years, longer than Emma herself.

But it was far from the only struggle to which Emma injected herself. In these six years, from 1879 to 1884, she championed the cause of shop assistants, forced opponents at the Trades Union Congress of women factory inspectors to reprise their stale arguments (and lose votes on the issue) and caused Henry Broadhurst to once again turn his eyes to the ceiling and sigh at the unwillingness of the women delegates to cede ground on issues close to them.

She also fought against the persistent idea among some of the men that justice would come if only the women depart their industry. We saw in the introduction her clash in 1884 with Richard Juggins of the Black Country metalworkers; in the same year, male weavers at Kidderminster went on strike against the introduction of women to a new branch of their trade. They marched through the town pushing prams, as a warning of what might happen next. Emma responded in the Women's Union Journal, first insisting that she had 'always declared against attempts to introduce women into trades at rates of wages far below those previously paid to men for similar work.'

Yet the strike, she added, was against women employed in 'a new branch of weaving, said to be better adapted for them than for men, on account of the lightness of the fabric and the need of special attention to the cleaning of the looms.' Getting rid of the women was not only unfair and wrong, but also (literally) unproductive. As you will see, she even courted controversy at the Trades Union Congress by suggesting that the awful conditions endured by young women in the Black Country metal trades and in other industries by suggesting that they were no worse than the average factory job.

Emma used the pages of her Journal in these years to bring the wider problems of working women into high definition. There are articles here on a saner and less restrictive form of women's fashion, and to urgent debates over the legal rights of married women through the Married Women's Property Acts. She urges greater access for working women to libraries and other sources of culture, and to real, restful holidays, and the ways by which her League could give working women the chance to take them. There are reports here of dinners and excursions enjoyed by members of the League, and the efforts of Emma and her co-agitators to make of the League a community that could raise the cultural and social life of its members as well as their standard of living.

This was, of course, the same period when she lost her husband Thomas, in 1882. The immensity of his loss, not only in personal terms, but also in how she was left with his debts and the need for strict personal austerity, makes the richness of her work in this period only more remarkable. And while there are signs in this chapter that the League was not progressing as far or as fast as she initially hoped – there are appeals here for help and support by women of the League – there is also ample evidence that the League's influence went far beyond the relatively small circle of its membership. Admiring letters from male trade unionists, and from the pioneering women's shoemakers union in the United States, the Daughters of St Crispin, must have served as partial compensation for her personal *tribulations during this part of her life. But first we return to 1879, and Emma's first encounter with the women of the Royal Army Clothing Depot in Pimlico.*

'Army Clothing,' Women's Union Journal, May 1879, pp. 41–43

All friends of the work of the Women's Protective and Provident League will probably agree that there could scarcely be a more fitting occasion for the intervention of the League than that afforded by the supposed 'Reforms' recently effected at the Royal Army Clothing Depot, Pimlico. Our Report of the Meeting convened by the League will be read with interest, as giving the women's statement of the case.

The present Government have been charged with extravagant expenditure of some millions of money. The attempt now made to save a few hundreds by reducing the already low rates of payment for making soldiers' clothing does not meet with public approval. Since the women have brought to light their grievances, the method of economy adopted has been severely commented upon by the Press. Mr Mundella's action in asking a question in the House and in promising to raise the subject again will be gratefully remembered. An effort to justify the reduction is being made probably at the instance of the authorities, by reference to the former earnings of some of the women, which reached occasionally 30s and 36s per week. We fail to see why it should be considered a preposterous thing, or an instance of extravagance, that such amounts should be earned, especially as it is stated that the pressing and all other branches of the work except cutting out are done by the women. Apart from this, however, when we learn *how* the amounts referred to were earned, we see at once the fallacy of quoting them in support of reduction. The women who spoke at the meeting convened by the League mentioned the old and the new rates of piece-work payment, and they showed that even at the old and higher rates, £1 25s, or 36s, could only be earned by taking work home at the close of the factory and working until midnight or early morning. The amount earned was to a great extent the measure of the time that a woman had been working when she should have been resting. Under the new regulations women who are employed in the factory are not allowed to take work home. If reform had not gone beyond this there would have been less cause of complaint. Since 'Alton Locke' was written, several high class tailors have boasted, though not always truthfully, that their work is 'done only on the premises.' All true friends of working women earnestly desire to see their work brought within reasonable hours; if more than nine hours' work daily is too much for a man, it certainly is too much for a woman. The authorities might even have been praised for evincing by this new rule, their desire to carry out the spirit of the Factory Act of the present Government, under which some sanguine persons think the system of late night work will be crushed. We find, however, that the soldiers' clothing is not all to be 'made on the premises,' for a good deal of work is still given out to women not employed in the factory. It is obvious, too, that the sudden withdrawal of home work from women who had long been accustomed to have that addition to their ordinary earnings, would alone involve a heavy loss, and when to this is added a reduction of payment, which brings down the amount it is possible to earn during the factory hours by 20 and 30 per cent, the loss is greatly increased.

The manner in which the reduction was managed though very ingenious would be scarcely creditable even to a firm of shop clothiers. On March 26th, the women, some 1,500 in number, were all discharged and were told that they might, at the end of a week, apply for employment under a pre-arranged scale of payment. No compensation whatever was given for the loss of the week's work. At the end of the week, some hundreds applied, but they were not then made clearly acquainted with the new terms and told that if they agreed to those terms, they would be at once re-engaged. Two or three price lists, badly written, were posted on the walls but there was no time to examine them. The women were told to pass before the managers one by one, and, if they wanted to be re-engaged, to sign the following paper.

> Application for Employment in the Royal Army Clothing Depot – I have made myself acquainted with the condition on which pieceworkers are employed in the factory, and subject to them, and any alterations which may be made to them from time to time, I request you will engage me – *To the Manager of the Factory.*

Having been out of work for a week, in many cases with nothing to fall back upon, they were, of course, anxious to regain what they had always supposed to be the steady employment of a Government Factory. No time was allowed them to consider the paper presented to them or to consult their fellow workers. They signed the paper, therefore, it may seem foolishly, but urgent needs were pressing them. A show of consent to the new terms having thus been obtained, the women were told to 'pass on' and to wait at home until they received notice to return to work. Within the next few days, a large number of the women received notices, but many others are still waiting. The convenience of the arrangement to the employers will be readily seen. The highly and regularly paid head officials of the Establishment were able at their leisure to send a summons to the workers they preferred to take on. It mattered nothing to them that distress was being occasioned in many households by the suspense. The troops dispatched to South Africa had been clothed, the pressure of work was decreasing, a smaller number of hands was required but it would be well, they thought, to keep the extra hands waiting – not to encourage them to engage themselves elsewhere; other little wars might suddenly arise and more clothing be required.

At the end of a week's work the women who returned to the factory, found on receiving their wages, how great the reduction was. The fact that upwards of 700 attended a meeting convened by the League at only two days' notice and took part in the outdoor demonstration the next day, shows how general the dissatisfaction had soon become.

In reply to Mr Mundella's question in the House, Lord Eustace Cecil said that time workers are paid 15s per week. This is but a small sum and the weakness of the statement as a reply is the fact that only about one fifteenth of the whole number of women employed are *time* workers. Payment by the piece is the prevailing system in the factory. Lord E Cecil promised that a Committee of enquiry should be appointed consisting of 'gentlemen conversant with the business.' We hope this does not mean 'sweating' tailors, conversant with slop shop prices. The publication of a report by the Committee will probably be asked for.

The changes effected have had one good result. The women now see that Government work is not so permanent as they have hitherto supposed it to be, and the idea of forming a Protective and Benefit Society, suggested to them at the meeting already referred to, was warmly taken up. A Resolution was at once passed that a Society should be formed and on the following Saturday large numbers enrolled themselves as members.

Report of the Trades Union Congress, 1879

(…) Mr Knight (Liverpool) opposed it [a resolution on women factory inspectors], on the ground that he objected to the appointment of ladies as inspectors unless he received an assurance that their views as to the hours of labour had changed.

Mr Broadhurst explained that he had had nothing to do with the omission of the word 'women' from the resolution, but he had the same opinion has he held last year – that it would be monstrous to agree to request the appointment of ladies as inspectors under the Factory Acts, when the ladies who would be appointed were the chief opponents of the regulations that were to be carried out under these Acts. Mrs Paterson had eloquently denounced the Acts from a hundred platforms; and in her little newspaper she had opposed them with marvellous ability, and she had not yet recanted. She was not a lady that made a recantation on anything that she had once expressed her views on (laughter) but until she stated that she felt she was wrong, and that the Congress were right, he felt it his duty to oppose the introduction of the word 'women' in the resolution. He could

not conceive any action which they could possibly take more calculated to defeat their object than to ask the Government to appoint lady inspectors to carry out the Factory Act. If they had any prospect of success last year, it was deliberately destroyed by the insertion of the word 'women.' If the Congress did include the word 'women' he believe they might not be concurred with by the Home Secretary. He, having a fair knowledge of the world and of men and women, might think the Government had already in their employment far too many womanly servants. (Laughter.) He thought it would be a misfortune to include 'women' in their resolution. (Laughter.)
(...)

Mr Pickard (Wakefield) advocated the appointment of female inspectors. They could not have the Act properly carried out if they prevented women from becoming inspectors. Was it not a fact that women were said to be the most curious class amongst them? If they got women inspectors they would find them poking into every hole and corner (Laughter). He thought if women were made inspectors it would be a great help.

Mrs Paterson (London) said there was a great difference of opinion about factory legislation, but it was not necessary for her to go into that to convince Mr Knight or Mr Broadhurst of her change of views in order to justify herself. The Factory Acts had been consolidated into one. They were to be put in force for some time, and it would be foolish and childish to oppose it. It would be like knocking their heads against a brick wall. Workwomen had desired that some additional inspectors should be appointed and that some of them should be women – not ladies, but practical working women. It had been said it was possible she herself might be the first lady who would be appointed, but she did not think it would be honest and straightforward in her to press this question if she had in view such an appointment. She might assure Mr Broadhurst that she would not accept any appointment of the kind, and she would be sorry if the impression were left on the Congress that she was a place-hunting imposter. She remarked that it was peculiar to observe that the strongest supporters of women inspectors were those in the trades by which women were employed. Mr Broadhurst spoke very dolefully about periling the question of an increased inspectorate with the Government by asking that there should be women inspectors, do dolefully that one could almost see the trembling in his eye (Loud laughter). The objection to working class inspectors, she considered, was owing to the deep-rooted class prejudice in the House of Commons (Applause). Mrs Paterson concluded by mentioning that Mr Stansfield appointed a woman as a poor law inspector, and she had discharged the duties most ably.

After Mr Davy had replied to the objections made to his motion, the President put the motion and amendment to the meeting. On a show of hands being taken, 49 voted for the amendment and 37 for the motion.

'Recent Strikes of Women,' *The Times*, 6 February 1880

Sir – I am very glad that the important subject of factory legislation for women is gaining attention in your columns. Nothing could be more conducive to a sound solution of a question which cannot yet be regarded as settled than to have both sides so impartially treated as in your article of yesterday. The public are too apt to forget one fact which you quote – that this legislation has been sought more by men for women than by women themselves. So far as my observation goes the 'protection' afforded to women by the Factory Act reaches them in the shape of deprivation and hardship. One out of many instances of this was the recent case in which a number of women were thrown out of employment because the hours of their work in folding newspapers, though actually of short duration, necessarily fell at other times than those particular hours prescribed by law. Yet, in the hours prohibited by law for this light work, women following what is supposed to be the specially feminine occupation of nursing the sick are continually engaged in exhausting labour.

The able letter by Miss Ada Heather-Bigg, also published yesterday, upon which I am anxious to offer a few explanatory remarks, lest a misconception regarding it should arise. The two recent strikes of working women are mentioned in such a connexion as to make possible the inference that the women's unions now in existence, of which the Women's Protective and Provident League is the centre and the Women's Union Journal the organ, had in some way originated the strikes quoted. The fact is, however, that during the whole four to give years of their existence these unions have had nothing to do with any strike whatever. I do not say that the unions are at all pledged never to enter upon strikes, but I may safely assert that they would not do so until every other effort possible had been made to settle a dispute amicably. It seems to use that the greatest strength of working women's unions – as it is acknowledged to be of working men's unions – lies in the fact that, so far from necessarily involving strikes, they afford opportunities of settling disputes by peaceful means.

Strikes of working women not connected with unions have frequently occurred during past years. The following extract from the first report of this League (1874) will show what is our view as to the influence which union exercises with regard to such disastrous action:

> The objection sometimes urged against women's unions that they will lead to strikes may well be answered by a reference to this (the Dewsbury Woolen Weavers') and similar cases. Up to the time of their strike the Dewsbury women had no union, but had it not been for the efficient organization commenced by them during the strike, it appears probably that the dispute would have lasted longer and not have ended

so satisfactorily as it did. A committee of 13 women (all weavers) was formed, and held frequent conferences with the committee of employers, by means of which an agreement was arrived at involving mutual concessions on various points, but establishing a fixed scale of prices acceptable to both parties.

I am, sir, yours faithfully, Emma A Paterson, Hon. Sec. Women's Protective and Provident League, 36, Great Queen-Street, WC, February 3.

'Lord and Labourer,' *Women's Union Journal*, April 1880, pp. 37–38

It is not within the province of this *Journal* to enter upon the discussion of political questions in any tone but that of strict impartiality towards the different political parties, for there are persons of all shades of opinion engaged in promoting the work of the League. Since strict impartiality can with difficulty be observed in such discussions, and upon the now all-absorbing subject of the result of the General Election we refrain from expressing an opinion.

But there was one contest which, quite apart from party considerations, must have been watched with intense interest by all who have welcomed, and rejoiced in, one of the greatest movements of the past few years, the awakening of the Agricultural Labourers into a new life of enlarged interests and intelligence. In the General Election now nearly concluded, Joseph Arch, the leader of this grand movement, made his first attempt to enter Parliament, and for the time he has been defeated. We cannot believe that more than a very short time can elapse before Mr Arch will be triumphantly returned, if not for Wilton for some other constituency. Sometime before the election, the Echo pointed out that Wilton was an unfortunate choice, as the Labourers' Union had always been weaker there than in many other parts of the county. That the great landowner of Wilton is strong, the result of the election has shown, but the nature of the efforts made to strengthen his position are not quite so well known as they deserve to be. The great landlord, whose brother, the Hon. Sydney Herbert, has been again returned, is an Earl possessing a park of many acres surrounded by a wall of great extent. This wall was turned to good account in the late election. Many days before the polling there figured on it, in elaborate and skilfully executed characters, not in the passing scribble of a boy or an idler, the following and many other polite intimations – 'Duck Arch,' 'Arch is a Rogue,' 'Herbert for Parliament, Arch for the Plough,' 'Useless Arch,' 'Don't vote for Arch the Robber,' 'No louts like Arch.' Of course to accuse the Earl of causing the notices to be written would be absurd; but it does seem surprising that his Lordship should suffer them to remain there for a single day: one would have supposed that he would have had them carefully washed off and would then have stationed a guard to see that they were not renewed. The printed papers scattered about the town were noteworthy but nothing could equal this remarkable exhibition of the way in which a noble candidate's walls may be turned to account in the advertising and vilifying arts.

One of the printed papers was in the form of a dialogue showing how a man who wanted to have his money back from the Labourers' Union could not get it, whilst a man who had placed his money in a Bank was at once able to draw it. The different principles of Unions, Insurance Societies and Savings Banks are well known in most places but possibly they need explanation in Wilton. Another placard asked whether the electors would vote for a stranger and ended 'Is this a proper rewards for all the kindness shown you, Shame upon you!' So by dint of libelling and scolding, if not also by threatening and promising, the great lord's brother is again returned.

It is almost needless to say that Mr Arch totally refrained from anything like personal abuse, even under this great provocation. An enthusiastic labourer at one of his meetings shouted out – 'There he is, now look at him those who have not seen him, there he is, every inch an English gentleman.' And Mr Arch's earnest and impressive speech indeed confirmed that view; though he has worked as a farm labourer, he is every inch a gentleman, an *honourable* man, one who would not bear false witness, nor consent, in fighting for a seat in Parliament, to fling about violent personal abuse. Another course pursued by Mr Arch was most praiseworthy though not worldly wise; as the Echo has stated, he totally refused to engage in personal canvassing.

We will quote in conclusion the closing words of one of Mr Arch's speeches; they afford a good type of the spirit in which he fought. He said

> he had never tried to be rich, or he might have been wealthier than at present, if he had felt disposed to take bribes, but he had refused them. He hoped that the poetry his mother taught him when he was a boy would ever be the pole star of his life. To live
>
> For the cause that needs assistance,
> For the wrongs that need resistance,
> For the glad time in the distance,
> For the good that I can do.

The Standard, 26 May 1880

Sir – My attention has just been called to your article of the 22nd inst., with reference to the sad death of Mary Williams and to the oppressive custom which obliges shop assistants to stand all day. Will you kindly permit me to point out that which I believe to be the only effectual way of bringing about the form, so much needed. It is by means of united protest among the shop assistants themselves. It has been proved, I think, that outside efforts can do but little in the matter. For several years, the Ladies' Sanitary Association has endeavoured to effect a change, even taking the very practical step of devising seats of a suitable kind and seeking to induce employers to use them. A memorial on the subject of shop seats, initiated by Lady Florence Herbert and bearing a large number of influential signatures, was recently handed over to the Association for use in this agitation. The National Health Society has also, I believe, made some movement upon the subject. All these efforts have been supported by pamphlets and newspaper letters, written by medical men of high standing, yet they have been unavailing. The employers frequently say, when they are appealed to, that the young women they employ do not wish for seats, and until the women themselves disprove this, probably nothing will be done.

The Women's Protective and Provident League would most gladly act as a centre for the united action which appears to be so desirable. I would suggest that any young ladies who feel the standing rule a hardship and wish to see it abolished should write to me. Their letters would be considered as strictly confidential, and when a few had been received the writers could be invited to meet here to confer about how to extend their effort. So general an appeal might ultimately be made as to induce the employers to concede to it; and if out of such common action should grow an attempt to form among female shop assistants a Protective and Benefit Society, such as our League seeks to promote, I think no one could object to this as being unnecessary or mischievous. Shopwomen most surely needs, as much as any other class of workers, to provide against times of want or work or of sickness. This League is ready to help any women who are obliged to earn their own livelihood to help themselves, by meeting and uniting together for mutual protection and aid. What it has already done in this direction may be ascertained by anyone who likes to apply for its papers.

I must ask permission to add one brief remark upon your reference to the recent demonstration of women, inconsistent as you may think it, I and several other women connected with this League were present. We do 'cast about for some measure of relief against the cruel customs of trade.' Some of us devote nearly every leisure moment to efforts to encourage and raise our working sisters; but many of us also 'demonstrated' on May 6th, for Women Householders' Suffrage. Let the oppressed shopwomen begin to demonstrate their wish for shop seats, and they can scarcely fail to meet with an attentive hearing.

I am, Sir, your obedient servant, Emma A Paterson, Hon. Sec. Women's Protective and Provident League, 36, Great Queen-Street, WC, May 25th.

'Shop Assistants,' *Women's Union Journal*, June 1880, pp. 57–58

A correspondence has been going on lately in some of the daily papers upon the subject of shop assistants' grievances. The suicide of a girl named Mary Williams – who seems to have complained bitterly of the long hours of work and to have lost all pleasure in life from sheer exhaustion – has drawn attention to this subject. One of the propositions which meets with most favour from the public, seems to be that of inducing the employers to provide seats for their assistants. A project is now started at the instance of a benevolent nobleman, to secure a pledge from ladies that after a certain date they will not purchase at any shops where seats are not provided for those who serve; a proposal in fact, that the customers, not the shop assistants, should 'strike' against the standing rule. These kindly intentioned efforts may have some effect, but we have very little hope of it. Ladies are ready enough to sign memorials to employers for provision to be made for seats, but to persuade them to give up a favourite shop will be a most difficult matter. We understand that seats have been provided for some time past at Mr Dobb's shop, Westbourne Grove, but we have not heard of any great rush to that establishment. To all such outside efforts the employers will return the answer they have frequently made: that the assistants do not wish for seats, that they do not ask for them. This is an answer not easily to be met; there are small means of knowing whether it is correct or not, but there seems some ground for it. The Honorary Secretary of the League, in reply to a letter written by her to the Standard, May 26th, suggesting combination, has received several letters from shop assistants, stating that seats would be of little use to them and that their urgent need is a shortening of the hours of business. These letters are chiefly from small establishments. The following is a copy of one very practical letter, signed by a number of young women employed in a provincial town; particulars of name and place are here omitted, because a promise has been made that all such communications shall be regarded as confidential.

To the Hon. Sec. of the Women's Protective and Provident League

> We the undersigned Drapers' assistants of – beg to offer our most sincere thanks for your letter in today's Standard; and to entreat you not to confine the proposed movement to London, but to remember the thousands of young women who, though living in country districts, have to bear nearly or quite as much oppression as our London sisters. We, the undersigned, work from twelve to thirteen hours a day from Monday to Thursday, and an extra hour on Friday, and from thirteen to fifteen on Saturday. If we had seats behind the counter we should seldom to be able to use them, so that what we really need is shorter hours of

business. We should be glad to join any Society which, in return for a moderate annual subscription, would strive to gain for us this great benefit.

On all grounds, it seems to be most desirable that the women engaged in shops should combine in an Association for their protection. The League would very gladly give advice and friendly aid in such efforts. All who are anxious to help shopwomen, could we believe do so far more surely by encouraging them to protect themselves than by any other outside action.

'The Army Tailoresses,' *Women's Union Journal*, September 1880, pp. 95–98

The present position of affairs at the Royal Army Clothing Factory, Pimlico appears to be but little known. An impression has been started and has gained ground, that the dispute was satisfactorily settled by the Committee of Enquiry appointed last Summer by the War Office. A strong and widely spread desire has however been shown for correct information regarding this dispute with the nation's workpeople, and it may be well to give a brief review of events which have occurred since the publication of the Report of the Committee of Enquiry in September last.

One of the first public condemnations of the Report, as well as of certain circumstances attending its publication, was embodied in a Resolution moved at the Trades Union Congress, Edinburgh, in September, by My Henry Broadhurst, now one of the Members of Parliament for Stoke upon Trent, and seconded by Mrs Paterson. That Resolution was reported by the Press and by comments on the whole case, with extracts from the Report of the Committee of Enquiry, also appeared, at the same time in many leading newspapers.

On the re-assembling of Parliament in February, a Conference was held at the Westminster Palace Hotel, under the Chairmanship of Mr Hodgson Pratt, when, by the unanimous vote of a large and closely crowded meeting, consisting, with only about a dozen exceptions, of women employed in the Factory, a resolution was passed, pointing out that in not one single point of complaint had the Committee recommended any concession to the aggrieved workpeople, and urging the necessity for a new enquiry – a Parliamentary enquiry – also deputing the Women's Protective and Provident League to act on behalf of the women. These Resolutions, with notes of the statements made by the workwomen who spoke at the Conference, were forwarded to Mr Mundella, who had given valuable help in the House of Commons last year and had referred in several of his vacation speeches to the great injustice done to the operatives by the serious reductions in their wages. Mr Mundella promised to confer with a few members of Parliament on the subject of the Resolutions. In the midst of these proceedings came the general election, which for a time necessarily suspended all action.

Many of the workpeople were among those who ardently rejoiced in the return of a Liberal Government; they looked forward to receiving justice at its hands. When things had settled down a little, Mr Mundella was reminded by the League of his promise and he replied that so soon as the appointment of the Minister of War should be decided on he would attend to the request. Closely upon the announcement of the appointment of Mr Childers as Secretary of State for War, came that of the appointment to office of Mr Mundella and of Sir Charles Dilke, who had also frequently spoken in strong terms of the grievances in question. Then occurred something of the sudden cooling which is well known to take place among even the best of men, when that eruption of the political volcano, a general election, is followed by subsidence into office. It certainly was something of a misfortune for the Army Clothing workpeople that two of their warmest friends were settled so near the summit of the mountain, instead of being toppled over into political insignificance at its base. Mr Mundella was not altogether despaired of. He was again appealed to, and he no doubt did what he could to bring the matter to the notice of Mr Childers. Possibly though he may have urged the question gently, exercising some of the tenderness naturally felt by one officer of State towards another, for we find Mr Childers saying, later on, that the War Office was ignorant of any dissatisfaction at the Factory.

While the League was endeavouring to find a Liberal Member of Parliament who would consent to put a question in the House of Commons, the workpeople, growing impatient and swayed by advice which did not emanate from the League, decided to hold a Public Meeting on July 8th at the Pimlico Rooms, with Capt. Bedford Pim – a somewhat unfortunate choice it appears to us – as Chairman. The Meeting was convened and the expenses were paid by the Westminster and Pimlico Branch of the London Tailoresses' Trade Union, to which several of the workwomen belong, but many women were present who have not yet joined the Union. A Petition was adopted praying for a Parliamentary Enquiry, and a Resolution was passed requesting the Members for Westminster, Sir C Russell and the Rt. Hon. WH Smith, to present it. A second meeting was held on August 11th at Portcullis Hall, when Mr WH Spink a Westminster Churchwarden presided. This meeting was paid for by a subscription raised by the women among themselves. On August 6th, after, as it would appear, numerous reminders, Sir C Russell presented the petition in the House of Commons, and on Thursday August 12th he asked Mr Childers a question concerning it. The following reply was given:

In the House of Commons on Thursday night, Mr Childers, in answer to Sir C Russell, said – My attention, Sir, has been called by the hon. and gallant baronet to a petition which he presented last night from Captain Bedford Pim, as the chairman of a public meeting of needlewomen employed at a Factory in Pimlico under the War Department. The petition states that a memorial was presented to Parliament last year by the petitioners praying from enquiry about their pay, although I cannot find that any such memorial was presented to the House of Commons; and it requests that the grievances of the petitioners may be investigated by a committee of this House. The facts are these: in April 1879, a revision took place in the wages and piece rates of the persons employed in the Pimlico factory, about one-fifth of whom are wives, widows or daughters of soldiers. A memorial on the subject of this revision was presented to my predecessor, and he appointed a committee to report upon the subject. It consisted of persons unconnected with the War Department, viz., my hon. friend the member for Oldham (Mr Hibbert), Mr Benjamin B Greene (Director of the Bank of England), and Mr Silver, a large employer of female labour, who was nominated by the colleague of the gallant baronet, the late First Lord of the Admiralty. This committee reported fully on 10 July 1879, and their report was laid before Parliament and published. With one exception – namely the conditions of the employment of women before and after childbirth, in which the advice of the Home Office was acted upon – all the recommendations of the committee have been adopted, and this was fully explained to the House by my predecessor on the 1st of March last, who congratulated the House on the satisfactory result of the inquiry. No complaint or grievance as to their wages or the conditions of their employment has been received either at the War Office or by the officers at the factory, since effect was given to the unanimous report of the committee. If any one of the operatives have any such complaints and will bring them before their official superiors in the manner prescribed by the regulations of the public service, especially before their subject has been brought before the responsible Minster in the prescribed manner, would be most dangerous precedent, and I feel certain will not be the wish of the House.

Upon this, the workwomen applied to Mrs Paterson, Honorary Secretary of the League, asking if she would accompany a deputation to the House of Commons. She consented to do so, and on Thursday August 19th, at 6:30 pm, nearly 400 of the factory women assembled in Westminster Hall, to show their interest in the object with which give of their number and Mrs Paterson were deputed to seek an interview with Mr Childers. The following report appeared in several daily and weekly papers.

Deputation of Female Operatives – Upwards of 300 of the female operatives employed at the Army Clothing Factory, Pimlico, assembled in Westminster Hall yesterday evening for the purpose of calling the attention of Mr Childers, the Secretary of State for War, to certain grievances which they at present suffer in regard to pay and other matters incidental to their occupation. Mr Broadhurst was requested by the War Secretary to see a deputation of the women, and several of them had an interview with the hon. Gentleman in the conference room. After stating the object of their visit, Mr Broadhurst advised them to draw up a statement and send it through Mr Ramsay, the director of the clothing department, to Mr Childers at the War Office. The women demurred, on the ground that their statement would not find its way to the War Secretary in the form they would wish, and they asked that a Parliamentary Committee should be appointed to investigate certain charges, to inquire into their pay, and into the working of the factory generally. One of the women said that they had been told that if they made any demonstration or went to the House of Commons they would be thrown out of work, and the establishment closed. They asked that Colonel Hudson might again become the director of the factory, for no one but a military man could understand the work. Mr Broadhurst said that no official dare alter their statement after it was addressed to Mr Childers; and the hon. Gentleman after some difficulty, being able to assure them on this point, they accepted his advice and promised to keep carefully a copy of what they sent.

At the close of the interview with Mr Broadhurst, the deputation met in the rooms of the Westminster Democratic Club, to consider and decide upon steps to be taken to draw up and present, through Mr Ramsay, a Memorial to Mr Childers. An adjourned meeting was held on Saturday, August 21st, when the following Memorial was despatched, bearing 263 signatures.

To the Rt Hon. Hugh CE Childers, MP, Secretary of State for War

The memorial of the undersigned workwomen employed in the Royal Army Clothing Factory at Pimlico Humbly showeth

1 That on April 1879 numerous and heavy reductions were made in the piece work rates of payment for our work, entailing in many cases a loss of five shillings and six shillings per week. That the withdrawal of the permission to take work home coming at the same time as these serious reductions in our wages greatly increased the distress caused by the said reductions; of this withdrawal however we should not complain if the old scale of prices could be restored.

2 That we feel it to be greatly to our disadvantage to be placed under a superintendent who is acquainted only with the ordinary tailoring trade and we earnestly desire the appointment of a military superintendent, who alone can fully understand the special character of our work and the need for care and thoroughness in its execution.

3 That the method of management under which these changes were brought about, and which was acknowledged by the Committee of Enquiry to be unnecessarily harsh, has been continued, and we have

been harassed by frequent and arbitrary changes in the Factory, changes of comparatively smaller importance than the reductions in our wages, but tending greatly to our discomfort. As one instance we beg to mention that during the winter, the windows close to the seats of a number of the workwomen were taken out and have not been replaced. The complaints we have made to our superior officers of this and of other hardships have been in most cases met by threats of dismissal or of the closing of the Factory.

4   That many of the outdoor workers are kept in a state of uncertainty as to whether they will receive work, and they are now told that all outdoor work will shortly be discontinued, a change which does not appear to have been proposed at the time of last year's enquiry.

5   That with regard to the enquiry made during the months of May and June 1879, by a Committee appointed by the War Office, we venture to submit that the evidence upon the prices paid by Contractors was too limited in extent to warrant the conclusion of the Committee 'that prior to the reductions the price of manufacture in the factory was much in excess of the trade price, and the cost of labour much above the market rate.' Only three contractors were examined, and one of these stated that his own prices were rather higher than those paid in the factory. The Committee refused to examine the late Superintendent, Colonel Hudson, who could have given important evidence regarding the bases of the former prices. The workwomen earnestly petitioned the Committee for the examination of Colonel Hudson but their petition was not granted.

We humbly and earnestly pray for a full and early enquiry with this statement.

August 19th 1880.

The acknowledgment received by Mrs Paterson, by whom, at the unanimous request of the women, the Memorial had been forwarded, was as follows:

War Office, August 25th 1880

Madam

I am directed by the Secretary of State for War to inform you that the memorial from Female operatives employed in the Royal Army Clothing Factory has been received by him, and he has intimated to the operative whose name heads the list that directions have been given to ascertain the exact nature of the grievance complained of by every individual who signed the memorial.

Although the memorial has been forwarded through you, Mr Childers feels assured that, when you consented to be the medium of communication, you were not aware of the Regulations which require that any complaints from individuals employed in the Public service can only be dealt with in direct communication with the persons so employed; and under these circumstances he can only deal with the operatives directly through their immediate superiors.

I am, Madam, Your obedient servant, Ralph Thompson

The enquiry promised in the above letter has been instituted, but the workwomen are disappointed about the mode of enquiry. They had hoped that if Mr Childers could not conduct it himself he would at least depute one of his Secretaries or Clerks to do so, from the War Office. Instead of this, Mr Quinlan, the storekeeper of the Factory, at whose recommendations all the reductions of wages complained of were made, has been deputed to investigate the complaints, by questioning the women who signed the Memorial, in the presence only of Mr Ramsay (the Director of Clothing) and a shorthand writer. This seems to be something like setting a defendant to assist in judging his own case. Shorthand notes of the statements made, are, it is said, to be forwarded to Mr Childers. The investigation was commenced on Thursday, August 26th. A paragraph went the round of the papers stating that Mr Childers himself recently visited the Factory for the purpose of receiving the women's statements, but this appears to have been incorrect, and the origin of the paragraph is unknown.

The following notice in the form of a large printed bill is now posted about the factory. The grammatical construction of the first part is peculiar, but we give it word for word, and we can vouch for the correctness of this copy.

NOTICE

The Secretary of State for War having intimated in the House of Commons that if any of the operatives have any complaints and will bring them before their Official Superiors in the manner prescribed by the Regulations of the Public Service, he will undertake to look fully and impartially into them.

Demonstrations are therefore unnecessary and that in Westminster Hall on Thursday afternoon having been followed by a counter-Demonstration in the Factory on the following morning which caused considerable excitement and loss of time.

He feels compelled in the interest of the women themselves, and for the maintenance of discipline, to forbid any further Demonstrations, and directs that the name of any operative taking part in them shall be reported to him.

By Order of the Secretary of State for War.
George D Ramsay
Director of Clothing, August25th 1880.

We hope to ascertain whether, even in Government service, there is any justification for interference such as this, to restrain the operatives from going where they like in their own time. The women who appeared in Westminster Hall did so after work time: viz. at 6:30 pm – the factory closes at 6. Their conduct was most quiet and orderly; no Demonstration was attempted.

With regard to the Memorial having been forwarded to Mr Childers by a person not employed in the Public Service, this could scarcely have been supposed to be contrary to the Regulations of the Public Service, for last year, the late War Secretary, Colonel Stanley, received and acted upon a memorial to a similar effect, signed only by Mr Hodgson Pratt on behalf of a Meeting of the women, and forwarded to Colonel Stanley by the Hon. Sec. of the League. It is quite useless now to attempt to confine interest in this question to the people actually concerned. A strong interest has been shown in it by the public, who have declined to say 'if you please' to the War Secretary, before taking the subject into consideration. It has been freely discussed by correspondence in the Press. English ratepayers feel, and we think justly, that they have a right to say something, about the workpeople employed by them, or in other words, by the State.

Two considerations present themselves very strongly in a review of the case. First, whether members of Parliament might not have been hastened in their very tardy action throughout the whole affair, had even but a small proportion of women possessed voting power; and secondly, whether some form of the principle of arbitration might not be applied for the settlement of this dispute. A Government by whom Mr Rupert Kettle has been knighted for his active labours in regard to arbitration, might perhaps fitly adopt this mode of settlement.

'Women's Trade Unions,' *Women's Union Journal*, October 1880, p. 108

(Excerpt from a meeting to promote Women's Trade Unions in Dublin)

Mrs Paterson, London, stated the objects of Unions in England. It was only about six years ago that the first movement was made towards establishing Unions. Many people sympathised with the difficulties of working women. A great deal of sympathy had been expressed with their condition, as in the 'Song of the Shirt,' and many articles had been written about the position they occupied, but it was only a few years ago that any practical effort was made to help them to a better position. A few friends joined together in London and formed what was known as the Women's Protective and Provident League. It was not a Union; it consisted neither of the employing nor the employed, but of a few men and women anxious to help working women by some practical method to better their condition. They believed that the best way of doing this would be to assist in forming Women's Trades' Unions, such as men had, with the same objects of protecting trade, providing members with assistance when out of work, and also with information where work might be got. The first Union formed in London was that among the women employed in the Bookbinding trade, ad after that the Upholsteresses formed a Society. Unions were subsequently formed in Yorkshire and Bristol and the Tailoresses, and other Women's Unions in London were established. Mrs Paterson impressed upon the Dublin working women the necessity of associating together, so as to get trade information, and by their organisation to promote a spirit of individual independence.

'Trades Union Congress,' *Women's Union Journal*, October 1880

Mr Broadhurst said that the Parliamentary Committee had on this [the issue of factory inspections], as on other occasions, drawn the attention of Parliament to this matter. In the early part of 1879, they had a very influential deputation to the then Home Secretary on the subject, and the cotton operatives of Lancashire were good enough to send them some very valuable delegates to accompany them to the Home Secretary. They, unfortunately, on that occasion had not the advantage of a personal interview with him, but they saw the second in authority. They, on that occasion, he (Mr Broadhurst) thought, made out a very good case for having an increased number of inspectors, and that a different class of men should be employed. It was perfectly true that the class of men from whom the inspectors were selected were not in all cases the most desirable for the work in which they were engaged that could possibly be selected. He was not going to say a single word to depreciate the good intentions of that staff of gentlemen. He had no doubt that, considering the peculiar circumstances and very delicate nature of the work they discharged they performed their duties as well as could reasonably be expected, when the very large area over which they had charge and authority was thoroughly considered.

When the deputation to which he had referred contended for on that occasion was, that they should have some practical workmen added to the staff – men who understood the way in which the provisions of the Act were evaded by the employers; but the result was that they got no great encouragement to persevere; and he sincerely trusted that now that matters had somewhat changed in the right direction, they might be more fortunate. He had an opinion that, if they carried this resolution today, as he knew they certainly would carry it, the best means the committee could adopt to further their views would be to again wait upon the Government by deputation. And in that case he sincerely trusted that the trades which were so deeply affected by the want of additional inspectors would do on that occasion as they did on the last – that was, to support the committee liberally by sending delegates from their trades to accompany the deputation upon the subject. They must be aware that he personally with other members of the Parliamentary Committee, had no very special knowledge of the subject, and it was by the delegates from the trades most affected by the Act accompanying the deputation that the strength of their case would be made out.

Now, with regard to the question of the terms of the resolution, he might say in the first place that he did not know anything at all about the preparation of that resolution. He was no party to the insertion of the word 'persons' in it. If he had been the author of the resolution he would have said distinctly 'practical men' so that there should be a distinct issue as to whether women should or should not be included. It was well known to nearly everyone present that to include the word 'women' in the resolution was practically to defeat the object in which they had in view. (No, no) That, he said, was a matter of opinion, and he said that the vast majority of the opinion of the meeting would be on his side. (No, no.) Then, if that were so, it would not be on the practical side but on the unpractical side, or he did not know what side it would be on. Of this one thing they might be perfectly certain, that working women would never be appointed factory inspectors. It had been said repeatedly, by high authorities – and he thought it had been said by a delegate at the Edinburgh Congress – that reasons of the most forcible character were given why it would be next to impossible for women to efficiently discharge the duties of factory inspectors. (Why?) The reasons were stated on the occasions to which he had referred, and he did not like to go into details of the very unpleasant and objectionable character of those which related to the greater part of the work of a factory inspector. He did not think it would be wise or right to do so in a mixed meeting. Mr Cook, of London, had said that women should be inspected by women, but he ventured the opinion that if the women themselves were canvassed they would rather be inspected by the men.

At all events, he only spoke from his own experience. This was a serious subject, and one which he thought should be treated seriously. The matter was now in the hands of the Congress. Unfortunately their lady delegates were as a rule possessed of great persuasive power and fascination. They had all great activity. They were delegates who discharged their duties most efficiently for the promotion of the objects they desired. He himself had not been canvassed to support their views on this subject, but he had been very energetically jogged in the ribs, if he might use such a vulgar expression – for the purpose of reminding him that they were not going to be put out by having the word 'person' used to throw dust in their eyes. He hoped that the delegates would this year stand firm by what they believed was a practical resolution – namely, one advocating the appointment of practical men to increase the staff of factory inspectors. He was certain that if they were ever to obtain what they sought it would be first through the means of obtaining the appointment of an extra number of men. And why would not ladies be reasonable for once in their lives (oh) – and agree that the first matter was to get more men appointed and afterwards consider whether the word 'women' should or should not be introduced into the Act of Parliament. But they all knew how unreasonable ladies were – (oh, oh) when a practical question was under discussion. They would have all or none of whatever they went in for. Half measures never satisfied them. (Laughter.) Although the increase in the number of factory inspectors had been deferred for years, they were determined to maintain their obstinate view of having the word 'women' passed into the resolution. He asked, in conclusion that a division should be taken, so that it would be shown that there were some members of the Congress who even in the presence of ladies were prepared to maintain a reasonable proposition.

[...]

Mrs Paterson, of London, in supporting the amendment, said that the word 'persons' would not be understood to include women. Some legal decisions with regard to claims made by women to vote for members of Parliament proved this. Mr Broadhurst had spoken of a deputation to the Home Office in 1879 on the subject of the increase in factory inspectors and had said that on high authority the proposition to appoint women as inspectors was regarded as impracticable. Why had no women been invited to join that deputation, so that objections raised might have been answered? The women's societies had heard nothing of the deputation until it was over. The Parliamentary Committee who arranged the deputation seemed to forget that this was a question more directly concerning women than men, the work of women, children, and young persons alone being regulated by law. Mr Shorrocks had referred several times to an interview which he had had in Manchester with Mr Redgrave, the Chief Inspector of Factories; but opinions expressed at a private interview could scarcely be regarded as authoritative. It would have been well if Mr Redgrave had met this Congress, when he could have conferred with women as well as with men. Mr Redgrave in his last report objected to the appointment of either working men or women as inspectors; he naturally wished to limit such appointments to men of his own class.

Working men should be the last class to use the argument of expediency, as Mr Broadhurst had done. They had often been told by the richer classes that they must wait for the granting of their just claims until it should be expedient to grant them. This question of factory inspection showed clearly the necessity for the representation of women at trade congresses. Even though eight women were now present, Mr Broadhurst appeared to think that he knew best what women's wishes were, for he said that according to his experience women would rather have their workshops inspected by men. She hoped that the Congress would adhere to the wording adopted at two previous congresses, and she could not believe that the large infusion of Irish delegates in this Congress would be the cause of the reversal of this act of justice to women.

Several delegates rose to speak, but the Chairman, who was supported in his view by other delegates, said they had heard enough on this subject.

'A House of Rest,' *Women's Union Journal*, December 1880, pp. 135–137

If Associations could become known and appreciated in proportion to the amount of good that they do, instead of according to the extent to which they are advertised or talked of, the subject of the brief sketch which we are about to give would hold a high and prominent position. In doing our small share towards spreading a knowledge of the House of Rest at Babbacombe, Torquay, we are guided by something more than printed papers. One of the printed papers we shall have occasion to quote, as well as some information afforded by letters received from Miss Skinner, a member of the Committee, but we have also the testimony of two members of the Women's Unions, who have been fortunate enough to spend three weeks or more at the house this year, and who speak in the warmest terms of the reception and treatment they met with, and of the enjoyment and strength gained from their stay in the beautiful region of Torquay.

The object of the House is to afford temporary rest and change of air to dressmakers, milliner, shopwomen and other women engaged in business.

> It is not intended to be a convalescent home, but simply a place of rest, to which overworked women can turn for a breathing time, and where also they may spend their annual holiday at small expense. The house is pleasantly situated, close to Babbacombe Downs, overhanging the sea, surrounded on all sides by lovely scenery. It is tastefully though inexpensively furnished, and is managed rather on the principle of visits to a large country house than as an Institution. The rules are only such as would be observed in an ordinary visit.

We are informed by Mess Skinner, one of the ladies most active in the good work, that the visitors, by their courtesy and their attention to the wishes of those by whom they are entertained, have fully justified the experiment of 'Trust, not watch'; we also learn that the visitors 'are very proud of their large, lofty drawing-room and handsome dining-room, which has beautiful pictures hanging on the walls, a present from a friend.' All the surroundings tend to rest the eye and refine the taste. Facilities are afforded for boating, bathing and driving, as outdoor amusements.

Seventeen visitors can be received at one time; the house is open all the year round and visitors may stay for a longer period in winter than in summer. The applications, during the summer especially, are naturally very numerous. A letter addressed to a Torquay newspaper by Miss Skinner, a member of the Committee, states, 'Many came almost broken down, and have been completely restored to health and the power of again earning their bread, by rest, change and medical care. It is probably not generally known that many women dare not consult a doctor whilst in a house of business lest they should be deemed incapable of work, and they gladly seize the opportunity offered them here. Some who come to us have never had a holiday in their lives; others not for periods of five or seven years. Some have never seen the 'real country.' They do not come in the way of ordinary help, and through lack of some special aid, often struggle on, and on, till they drop. How eagerly they embrace it when it is offered is shown by our having had between sixty and seventy applications within three months, chiefly from London.

We now come to the important point of the provision of means for this admirable and much-needed house. Feeling most strongly the importance of self-supporting and independent associations of women we should hesitate to recommend any ordinary Society aided by outside subscriptions. This effort, however, is one which it would be scarcely possible to make wholly self-supporting, at all events in the first instance, and while the wages of women are so inadequate to their wants. Subscriptions of one guinea a year are invited; and each subscriber is entitled to a ticket of admission for three weeks; the women to whom these tickets are given are required to pay 5s per week each during their stay in the house. This payment is never remitted, for, as Miss Skinner justly says, 'the idea of charity would upset our prime principle in beginning the work, and would be much resented by the class for whom we began it.'

There is another excellent arrangement by which, on payment of 12s per week, a visitor is admitted without obtaining a subscriber's recommendation; this arrangement will probably help to make the house ultimately self-supporting – though 12s is but a very small payment for board and all the comforts and advantages afforded. The visitors of course pay their own railway fares, but 'through the kindness' return railway tickets are supplied to them for single fares (from London 1s 6d third class).

We must now conclude this notice without a reference to the untiring and earnest labours of the Misses Skinner. These ladies, two of the founders of the house, live near it and give a hearty welcome to the visitors. They also give much assistance of other kinds. The great success of this experiment is without doubt due to the large amount of friendly help given by the

94   *Societies and Struggles: May 1879–1884*

Misses Skinner. The numerous letters received are answered by one of the ladies referred to, who very wisely says, 'we feel it best for the communications at present to be made by ladies on the committee, not by officials.' We must add that the lady who acts as paid superintendent of the house seems to be admirably suited for the position.

Such work as we have described needs no comments; its value must be at once recognised by those who are acquainted with the lives of workwomen. We earnestly hope that all sympathisers will give any help that they can. We shall look forward to the desirable, and not impossible, event of the self-support of the house being finally arrive at; in the meantime we are willing to regard the subscriptions which are contributed as a substitute for the invitations to their country houses, which ladies gladly give to their personal friends, and as a small compensation for some of the thoughtlessness of fashionable ladies about work relating to their dress, which often tends to make the lives of work women, or of shopwomen, harder and more irksome than they might otherwise be.

'Correspondence,' *Women's Union Journal*, December 1880, p. 141

To the Editor of the *Women's Union Journal*

In reading over your issues from time to time, I am struck forcibly with the idea that so far as being able to manage and support a 'Trade Journal' the women are far ahead of the men.

Many a time during this latter half of the 19th century have workmen essayed the issue of a Trade Journal, but I believe in every case they have failed miserably.

I need not point out the names of those papers and their managers, it is enough to say failure has overtaken both paper and management.

When I compare 'The Women's Union Journal' with most of the Journals started on behalf of the workmen, the conclusion is forced upon my mind that men have wished to soar too high and as a natural consequence have overshot the mark aimed at.

Men could not do to walk slowly and read carefully a small sixteen page Journal; no, they must have a large sized paper six times the size of one they knew they could support. They must also go in for a highly paid editor, sub-editor and staff in proportion, which caused expenses to run in almost every case to enormous losses on the sales.

Again, they could not be content with reports and notices of Meetings and authentic news, especially applicable to their state and condition, but they must have high flown leading articles far beyond the grasp of the comprehension of more than two-thirds of their readers. Many other faults might be found with all the workmen's attempts to secure a medium of communicating one with another, learning the state of trade throughout the country and aiding each other both morally, socially, politically and pecuniarily.

I am glad to see the women use greater wisdom in the selection and management of their Journal than the men have up to the present moment. I am glad to see that, as a rule, the short but pithy leader is also practical in its scope and tendency. I feel certain that if it continues its present course and does not seek to compete with other and more wealthy Journals, there is a bright and successful future before it.

Women everywhere should give it their best support, and their best support is to buy it, read it, follow its advice, and to secure its purchase by their sisters in their own immediate neighbourhood.

You have still grievances to remedy, disabilities to remove, inequalities to level, and much work to do, which can only be done by earnestness sociability, intelligence, money and a thorough organisation.

There is work connected with your homes, your workshops, the management of your towns and that of the country generally, which you will do well to look after, through your Journal and Trades Union.

I was glad to see and hear your representatives at the Dublin Congress. They discussed your cases both eloquently and intelligently and created a very good impression upon the men delegates, notwithstanding the adverse criticisms of Messrs Broadhurst, Knight and Shorrocks.

Let me say to the women, unite, unite and keep united.

Yours, etc., Benjamin Pickard, Miners' Offices, Wakefield, November 18th 1880.

Durham Miners' Association, 16, North Rd Durham, December 3rd, 1880.

Enclosed is 18 stamps being twelve months' subscription for the 'Women's Union Journal.' I am very pleased to see such a useful periodical, devoted to the interests and social emancipation of women. It is much required. Wishing you every success.

I am very truly yours,
William Crawford.

'Women's Unions in America,' *Women's Union Journal*, January 1881, pp. 4–5

Labour Bureau Office
St Louis, MO, U.S.A.
November 20th 1880
To Mrs Paterson, London

Madam, Through the valuable columns of the Co-operative News I am enabled to write to you, seeing your name in connection with those of

Miss Whyte and Miss Geary as delegates from your respective trades societies to the Trades Union Congress held in Dublin in September. And now for the object of my writing to you. About a month ago I addressed a society of the Daughters of Crispin in this city. In the course of my remarks I referred to yourself and colleagues as present at that Congress and suggested to my hearers the advantages and benefits of corresponding with associations so much older and more experienced in trades organisation. As my audience were all young and inexperienced in work of this kind I volunteered to write and open the way for a mutual interchange of opinions. If you have anything in the way of trade reports, (women's) results of organisation, financially, socially and educationally, by addressing them or any communications to my address I shall take pleasure in placing them in the hands of the above society. Hoping to hear from you in reply, I am, Madam, Respectfully Yours,
John Samuel

(The Honorary Secretary of the League in replying to this letter, has begged for some information about the Daughters of Crispin, for publication in the Journal.)

'The Daughters of St Crispin,' *Women's Union Journal*, March 1881, p. 27

(This letter, received by the Honorary Secretary of the League, will, we are sure, be read with much interest. – ED)
St Louis, February 7th 1881.
Dear Mrs Paterson

Your letter of the 22nd of December which you sent to Mr Samuel was read before the Delegates of St Crispin and we were all very much pleased to hear from you and the Women's Union.

I will now give you some particulars concerning our Union.[1] We organised in June 1880 and have now about 80 members; there is no other Union among the working girls except our own. And we are all working hard to unite the other working classes.

I almost think it impossible if only girls knew what a benefit it would be to them, that they would hesitate an instant. All the first class shoe fitters get very good wages, 8 dollars to 9 dollars per week and steam power. The second class from 5 dollars to 7 dollars; the girls that work piece work make more, but 9 dollars a week is good wages. The Knights of St Crispin help us along, and it if were not for them I know there would be no Union, for they encourage us. There has been a reduction in two of the Factories; we were not strong enough to withstand it, but the girls left and got other places and got their prices.

The papers which you went were distributed among the girls of the Union and they were all very interesting. The Knights publish a paper which is very interesting also. I have no more information to communicate at present.

We all send a vote of thanks to you for your kindness, and hope your Union will succeed in all her undertakings, hoping to hear from you soon.

I remain, yours truly,
Annie Shaw
Corresponding Secretary, Daughters of St Crispin.

'Workshops in Towns,' *Women's Union Journal*, August 1881, pp. 79–80

We publish this month a valuable communication upon the sanitary condition of London factories and workshops. The subject is one of the greatest importance and we should be glad to have it frequently considered in these pages.

Recent experiences in visiting a number of tailoresses' workrooms in two large towns of the North of England, have shown us that the evil now referred to is not confined to London. The front part of a grand tailoring establishment, with its granite pillars, expanse of plate glass and lofty showrooms, is all that is visible to the customer who enters for a few minutes, or to the passer-by. At the back of this respectability are often to be found, after giddy ascents of spiral iron staircases, or crazy outside ladders, or gropings up pitch dark steps, the lofts in which the men and women who produce the articles sold in the front shop spend the greater part of their lives. The overcrowded and stifling state of many of these rooms (there are a few notable exceptions) must be a fruitful source of disease and misery. There are legal regulations as to the number of cubic feet to be allowed to each person in lodging houses and in many other places liable to inspection, but no limit with regard to crowding in workrooms appears to be thought necessary. The section of the Factory Act to which our correspondent refers, leaves it at the discretion of the Inspector to say whether a workshop is so overcrowded as to be injurious to health. That the Inspectors have paid very little attention to such matters is, we think, shown by a glance at the lists of prosecutions under the Factory Act, given in the Reports of the Inspectors for several years past. Only about 5 per cent of the indictments are for infringements of sanitary regulations, such as neglecting to limewash the walls; the others are for work beyond the legal hours, or for employing young persons without entering their names in the register, or without getting a doctor's certificate as to their fitness to work, and so on.

We have always strongly urged the necessity for the sanitary inspection of factories and workshops. Legislation with regard to hours of work can, we fear, make but a slight impression upon the great evil of overwork, in consequence of the ease with which it may be evaded, and of the impossibility of the frequent, almost daily, visitation necessary for effectually carrying out the law. There may also be brought against it the serious objection that it weakens the self-reliance of workwomen, by seeking to do for them that which the experience of men's Unions has shown can be better done by means of trade organisation. The hours of work in any particular trade are to a great extent governed by similar conditions and may be regulated by mutual agreement all through the trade; but the construction and internal arrangement of workshops vary widely, as our correspondent shows, the buildings being frequently intended for totally different uses. Agreement and common action among workpeople with regard to sanitary arrangements are scarcely possible and the necessity for inspection is therefore obvious.

Many London workwomen complain of insufficient ventilation and of the want of attention to other sanitary matters, but very often they are indifferent upon these points, because they are not conscious of the evils existing. It is only after work has been going on for some hours that the bad air of an ill-ventilated room becomes felt, and then it is less noticed by a person working in the room than by anyone entering from the fresh air.

It is surprising that customers do not sometimes ask to see the rooms in which their work is being done. Ladies, especially, could do much good in this way. The separation of the customer from the worker is unfortunately every day widening. We have heard of one large establishment in the West End of London, where, as there is no back entrance, the workwomen are not permitted to go out at all during the day, because it is supposed that the customers would dislike to see them.

We believe that the system adopted in Paris, the employment of a staff of women as Factory Inspectors, would, if tried in this country, lead to great improvements in women's workrooms.

'Women's Trade Societies,' *The Times*, 15 September 1881

Sir – will you kindly grant me space for a few words with reference to the mention made in The Times of yesterday of the women's trade societies represented at the Trades Union Congress? The statement is that 'the women's societies appear to be numerically the weakest, the smallest numbering only 30 members, the largest but 460 members, while the largest workmen's association represented, the amalgamated Society of Engineers, returns 45,000 members.'

I wish to point out that the women's trade societies are but recently established, the oldest – of which I am one of the representatives – having been formed only in 1874, and that they are at present limited to the places in which they were started. The Amalgamated Society of Engineers has been in existence 30 years, and its 45,000 members are made up by branches all over the country, some of the branches having, however, but a very small number of members. I may also point out that one of the men's societies represented at the Congress has only 40 members – a fact not mentioned in the paragraph I have quoted – and that many of these societies are much older than the Engineers' Society.

From the progress already made in the women's union movement, with all its special difficulties and drawbacks, there is every reason to hope that in 20 years' time the numerical strength of the women's societies will have largely increased.

I am, Sir, your obedient servant, Emma A Paterson, St Andrew's-hall, Newman-Street, W, September 14.

'How to Help Our Work,' *Women's Union Journal*, January 1882, pp. 1–3

An Appeal. But not an appeal for money! We hasten to explain this, for we have no wish that the League should be included among the numberless societies which at the present season advertise, circularise and beg in every possible form. It is true that the League is obliged to receive money help, although its main object is to assist in organising self-supporting societies of working women. But the Committee seldom ask for money; they go on working, literally interpreting the motto that 'to labour is to pray.' They wish the work to be its own recommendation, and they have adopted this monthly Journal as a means of making it known.

What we now suggest is that every subscriber to the Journal should help by forming in her or his own neighbourhood, wherever it may be, a Committee of friends of our movement, men and women, whose business should be to consider in what way they can best encourage the working women of their town, or even village, to join together for mutual protection and support in times of difficulty.

There need be no idea of patronage or charitable aid in such efforts. It might be found desirable for one of the members to invite, in the name of the Committee, a few working women to her house, or to some room lent for the purpose, to talk over plans. At first, it would probably be difficult to get the names of more than a few women, but as soon as these became interested they would bring others. When twenty, or even a dozen, had expressed their willingness to join a Society, a start might be made. Then the work of the local Committee would be to help and advise the women in drawing up rules and making arrangements for the business of the Society. In these matters, the aid of the London League Committee would be most readily given, if desired. This Journal could be used as a means of communication between all helpers in the work. The Journal has subscribers in Ashford,

Brighton, Birmingham, Birkenhead, Belfast, Barnsley, Bideford, Cambridge, Corsham, Cheltenham, Darlington, Derby, Devonport, Dorking, Durham, Dumfries, Edinburgh, Huddersfield, Hartlepool, Horsham, King's Lynn, Kilmarnock, Leeds, Leicester, Newcastle, Portsmouth, Pontypool, Stockport, Scarborough, Stoke-on-Trent, Sandy, Tunbridge, Wolverhampton, Wokingham Woodford and Windsor, besides many smaller places and the various districts of London.

In all these localities, there must be workwomen who would gladly welcome the friendship suggested. In different districts of London too, such attempts might well be made, for it is not to be expected that the central organisation can reach dwellers in all parts of the big city. If in any non-manufacturing locality classification into trades seemed impracticable, a general Society might be formed, of women earning similar rates of wages. This plan has been successfully tried in Oxford. In large towns, however, division according to trades in always found to be the best method. We are glad to say that in Bristol, Dewsbury, Dublin, Folkestone, Leicester, Liverpool, Manchester, Nottingham and Oxford, where the Journal also has subscribers, local League Committee and Unions of working women have been formed, particulars of which may be obtained of the Honorary Secretary of the League.

It may be objected that working men's societies were not started in the way we have indicated; that they were almost entirely of spontaneous growth; but it must be obvious to those who are at all acquainted with the circumstances of working women, that a certain amount of outside sympathy and counsel is required by them. The depression, and the lack of energy and enterprise, resulting from low wages, and the want of leisure arising from excessive hours of work, prevail among working women to an extent seldom realised by workmen even in the worst days of their trade disorganisation. Then, too, the increase in the employment of women during the past thirty years, has been so rapid that only lookers-on can well realise the extent to which women are beginning to influence the labour market, and the serious evils attending their disorganised condition. On-lookers deplore the evils but do not always see any remedy. As an instance we quote a paragraph from the Ladies' Pictorial (of Dec 17) a newspaper which we may remark, by the way, appears to take usually a more sensible view of questions relating to the position of women than most of the fashion papers of the day.

> How many poor and industrious girls are living by their needles in our own metropolis we are not aware, but from a French return we gather that in Paris there are no fewer than 12,322 patronnes or employers of female labour. Allowing to each an average of eight workers, we reach the total of close upon 100,000 young women gaining a livelihood in

this way. From the same source we learn that their average earnings amount to only 2fr. 50c., or about two shillings a day, while some are paid no more than a franc and a half. The worst feature in the existence of these poor creatures is its utter hopelessness.

We venture to dispute the hopelessness above lamented. We point as an answer to the very encouraging notice just issued in a handbill by the Society of Women employed in Bookbinding: it will be found on another page. Many of the members of that Society do not receive more than 12s a week as wages, yet they have been able to establish, with the little help that the League gives, a thoroughly sound and self-supporting Union, as a provision against times of difficulty arising from fluctuations of trade, or from illness.

With needlewomen the obstacles in the way of association are no doubt greater than in any other occupation, and such an appalling case of poverty, as that concerning which we reprint an article from the Daily Chronicle, may indeed seem almost hopeless. The miserable earnings of 5s per week would appear to be too low to make any provision possible; yet a large number of women joining in a Society and paying but a penny a week, might provide 2s or 3s a week for times of distress. It is evident that the 'benevolent people' indicated by the Daily Chronicle cannot reach such cases. There is frequent proof that men and women will starve to death upon honest labour (paid for, unfortunately, at dishonest prices) rather than apply for charitable or poor-law relief. The true way to help them seems to be to induce them to help themselves; 'to make the weak strong to stand.' We hope that this appeal may bring to the League Office many inquiries and promises of the aid that is so much needed in all parts of the country.

'Rational Dress,' *Women's Union Journal*, February 1882, pp. 9–10

We have seldom ventured to touch upon the weighty question of women's dress. The long description of 'Fashions for the Month' from *Le Follet*, presents a tempting piece of padding when matter runs short, but we have resisted the temptation; we observe however that our big and excellent brother, *the Labour Standard*, has succumbed to it. Upon opening a recent number of that paper to look for news of a different character, we came upon *Le Follet*, which the editor, with a due sense of the fitness of things, had placed immediately under a number of extracts bearing the heading 'The Comic Papers.' Very comical sense of the new mandates of fashion are, although this first sentence seems reasonable enough:

Our readers will own they have cause for congratulation when we inform them that, whatever may have been the façon, the trimming or the colour most becoming and attractive to them, during the last few months, may be still as effectively worn, for all the attractive features of the modes of the past year as to be retained.

An inexperienced reader would suppose that no more need be said and that having graciously permitted women to continue to wear what they had found becoming and attractive to them, Le Follet would take his leave, at least for another month. Instead of this he proceeds to put forth numerous instructions. 'Skirts are held back in three places.' 'Some of the trains are very long and full.' 'Panels (what can these be in dress)"' 'separating the fronts and backs of skirts must always be of a richer or more ornamental material than the dress itself' 'The long cuirasses and the paniers pleated or gathered to the edge, drawn away from the front, and draped at the back, accompany very well the pleated skirts.'

It is pleasant to turn from these tedious and puzzling technical details, to a movement for dress reform, which we rejoice to know has at last been inaugurated, not by Mr Worth nor any other male purveyor of fashions, but by women. The Rational Dress Society was formed last year 'to promote' as stated in its Rules 'the adoption according to individual taste and convenience, of a style of dress based upon considerations of health, comfort and beauty, and to deprecate constant changes of fashion, which cannot be recommended on any of these grounds.' The Society has issued a protest against 'Crinolines or crinolettes of any kind, as deforming, indecent and vulgar.' This protest has, we believe, conduced largely to the recently announced failure of efforts to reintroduce crinolines.

At the Brighton Health Congress held December 13th to 21st, the Society obtained a silver medal for its 'Improved Costumes for Ladies,' and the Honorary Secretary, Mrs EM King, read a paper on 'Women's Dress in relation to Health.' The adoption of the improved costume is, we must mention, an entirely optional matter for members. Simple approval of the objects we have stated, is all that is required for membership. The new costume is however rapidly gaining favour. It is devised so as to get rid of undue weight and tightness, which the Committee considers injurious, and also to avoid the uncomfortable and inconvenient clinging of the ordinary skirt. It bears no resemblance to the much abused 'Bloomer' garment, and we understand that it has been devised by one of our countrywomen, to whom the gratitude of many other women, who have been longing for some revolt against the extremes of fashion, is due.

For women who are obliged to go out in all weathers to their work, this improved dress would have special advantage, in abolishing the discomfort of clinging skirts in wet or windy weather.

The attack upon constant changes of fashion seems to us the most important of all the objects of the new Society. If only some rational, national dress in which a woman could always be 'in the fashion' were to be adopted, the reform would indeed be a great one, not only for health but also for the pockets of both men and women.

We hope that the revolt against 'the folly' has commenced in earnest and that the new Society will speedily find numerous and firm supporters, who will not only protest but will also carry their protests into action.

'Correspondence: Working Women and Trade Organization,'
Women's Union Journal, February 1882, p. 15

To the Editor, *Women's Union Journal*

It is some time ago since I wrote a short note to your very useful Journal. The first time I wrote, it was to congratulate the promoters of the Journal on its apparent success, and I now write to state I am of opinion the Journal has made its mark in the literary world another year. During the year 1881 the paper has been read with interest by many who are not intimately connected with women's work, and who do not know accurately the struggles going on daily in many workshops where they are employed, for all the various kinds of improvements sought in the social, moral and pecuniary respects so desirable for them as a class.

It appears to me that the sanitary arrangements of the different kinds of workshops should be more closely looked after than at present. In order to bring this about there needs a greater number of practical inspectors than we now have, not merely of the male but the female sex; the inspectors we now have may be, for aught I know to the contrary, very excellent persons, whilst, on the other hand, they may be quite the opposite. Inspectors should be practical persons and not given to express too many theories of their own or other people's work. They should not listen to extenuating pleadings in the employer's office, neither advise leniency to workpeople in matters relating to the carrying out of the laws regulating their labour. My opinion is, that practical inspectors could be met with, both in the ranks of ordinary workmen and workwomen. Persons who hold the opinion that women should be excluded from such an office should go a step further and say that all women's labour should be prohibited, then they would make themselves consistent and logical. Where we have women working in large numbers in factories and other workshops, there should women inspectors be found, because who best can deal with a woman's question in such delicate matters as are known to exist in all their various classes of employment? When I refer to this vexed question of women inspectors, I know I lay myself open to severe criticism from certain trade union leaders and trade unionists; therefore I desire to look at this question as broadly as the case will admit, without in any way committing myself to any principle which would lead me into a far more vexed question than that of placing women in the position of inspectors of factories and workshops.

Women, as we all know, know more of the practical part of inspecting the sanitary state of our homes than the man. They also know more of the real wants and desires of their class than ever a man can expect to learn in a life-time. That being the case one would imagine they could easily fit themselves in the other branches of a practical nature, for the work necessary to the position of inspectors. So far as I am able to judge, so long as our womenfolk procure a livelihood in our mills, factories and different kinds of workshops, the legislature of this country should enfranchise the working women by placing no bar to their fitting themselves for the office of inspectorship, now open to the male population of this country. What then is the power to raise woman to this position? Union, Union and nothing else but Union.

There is another question I would briefly refer to, and it is this. So long as woman is in the field she should have a fair field and not be handicapped as she now is. If the husband will place his wife in the mill, if he will allow his own offspring to compete with him in the market, he should do so on equal terms.

If the lords of creation will not unite together to obtain a wage sufficient to keep themselves and families respectably without the adventitious aids of unnatural labour, they should do so on conditions which would allow the weaker sex the privilege of competing for a living in such a way as they would not have to complain that the workman stands back to back with a woman, and only does the same amount of work she does, but for his work he often gets 1/ and more per day.

Women will enquire what is to alter this state of things. My answer is, Union, Union.

If the workmen of this country, I again repeat, continue allowing their small children and wives to perform work which should be performed by themselves, the work should be equal to the pay and the pay equal to the work, and no man should receive more money for the same work done by a woman. Let the women take it to heart this great monetary and humane question, and in doing so let them deal with it purely as a labour and worth question.

I contend that the wages of both men, women and children in our mills, factories and workshops are far too small, and that they should one and all go in for a fairer share of the wealth they are constantly aiding to create. What is the condition of things now? Why we have the millionaire owner of large factories and workshops whilst the poor are gradually becoming poorer. Workers have enough to do to pay their way without laying aside sums of money for a rainy day in the sense of being able to keep them in a green old age. No, whilst the owner looks forward to a mansion here on earth, as a rule the workman's, if he looks for one at all, is beyond this vale of tears, a mansion in the skies; no, whilst the owner is laying up treasures for the evening of life, his workman is laying them up where neither moth nor rust doth corrupt and where thieves do not break through and steal. The mansion the worker may hope to rest in here on earth is the union house, the bastille or workhouse.

Now what is to aid workers to secure more of the wealth they create? Why organisation, to be sure. Then women of England some to the rescue, girls of England come to the rescue. Join your local unions in the counties, in the boroughs, and federate into one grand union for mutual protection both socially, pecuniarily and legally, and for any other object you consider worthy of attainment, and call upon your fellow helper, man, to assist in breaking the chains and fetters which now enthral you.

I was at a meeting at Huddersfield on the night of the 10th December, connected with the weavers of that and other towns. The meeting was a great success, about 2,000 men, women and children were present. Mrs Ellis spoke with her usual practical common sense, and I spoke a short time on the advantages of union. I have no doubt if the people there follow up the results of that meeting it will be felt for a long time.

Then in the name of the poet let every woman and girl strive to make her place in the niche of time, and in that of another, as follows.

> The hills have been high for man's mounting
> The woods have been dense for his axe,
> The stars have been thick for his counting
> The sands have been wide for his tracks
> The sea has been deep for his diving
> The poles have been broad for his sway
> But bravely he's proved in his striving
> That where there's a will there's a way.

I am, &c, Benjamin Pickard, Barnsley, Jan 1882.

'The Shop Hours Bill,' *Women's Union Journal*, March 1882, pp. 17–18

The Shop Hours Regulation Bill introduced by Earl Stanhope in the House of Lords, was withdrawn on February 28th, after a debate of considerable interest. To those who think that legislative restrictions upon women's work should now be diminished, or should not be increased – so long as women have no means of making known, through the franchise, their wishes upon such questions – the debate, of which we give a report, is highly satisfactory. Earl Stanhope's opening proposition, that the Bill was designed for the protection of those persons who are not able to protect themselves, we of course demur to – at least so far as women are concerned. Women are now showing that they can successfully unite for mutual protection and aid, but every additional restriction by law tends to discourage rather than to promote such efforts. Moreover as all attempts that have been made to organise male shop-assistants have failed, Earl Stanhope, to be consistent, should have made his Bill apply to them also, in which case it would probably have met with less opposition from advocates of the employment of women. The injurious tendency of special legislation for women is beginning to be recognised, and there are indications that it will gradually be removed. It is important to notice that four of the speakers in the debate, whilst disapproving of the proposed legislation for shopwomen, expressed approval of it for young persons.

This, we believe, is the most desirable conclusion that can be arrived at in regard to all legal restrictions upon employment, and under the French factory law it has been carried out. Girls employed in French workshops are subject to legal protection up to the age of sixteen, but adult women are free to make their own terms. This system may, it is to be hoped, be ultimately adopted in our own country. It would be a change which would not be likely to meet with much opposition from the Factory Inspectors, because there would still be ample employment for them inspecting factories and workshops where boys and girls are employed. With this change, and even before it takes place, we may hope that the French system of the inspection of girls' workshops by women, will also be adopted. Earl Stanhope's suggestion that policemen should act as Inspectors of retail shops, was scarcely calculated to commend his Bill to support.

With regard to long hours in drapers' shops, and in many other retail shops, there is no doubt much to be done and many evils have yet to be removed. We believe that combination by the assistants, side by side with the earnest efforts of women of all classes against late shopping, will accomplish the desired end. Already great improvements have taken place, by means of the Early Closing Association and other voluntary Societies.

If in some localities a late Saturday closing is found necessary – though with the early payment of wages now adopted, we doubt this – an agitation should be commenced for early closing on some other afternoon of the week. This plan is very successfully carried out in many watering places during the summer, not only by drapers but by shops of all kinds, and the employers as well as the assistants acknowledge the benefit of it. We hope that Ladies' Committees will be formed in all parts of London and in all large cities to promote early shopping. In the smaller towns, early closing has already been very generally adopted.

'Women as Inspectors of Factories and Workshops,' *Women's Union Journal*, June 1882, pp. 46–47

(From a meeting on the subject, called by the Women's Protective and Provident League at the Westminster Palace Hotel)

Mrs Paterson then made an introductory statement, of which the following is a summary. The first movement in the direction of the appointment of women as Inspectors of Factories and Workshops, was at the Trades Union Congress in 1878. Upon a resolution being then moved in favour of the appointment of working men as Assistant Inspectors, one of the give women delegates moved, as an amendment, a recommendation for the appointment also of working women, and quoted in support, information she had just received from France, announcing the appointment of seven women as Workshop Inspectors in the Department of the Seine. The amendment was carried by the Congress, with a majority of 13 votes. At each succeeding Annual Trades Union Congress, the same amendment had been carried by an increasing majority, and last year, at the London Congress, almost unanimously. The great body of the Trade Union representative of the United Kingdom had thus clearly recognised the claims of women, in a matter so directly concerning the interests of women.

It was now thought advisable to make an effort to place the proposition before the public, and before the Home Secretary, and with that view the Women's Protective and Provident League had convened this meeting. They were fortunate in having a Chairman whose noble efforts on behalf of factory children many years ago would long be gratefully remembered (hear, hear). It should be borne in mind that the proposition to be brought before the Conference did not imply a demand for further legislation regarding the work of women, but simply put forward the view that so long as the Factory Act, which very closely affected the interests of all working women was continued, some at least of the Inspectors under the Act should be women. Statistics had shown the proportion of women, young persons and children employed in Textile Factories to be 75 per cent, whilst in several large industries such as dressmaking, shirtmaking and straw plaiting, almost the whole of the workers are women and girls. The present staff of Inspectors for 126,000 establishments numbered 49. The convenors of the Conference did not wish to express any opinion as to whether the number of Inspectors should be largely increased; they simply urged that, whatever the extent of the staff, some of the Inspectors should be women.

The Council General of the Department of the Seine, had adopted a very complete system, in appointing an equal number of men and women as inspectors, on an equal footing, with this division of duties that the men inspect the boys' and mixed workshops, and the women inspect the girls' workshops, a difference between the French and English Factory law being that in France women are protected up to the age of 21 only, whilst in this country women of all ages are subject to Factory and Workshop legislation. Letters had been received by the League, and would be read by Mr Hodgson Pratt, reporting most favourably upon the results of inspection by women. It would perhaps be too much to expect anything like so complete a system to be adopted in England; the promoters of the movement would be quite content to have the experiment tried gradually; they were especially anxious that women who have actually worked in Factories and Workshops, should be appointed to assist in the work of inspection. It had been said in many quarters, by people of all classes, that the sanitary condition of workshops urgently required improvement, and for this work, in shops where girls and women are employed it would probably be readily admitted that women were most suitable.

One of the Inspectors in the North, Mtr Whately Cooke Taylor, who has advocated the appointment of women as Inspectors, stated in his evidence before the Royal Commission in 1875 that 'the present state of things as regards decent accommodation for workwomen is in many cases horrible.' Workwomen have frequently endorsed this statement, but they have added that they scarcely ever saw an Inspector and when they did they felt it difficult to talk to a man about these matters. There had recently appeared in the newspapers a full extract from the last Report of the Factory Inspectors, which gave an account of Mr Whymper's inspection of several large Drapery Establishments in London. The information was chiefly about the clean, airy and tidy appearance of the bedrooms, the food and recreation of the shop girls, and other decidedly domestic matters, which everyone must admit to be eminently suitable for women to report upon.

Various objections had been raised to the proposal that women should be appointed Inspectors; the two principal ones might be briefly mentioned and answered. More than one speaker at the Trades' Union Congress had urged that it would not be desirable for women to go back into back slums and into lofts up dark stairs, or through men's workshops, to inspection women's workrooms. The reply to this was, that the very fact of the roughness and repulsiveness of the places in which some women worked, and of their being surrounded by men's workshops, and superintended by men as employers and overseers, rendered inspection by women the more necessary. It was bad in every respect for women and girls to be cut off, by the conditions of their work, from the sympathy and help of other women. An objection raised by Mr Redgrave, the Chief Inspector of Factories, in one of his Reports was 'that the general and multifarious duties of an inspector would be incompatible with the gentle and home-loving character of a woman.' To this, it might be answered that working women appeared to love their home, when they had any place worthy of the name, quite as much as other people; also that women ready to take Inspectorships would probably be in a position which made it necessary for them to support themselves in order to keep a home together, and that a closer acquaintance with the interior of many place in which women are obliged to work, would tend to make the women who inspected them more home-loving than ever.

'Workshop Inspection by Women,' *Women's Union Journal*,
August 1882, pp. 63–64

Many of our friends have expressed a wish to know what has been done towards carrying out the Resolutions passed at the Conference held by the League last April, on the subject of Factory and Workshop Inspection by women. We will now give them an account of the position of affairs.

The Earl of Shaftesbury, who presided at the Conference, undertook to ask the Home Secretary to receive a deputation on the subject, and some weeks afterwards his Lordship informed the Honorary Secretary of the League that Sir William Harcourt has consented to see a small deputation, on June 19th. The members of the deputation were then duly elected and, as the number was to be limited, it was arranged that the majority should be Secretaries of the Women's Unions, who could speak from actual experience as to the needs of workwomen. On the morning of the 19th a letter was received from the Home Office, stating that, with much regret, Sir William Harcourt was obliged to postpone the reception, in consequence of a Cabinet Council having been called for the afternoon. Shortly after this the Egyptian complications increased and there arose the usual difficulty of gaining attention for home affairs in time of war. The last communication received by the League, in reply to an application made to the Home Secretary at the end of July, expresses his regret that 'he is unable, at present, to fix a time for the deputation.' We are however led to hope, on high official authority, that the reception will take place when Parliament re-assembles in October for the Autumn Session.

On June 16th, the Home Secretary received a deputation from the Parliamentary Committee of the Trades' Union Congress and from various Trades Union, 'for the purpose of urging the government to increase the staff of Factory and Workshop Inspectors.' So long ago as last February, Sir William Harcourt made a promise to receive that deputation. The printed Report of the interview, with the Memorial presented, has lately reached us. We observe that the Memorial recommends the Home Secretary to 'double the present staff by appointing as sub-inspectors 50 *persons* having a practical knowledge of manufacturing processes. Each of the sub-inspectors to be under the supervision of the inspector of the district to which *he* is appointed.' The two words we have given in italics very much surprise us. Our readers may remember that the Trades Union Congress, from which the Parliamentary Committee receives, or is supposed to receive, its instructions, resolved almost unanimously at their Meeting last September, and for the fourth time, to recommend the appointment of working men and women as sub-inspectors, the word 'persons' first proposed being rejected. Why the framers of the Memorial should have so completely disregarded the distinct wish of the Congress we cannot understand, and we hope this question will be asked at the Congress to be held in Manchester next month.

In the last debate it was urged that the word 'persons' was meant to include women as well as men, but if the framers of the Memorial also intended this, they have quite contradicted it by using the word 'he' almost immediately after. Mr Broadhurst, too, in introducing the deputation said he believed that 'a commencing salary of £100 per annum with prospects of advance, would attract many superior working men, as candidates for the office of sub-inspector.' We recommend these facts to the consideration of the Congress, in which, fortunately, a number of working men are to be found who are 'superior' in the sense of liking justice and fair play.

'Married Women's Property,' *Women's Union Journal*, September 1882, pp. 71–72

The passing of an Act of Parliament which will give married women entire control over their own property and earnings, of whatever amount, is a step of profound importance to many thousands of women. Sir George Campbell, in opposing the Married Women's Property Bill during the last debate upon it, on August 11th, said that it would effect a 'complete social revolution.' This was an extreme view of the matter, but in the expression of belief with which Sir George Campbell followed it 'that not one woman in a million had the slightest idea of what the Bill proposed to aid' he and those who share his fears may find comfort. If he is correct, the revolution will be but a slow one. We are inclined to think that many more women than one in a million have anxiously watched the progress of the Bill and know very well what it means. They may, it is true, be surprised at the thoroughness of the reform. Even those who have most actively worked for it, and who commenced their labours 15 years ago – Mrs Butler, Miss Wolstenhome, (now Mrs Elmy) Miss J Boucherett, Mrs Jacob Bright and others – could scarcely have contemplated so triumphant a conclusion to their unceasing efforts.

The Married Women's Property Act of 1870, introduced by Mr Russel Gurney, but much cut about by the House of Lords, which is now repealed and consolidated in the new Act, was a smaller measure, limiting the property right up to £200, though initiating the great boon of giving a wife control over her own earnings. Many practical difficulties were found to arise in administering that Act in consequence of its incompleteness. The new Act introduced by Mr Osborne Morgan, abolishes all former anomalies, and by it, after 1 January 1883, a married woman will stand in precisely the same position as a single woman, with regard to the holding, investing and disposing of her property, unless special settlements and agreements are made at the time of marriage.

We observe that Mr Wharton, the famous universal obstructor, proposed an amendment, which was negative, limiting the operation of the measure to women married after the passing of the Act. Mr Warton also opposed the Bill on the ground that it would act in restraint of marriage; no man, he said, would marry a woman with property, knowing that she could set him at defiance so long as the marriage continued. This remark points to what we consider will be the most valuable effect of the Act. It will restrain mere money hunting marriages, whilst, however, it will not in the last degree deprive a woman of the power to give her husband the whole of her property or earnings should she wish to do so. It will have no injurious effect when the marriage is a happy and mutually trustful one, but it may prevent many mere mercenary matches and the miseries which arise from them.

'Reported Congress of Working Women,' *Women's Union Journal*, November 1882, p. 87

Reports have appeared in certain newspapers during the past few months, of a Congress of working women, sewing machinists, cigar makers and others, held at Brystone Hall, St Luke's. The latest of these we read as recently as 21st October. There have also been accounts of barmaids' and shop girls' Conferences, held after midnight at a Hall in Bloomsbury which no one we know has ever been able to find. We are informed by a gentleman connected with the press, upon whose word we can rely, that the reports represent nothing more than a discharged printer's devil's fertile brain and his desire to turn an honest penny-a-line. We are therefore no longer surprised that the promoters of the Congress did not seek the co-operation of the Women's Protective and Provident League, and we are again reminded that everything in the papers – the Women's Union Journal except – must not be believed.

'Women as Nail Makers,' *Women's Union Journal*, December 1882, p. 97

Now that we are at last again at peace with all men, home matters are beginning to receive some attention. One of the evils, or supposed evils, at present under consideration is that of the employment of women and girls in the work of nail-making and chain-making. The agitation for the legal prohibition of the work of women in these industries is no new one. As long ago as 1874, a Midland newspaper started the subject, at the instigation of some local Trade Unionists, and painted the work and its surroundings in the blackest colours. More important questions having intervened, this one was dropped for a time, but it has now been revived in a letter sent to fifty members of Parliament, one of whose letters in reply (Mr Charles McLaren's) we now reprint.

Some leaders of men's Trade Unions are again the chief movers in the matter. We regret exceedingly that the only remedy our friends recommend is the passing of a law which should forbid women to work at nail-making. Why do they not make an attempt to induce the women to form a trade organisation for protection against 'foggers' (Middlemen) and other wrongs? The Women's Protective and Provident League would very gladly help in such efforts, but the proposed repressive measure must meet with strenuous opposition from the League and from all who believe that to shut women out from honest work by an unbending law is to bring about grave evils. There may be women and girls in the Black Country districts who are compelled by the idleness and neglect of their husbands and fathers to work at nail-making, just as in all districts there are women who are obliged, from similar reasons, to go our charing and washing, but we cannot believe that this is invariably the case. A law which would turn out all women from the nail and chain trades, whilst there are no other local industries to which they could go, would almost certainly drive many to starvation, or to a life of shame.

'Workmen as Factory Inspectors,' *Women's Union Journal*, February 1883, p. 9

We learn, with regret, that Mr JW Davis, of Birmingham, has been appointed one of HM Inspectors of Factories. We say with regret, because we had hoped, for Mr Davis, greater things than the domestic duties of Factory and Workshop Inspection, having much respect for his ability and courage in public life. The *Labour Standard* and other papers rejoice over the appointment and relate, without a sigh, that Mr Davis has resigned his seat on the Birmingham School Board and Town Council. His position as a member of the Trades' Union Congress Parliamentary Committee, and his Secretaryship of the Brass-founders' Trade Society, must also be vacated. All these are acts of public suicide, but are required by the acceptance of the official appointment. Mr Davis's fellow workmen have decided to present him with a testimonial, usually the final act of retirement from public work, on account of old age or infirmity, but Mr Davis is yet young in years. As 'lookers on,' are proverbially credited with long sight, we ask our brethren to consider whether the course they are pursuing is a wise one, in the interests of working people; whether to select foremost men like Mr Prior and Mr Davis for official births and deaths, is not seriously to endanger future reforms, especially that of labour representation in Parliament? With only a slight parody we may say,

> They're dropping off, the leading men,
> They're going one by one.

We sincerely trust Mr Arch will not be captured next. What, we ask, will the Trades Union Congress of the future be, if only the pigmies remain? Now that two workmen have become Inspectors, we advise our brethren to turn their attention to the last part of that famous resolution of the Congress and get some women appointed. Women are not yet politically alive, being voteless and are not likely to become Labour Candidates; consequently their extinction in office will be of little moment.

'Women as Employers,' *Women's Union Journal*, February 1883, pp. 9–10

Hamilton and Company, Co-operative Shirtmakers and Dressmakers, have published a Report of their trade position at the end of the seventh year since the firm was established. We give, with permission, several extracts from the Report, believing that they will be of interest to our readers and will also appropriately follow SGL's article in our last number, suggesting Women's Co-operative Workrooms in the Seaport outfitting trade.

The Report, which is entitled Rem Acu, is, we believe, written by Miss Edith Simcox, who with Miss Hamilton founded the establishment, and in our opinion its authorship is not the least of its attractions. All who have at heart the welfare of hard working women, must feel thankful that the organisation of women's trades is beginning to receive, not only attention, but also what is far more necessary whilst more difficult, practical solution, from women with so wide a sympathy and of such high intellectual power as Miss Simcox possesses. The innovation gives promise of a brighter day for workwomen, who have long been too often wholly at the mercy of unprincipled and tyrannical overseers, led by employers of a similar kind. Miss Simcox will, we venture to think, infuse into the work of women much of that striving after a high ideal and a nobler industrial future, which Mr William Morris earnestly advocates in his Lectures relating to Art Workmanship. A Review by Miss Simcox of those very Lectures appeared not long ago in one of the principal Magazines and clearly showed how deeply she sympathises with the views of Mr Morris.

The ordinary trade in which women engage are, it is true, of a more prosaic kind than art workmanship, but there is consequently the greater need of elevating influence. Such influence, too, may do more than anything else to humanise customers. We most earnestly commend to the consideration of all men and women who are in the position of customers, those parts of Rem Acu which refer to sudden pressure of orders for work. We are sure that serious evils arise from thoughtlessness in these matters. We have heard, for instance, from a tailoress, of a certain Member of Parliament, a most benevolent man and foremost in advocating the Factory Act because he believed it would protect women from overwork, who yet ordered a travelling coat for his summer holidays at such short notice that to get it completed would have been impossible, except by a breach of the Factory Act. It may be said that the employer should have refused to carry out the order, on the ground that overtime work by women was illegal, but it is well known that most employers will usually run the remote risk of discovery and of a fine, to accommodate an influential customer.

We are always ready to make known the grievances of workwomen; it is only fair, however, to admit that employers have many anxieties and difficulties to cope with, the thoughtlessness of customers being not the least of these. One form of worry and hindrance, that of requiring estimates for sometimes even the smallest orders, has been lately dealt with by the Typographical Circular, which is the organ of the journeyman printers' Union, and is therefore not altogether written in the interests of employers. We reprint the remarks referred to and commend them to the consideration of those whom they may concern. They are not out of place in our columns, because we hope to give, in an early number, some account of the progress of the Women's Printing Company at Westminster, which was established about the same time as Hamilton and Co. and in whose office this Journal has from the first been printed.

'Nail Making by Women,' *Women's Union Journal*, May 1883, pp. 33–34

The publication of our present number has been delayed for the insertion of Reports of a Meeting of Women working in Nail-making, held at Lye, near Stourbridge, on Monday, May 7th, and the Debate, upon Mr Broadhurst's Bill, in the House of Commons on May 9th. Mr Broadhurst's speech clearly showed that his efforts were directed against the work of women in the nail and chain trades, but in other trades also. We are therefore glad that his Bill met with a decisive defeat. The scarcity of his information upon the subject may be judged from the fact that his arguments, and the story about the woman who thought he had 'married a swell' appeared in the Factory Inspectors' Reports of April, 1875 – eight years ago! If the men who are agitating for the exclusion of women from their trade can supply Mr Broadhurst with no more recent, or more striking arguments, their case must indeed be a poor one. Unfortunately, many women think they have married swells and find out, too late, that they have to keep them, not necessarily by nail-making, but by washing, charing, needlework, nursing the sick or other occupations, acknowledged to be strictly feminine. Mr Broadhurst's illustration, therefore, was a weak one, besides being considerably time-worn.

We readily admit that there are evils connected with the employment of girls and young women in the trades referred to, one of the greatest being that their excessive competition keeps down the wages to a very low rate. It is generally agreed, as will be seen by the various reports we quote, that new fields of work are much needed, for the younger generation of these women, and earnest attention cannot be too soon turned to that question.

The following impartial notes and practical suggestions of two ladies, members of the Committee of the Women's Protective and Provident League, who have recently visited the much-debated districts, will be read with interest.

Miss A Heather-Bigg reports;

> There is great need of unionism, as the people undersell each other, and then of course, the large employers have to reduce wages to the level of those which the small employers are giving. A workers who gets a decent price for the nails from one employer will, in spare time, work up nails at a cheaper rate for another (unfair) employer. Then the two employers, when they sell the nails to customers do not charge the same price, and the first employer has to come down in his payments to the people who work for him, in order to keep the market. The women ought to combine, so as not to work at less rates than the better employers give, and the employers ought to adhere to a fixed price list. Unionism, too, would enable the women refuse to do men's work (i.e. heavy nails and chains) unless they are paid men's wages. It is better they should not do the heavy work at all, but they want money badly. I think that if an attempt could be made to help some of the nailers to get their girls out into other occupations, it would be well, and I told several of the women that that when the deputation from London came to the Meeting, they would discuss this point. I told them, also, that through Unions you got people to give information about openings for employment in London and elsewhere, and other trade matters. I threw out the suggestion that I might be able to get up a small Society of ladies, to work to provide outfits for the girls desirous of going into service. Half the women do not want to have their trade interfered with, but a good many would like to get their girls into something better. There is nothing objectionable in the trade except its starvation wages.

Miss Edith Simcox says:

> We went round with Mr Pipe to some of the forges on Monday, but as few work on that day we saw some of the women at home washing; they also all bake at home. No doubt we saw the best specimens, tidy sensible, energetic women, who would make excellent Unionists. They all had it in their heads that we wanted to stop their working, and met us everywhere with explanations that they must all "clem" if they

didn't work. When the evening came, by a ¼ to 8 the schoolroom was packed full, a score or so of men in the background. At one time it got very noisy, all talking to their neighbours at once, but they were quieted and finally voted, the women unanimously for a resolution against legislative interference, and the men 7 for and 3 against an amendment in favour of further legislation. By the help of one Sarah, a very ladylike looking girl, whom we saw making nails in the afternoon, several verses of one of our Union Songs were sung, and the chorus was well taken up. The day was somewhat unfavourable for the Meeting, as several of the "May Clubs" were being held; and there was much excitement. Few, either men or women, want to limit the work of the "wenches," but there is a strong feeling, amongst both, against the women doing work above a certain size, and if they had a society they would probably make a rule against it. For the smaller work, men and women get the same price, but apparently the price of the larger nails and chains has been reduced, in one case from 2s to 4 1/2d, partly, it is thought, by the women taking to it. One of the chief grievances is having to give from 10 to 20 per cent discount off their wages on Saturday, so that they receive only 18s or 16s out of the 20s due according to the low price lists followed. They also have to make good any deficiency arising in the nails from faulty iron.

'Seaside House for Holiday Visits of Members of the Women's Unions,' *Women's Union Journal*, August 1883, p. 63

Lady Goldsmid and Miss Montefiore having again very generously given special donations for the above purpose, the Committee of the League have taken a furnished house at Brighton, for eight weeks, from August 3rd to September 28th. The house is very pleasantly situation and has a large garden and croquet ground, a drawing room with verandah, a dining room and five bed rooms, accommodating eight visitors. It is a private residence and is therefore in many respects more comfortable than a lodging house. Attendance will be given the housekeeper, and during part of the time by a servant also.

Early application should be made to the Honorary Secretary of the League by those wishing to use the House. The charges to members of Unions are 3s and 4s a week for bedroom, use of other rooms and attendance; to friends of members (women) 5s and 6s. All payments to be made in advance at the League Office. Visitors must make their own arrangements with the housekeeper, about Board. Return tickets (3rd class) for 8 days, L. B. & S. C. Railway, from Victoria or London Bridge, cost 7s 6d, single fare, 4s 2 1/2d.

'Dining Halls for Women,' *Women's Union Journal*, October 1883, p. 81

We have great pleasure in announcing that a Working Women's Dining Hall has been opened at 57, Marsham Street, Westminster. The prices charged are remarkably low, a dinner amounting to only fourpence or sixpence, but it has been found that food of good quality can be sold at these prices, with a small profit.

This has been proved to be the case at 'The Welcome' in Jewin St, Aldersgate Street, Manageress, Miss Somerville – where from eight to nine hundred women and girls dine daily. We recommend our readers to try this Dining Hall; both the food and arrangements are excellent, the only thing to complain about being the unavoidable crowding occasioned by the great numbers attracted by the good food and low prices. There has for some years been a similar Hall in Nottingham.

Both 'The Welcome' in Jewin Street, and the new Hall in Marsham Street are for *women only*. In the present day when so many clubs and other places are opened for the exclusive benefit of men, we are glad to find that efforts are being made to meet the great need that working women have long felt of wholesome food, cleanliness and comfort at a price within the reach of all. A noteworthy fact in connection with the Marsham Street Dining Hall is that a member of the Committee of ladies who have established the Hall, has generously given up a great part of her time for some weeks to supervise the cookery and other arrangements. There is almost endless opening for the energies of ladies, in work of this kind.

'Lady Brassey's Dinner,' *Women's Union Journal*, October 1883, pp. 81–83

When presiding at the Annual Meeting of the League in June, Lady Brassey said that she hoped to arrange an excursion for members of the London Women's Unions, before the close of the summer. Lady Brassey is never known to fail in any promise she makes, and this one has been well fulfilled, though not quite in the form at first proposed. The uncertainty of the weather near the end of August, and the shortening days, were considered to be unfavourable to a country excursion; Lady Brassey therefore decided to invite a party of 250 members of the Unions to a Dinner at the Fisheries' Exhibition, and to give them also tickets of admission to the Exhibition. Tuesday, September 18th, was the date fixed for the entertainment. For various reasons, it was not possible to give more than about two days' notice that members of the Unions who wished to have tickets must apply to them to Mrs Paterson at the League office on the evening of Monday, September17th. The crowd of applicants who besieged the office on that evening showed how welcome the invitation had been. Fortunately the number of tickets exactly met the demand, and by 12 o'clock every applicant had been supplied.

The arrangements of time for the visit gave general satisfaction. A late hour, 6 pm, was fixed for the dinner, as Lady Brassey with her usual thoughtfulness wished the visitors not to be obliged to lose much time from their work, but the tickets of admission were available for the whole of the day, so that each visitor could go into the Exhibition at the hour that suited her best. However much they had been scattered during the day, nearly all assembled outside the dining hall shortly before 6, and upon the arrival of Lady Brassey and her party, all but about seven of the 250 chairs were rapidly filled. The tables were tastefully laid out and decorated with flowers, and the gathering around them of a large number of what were justly termed 'respectable well behaved workwomen,' presented a novel and pleasant sight. Lady Brassey presided and placed Miss Brassey, Mrs Roger Eykyn and other ladies at the ends of the tables.

The guests with members of the
Society of Women employed in Bookbinding, 91
Upholsteresses' Trade Society, 42
Westminster & Pimlico Tailoresses' Union, 49
West End Tailoresses' Society, 17
Shirtmakers' Society, 20
Dressmakers, 7
Women's Union Swimming Club and other friends, 24
[total] 250

After justice had been done to the substantial joints on the tables, and to the tea, coffee or beer which each guest could order if she wished, Mr Roger Eykyn proposed a vote of thanks to Lady a Brassey and said he thought every one present would agree with him in regretting that Sir Thomas Brassey could not be there, to join in welcoming the guests. Lady Brassey was constantly forming some plan to promote the happiness of others, and he knew it gave her great pleasure to arrange for this entertainment. The objects of the Women's Unions and of the League, which helped to form Union, were, he thought, highly important; he was exceedingly glad to hear that the Unions were in a satisfactory and self-supporting position. In the past, Trades Unions had been much misunderstood by many persons, but opinion was rapidly changing upon the subject, and the claim of the workers to participate in the profits of a business was becoming recognised. He had not before been aware of the very large extent to which women were employed in trades; the Secretary of the Tailoresses' Union who had been seated next him at dinner had enlightened him upon this matter and had also asked him if he had studied the Census Returns; he must confess he had not done so with regard to the employment of women. He heartily wished the Unions and the League prosperity; it was a true saying that 'those who sleep by day must hunger by night,' but the members of such Societies as these were in no danger of doing either.

Mrs Paterson, in seconding the vote of thanks to Lady Brassey, said she knew all present would concur in thinking that the Entertainment would have been incomplete without the presence of their kind hostess, who had come from Hastings at considerable inconvenience in order to preside over this large dinner party, and who indeed worked so hard in giving pleasure to others that the holiday tour she was about to make in the famous 'Sunbeam' would be well earned. Next to going to the seaside, a visit to the Fisheries' Exhibition seemed to be the best thing; for there were reminders of seaside sights in all directions. The visits would long be pleasantly remembered in connection with the League. The vote of thanks having been carried amid loud applause,

Lady Brassey responded and after thanking the guests for the heartiness of their reception, said she did not intend to give them another long Address upon women's work and wages, such as she had delivered when last they met at the Annual Meeting of the League; they would not want to sit listening to speeches, but would like to disperse soon into the Exhibition, where there were so many objects of interest, and where she trusted they would spend a very pleasant evening. It had given her great gratification to receive them at dinner and had Sir Thomas Brassey been able to attend he would gladly have done so. They might be sure that they had his very best wishes for their employment. In conclusion she desired to propose the health of Mrs Paterson, the Honorary Secretary of the League.

Mr RT Pritchett said he had pleasure in responding for Mrs Paterson, though he was sure she was capable of doing this herself. He wished to thank Lady Brassey for inviting him to so enjoyable an evening; several members of the Unions had been giving him accounts of their Societies during dinner; the movement appeared to him to be admirable in its aims and working. After what Mr Eykyn had said, he felt some trepidation and unworthiness in speaking, for he had not studied the figures of the Census upon the employment of women; but he would try to do so in future. (Laughter.) He should also certainly try to attend the Social Meetings to which the members had kindly invited him. He was glad to see that three or four of them had brought very young contributions to the movement, who would he hoped grow up to appreciate the advantages their mothers had so wisely sought to secure for themselves and for working women generally.

The proceedings were now brought to a close, and Lady Brassey and Miss Brassey on leaving the tables to visit the Exhibition, received many round of hearty applause.

'Meetings in Nottingham on Women's Trade Unions,' *Women's Union Journal*, October 1883, pp. 83–84

A public meeting of women employed in warehouses, factories, and workrooms of any kind was held on Thursday night, September 13th, in the Lecture Hall of the Mechanics' Institute, Nottingham, for the purpose of the advantages and progress of Women's Unions being explained and discussed. There was a good attendance.

The Rev. Professor Symes, MA, who presided, said he had received letters from Mr Ald. Cropper, and from Dr Paton, regretting their inability to attend. The Chairman then said that he believed there were 3,000,000 women engaged in wage-paid work in the United Kingdom; unfortunately they could not be described as a vast army of workers, for they lacked organisation, and consequently had to endure many evils that might be prevented by Union. They were not met to speak against the employers, because he believed many of the employers were doing much for those who worked, but what was needed was that women should combine for self-help and protection. The question remained with the women workers' all that outside friends could do was to bring it before them and give them encouragement and advice: he hoped that that night would see the beginning of a society in Nottingham. He did not suppose that the society would suddenly revolutionise the loss of the women workers. The beginnings would be very small. The benefits would be explained by the ladies who were present for that purpose.

Mrs Paterson, of the Women's Trades Council, London, said that the women who were attending the Trades' Union Congress had ventured to convene this meeting, as they had been much struck with the number of women workers in Nottingham. From all they had seen of the splendid public buildings in the town, and of the 'go-a-head' and sociable character of the people, she believed that societies of working women in Nottingham would be even more successful than they had been in London, where the work and workers were less concentrated. It would be for the meeting to consider whether it would be best to form a society for each trade, or to form one central society, with some such title as, 'The Working Women's Mutual Benefit Society.' She then proceeded to explain the working of the Unions in London, the objects of which were to maintain and protect the rights and privileges of each trade, and to grant relief to such members as might be out of work, or disabled by sickness. The Unions had been instrumental in preventing reductions of wages. Another very important object of the London societies was to help the members to obtain employment. She suggested that a general society should be first of all formed in Nottingham, and then when they became stronger, branch societies for the different trades could be formed.

Mrs Ellis, of the Huddersfield Weavers' Union, was the next speaker. She believed that the lace firms in Nottingham did not pay the same prices for the same class of work. She considered that was very unfair, and a society would prevent anomalies of this kind. Although the heavy Woollen Weaving Trade in which she worked was altogether different to the lace trade, they had to meet with similar difficulties. The Union she belonged to was formed eight years ago, after a strike had taken place, and was in a very prosperous state. Nottingham was a splendid place for Trades Unionism; the men had strong Unions in the town, and she did not see why the women should not have equally large societies. (Applause) If they tried she believed they would succeed.

Mr Oscroft, a delegate from the Nottingham Carpenters' Union, said he had been interested for the past two years in Women's Trades Unions. During that time they had tried to start a Women's Union in Nottingham, but they could not get anyone to come forward to act as secretary. They had been promised assistance from Mr Ald. Cropper, Mr SG Johnson, the respected Town Clerk, and other ladies and gentlemen in the town; but what was the use of such assistance if the working women would not help themselves. He would advise that a United Women's Benefit Society should be formed rather than a separate society for each trade in which women were engaged. Young women engaged in the lace trades were better off in one respect than those engaged in millinery, dressmaking and some other trades, because under the Factory Act they could not be made to work more than a certain number of hours per week, and were sure of giving over work at the dinner hour on Saturdays. The trades in which women were engaged in Nottingham, were the lacy and hosiery trades, millinery and dressmaking establishments, tailoring and cigar establishments, so that there was goods cope for women's unions. They need not be afraid of strikes, because anyone acquainted with Trades' Unionism would tell them that strikes were going out of fashion. That was the case with men's societies, and he did not see anything to prevent the same result attending women's societies.

Mr Bailey, the President of the Amalgamated Society of Tailors, said he hoped none of those present would consider it in any way a disgrace to belong to a trade society; there was nothing derogatory about it, as some women appeared to think. Trade organisations were recognised by the State, and they were conducted more and more on the principles of arbitration and conciliation. A large number of women worked in the tailoring trade all over the country and if they had an organisation with branches, their position would be greatly strengthened, because when work was bad and funds were low in one place they could be helped by tailoresses in other places where trade was better. He hoped it would be at once decided to commence a Women's Union in Nottingham.

Miss Wilkinson, of the Upholsteresses' Trade Union, then moved 'That this meeting approves of the establishment of a Workwomen's Mutual Benefit Society in Nottingham, and pledges itself to promote the formation of such a society.' She referred in an impressive manner to the desirability of putting the resolution into practice. There was no feeling so bad as that of utter helplessness which came over one when it was known that there was no work to be had, and no one who could be depended upon for help. That was the time when societies such as they sought to establish were so beneficial. She should like to leave Nottingham carrying away with her the knowledge that a working Women's Benefit Society had been formed there, and entertaining the hope that it would be very prosperous.

Miss Whyte seconded and gave an account of the formation and sound financial position of the Society employed in Bookbinding, in London, of which she is the Secretary.

Mr King, Secretary of the Consolidated Bookbinders' Society, London, supported the Resolution and showed how greatly the men in his trade had improved their position, both as to wages and hours of work, since their society was established. He said it was quite an important to prevent reductions as to gain rises of wages: women had to be on their guard against the frequent attempts at small reductions, which in the end meant great losses. He felt sure that they would have the sympathy of all good employers in efforts to protect and help themselves.

Mrs Heatherley supported the Resolution, from the body of the Hall, and spoke of one benefit of the Societies which had not been mentioned by other speakers, viz., the grant at a members' death.

The Resolution was then carried unanimously.

Mr Mawdsley, of the Amalgamated Society of Cotton Spinners, expressed his cordial sympathy with the objects of the meeting and proposed a vote of thanks to their Chairman which was carried with applause. Before the meeting separated, a number of the workwomen present gave their names, as intending to join the Society.

'A London Free Library,' *Women's Union Journal*,
December 1883, p. 101

The Committee of the Free Library in Great Smith Street, Westminster, have lately given two proofs of their desire to increase the usefulness of this already invaluable institution. One is the opening of a Ladies' Reading Room, well supplied with newspapers. There has been no rule against the use of the general Reading Room by women; some years ago when the librarian disputed their right to admission, it was soon announced that he had been mistaken; the disputed visitor happened to be Mrs Fawcett, who took care to get the doubt investigated. The very large attendance of male readers, averaging, the last Report states, 520 daily, has probably acted as a deterrent upon the use of the room by women, for one of the few things that makes an ordinary man surly is to find that a woman is reading a newspaper he wants himself. Perhaps when women have the suffrage it will be believed that they require to read something of wider interest than the births, marriages and deaths. For the present, the provision of a separate Reading Room is a wide and thoughtful action. We hope it will be well responded to.

Another reform is that the Library and Reading Rooms are now open from 9 am to 9 pm, instead of for only part of the day.

This Institution, of which Westminster may well be proud, was the first rate-supported Library in London; and we believe there are still only two or three others; it was opened 25 years ago by the united parishes of St Margaret and St John. The rate seldom exceeds one halfpenny in the pound and by it an income of £1,209 was raised last year. The selection of newly published books, constantly added to the Library, is admirable, and nearly all the high class (and high priced) Reviews and Magazines are also taken and are lent out for four days at a time. The present Secretary and Librarian, Mr HE Poole, appears to have introduced several improvements, and he and his assistants are attentive to all comers. At the Branch Library, 3, Trevor Square, Knightsbridge – a distant district of the two large parishes named – the Library is a lady, Miss Elizabeth Smith.

The classified list of borrowers of books from the chief Library shows a total of 568 males, following 131 different occupations, and 231 females having 28 occupations. The total number of issues of books during the year, from the both the Libraries was 76,210.

'Our Prospects,' *Women's Union Journal*, February 1884, p. 11

With much gratification we are able to announce, as a result of our appeal last month, an accession of 57 new subscribers for this year's Journal, 43 in the provinces and 14 in London – a far larger result than we expected in so short a time. Many of the letters received, from both old and new subscribers, are so cheering that they will repay us for a fit of despondency. We have asked permission to publish the two following. Mrs Tyndall Johnstone of Alloa, Scotland, writes:

> I enclose 1s 6d, my subscription for 1884. I see the Women's Union Journal is in difficulties; I forward you 5s for it and I trust you will soon have a largely increased roll of subscribers to it. I am sure it does a most useful work in awakening and keeping alive sympathies in many directions.

The Rev. VG Borradaile, a London clergyman who works untiringly in a poor district of the west, says:

> I enclose herewith a donation of £1, to the funds of the Women's Protective and Provident League. I feel more and more, that combination is the only way by which women will obtain proper remuneration for their labour. I enclose 1s 6d my subscription for the Journal. I should be glad to know whether there is any Benefit Union to which women who have no particular trade can belong.

We hope our friends will remember that we are always very glad to receive contributions to the Journal's pages, in the shape of information about women's work in different parts of the country, or letters and articles upon that and kindred subjects.

There is at present no general Union, such as Mr Borradaile asks about, but the League Committee would gladly assist in organising one if a sufficient number of names to start with (not less than twelve) were sent in to the Honorary Secretary.

'Important Notice,' *Women's Union Journal*, February 1884, p. 14

Any correspondents who within the past few months have addressed letters to the Honorary Secretary or Treasurer of the League, and have not received replies, are earnestly requested to write now stating this fact, and giving particulars. During the month of October, some letters which came to hand appeared to have been tampered with, and it was soon afterwards ascertained that two had been altogether lost. One of these contained a donation of 5s in postage-stamps from Mrs and Miss Wade. In the other, seven stamps were sent for copies of the Journal. It was hoped that only these two letters had been actually lost, but it now appears that two others sent about the same time were also not received, and it has therefore been thought necessary to insert this notice. The Post Office authorities were applied to without delay but all their efforts to trace the letters failed. By their advice a lock was placed on the letter-box and this precaution, taken early in November, seems to have been effective, as no losses since that time have been heard of, but the Committee are anxious to learn as far as possible, the extent of those which occurred previously.

'The Carpet Weavers,' *Women's Union Journal*, March 1884, pp. 19–20

Although it is the object of our paper to advocate the industrial interests of women we have always declared against attempts to introduce women into trades at rates of wages far below those previously paid to men for similar work. We have therefore never joined in, or expressed approval of, the abuse heaped by certain middle-class papers and economists, upon workmen who have struck against unfair competition of this kind. But the strike in Kidderminster, commenced last month is altogether a different matter, since it is directed against the employment of women in a new branch of weaving, said to be better adapted for them than for men, on account of the lightness of the fabric and the need of special attention to the cleaning of the looms. The following, taken from the Pioneer, seems to show that the Weavers' Association is not likely to be supported in its present action by workmen of other trades:

> Unless there are reasons which have not yet appeared in any of the accounts we have seen of the carpet weavers' strike at Kidderminster, we fear the men who have this week left Messrs Dixon's Brussels and tapestry works will find they have made a mistake. The facts of the case, as reported, appear simple enough. A firm of carpet weavers has introduced into the town a manufacture – that of Medici velvet – which had never been carried on in England before. The firm has always employed men and boys in carpet weaving, but in this new business, which has nothing whatever to do with carpets, they engaged women as weavers. Thereupon the carpet weavers informed their masters that if they did not dismiss all the women and employ only males in the new branch, they would strike. The masters declined, and the carpet weavers this week carried out their threat, and are now idle. We fear that the position the weavers have taken up in the matter is untenable. Suppose for a moment the new industry had been started in Kidderminster, not by Messrs. Dixon, or any other firm of carpet weavers, but by utter strangers – a firm of enterprising Germans, for instance: of what avail would it have been for Messrs. Dixon's carpet weavers to strike in that case? And if there is any more reason in the course they have actually taken, we should like to know what the logic of it is.

A friend of the League who has just returned from Kidderminster, reports that the town is in an uproar with the men on strike who were perambulating the streets with bands and boards on which were drawn men turning mangles and men washing and then came a procession of perambulators wheeled by men, containing infants.

'Women Who Work: II, Women's Trade Unions, and Their Founders,' *Pall Mall Gazette*, 10 April 1884

Every Monday night at eight o'clock there assemble at the rooms of the Women's Protective and Provident League, in Great Queen-Street,

Lincoln's-inn, the secretaries of the Women's Trade Unions of London. Here they meet Mrs Paterson, the hon. Secretary and the presiding genius of the League, together with many members who call to pay their subscriptions. There is a strictly business-like aspect about the large assembly room. Its chief furniture consists in a small desk for the presiding lady and a large counter, behind which each of the secretaries has her special place where to keep papers and account-books. There in the corner sits the secretary of the bookbinders' union, a middle-aged woman busily engaged in sorting papers. Next to her the intelligent-looking head of the tailoresses, who bustles to and from between her desk and that of Mrs Paterson. The shirtmakers are represented by a pale woman who is quietly examining her papers. The upholsteresses' secretary, next to her, is busily adding up current expenses on the back of an old envelope. Since the formation of the League in 1874, Monday night has always been set apart for these meetings. Before describing the work of the unions whose representatives meet at Great Queen-Street, it may be well to say something about the origin of the League.

Until ten years ago nothing very practical had been done to ameliorate the lot of the thousands of women employed in industrial trades, often at starvation wages. Now and then, when some terrible case of starvation or suicide came to light, a stir was made by newspapers and benevolent societies, but it died out before long, and no active permanent help, such as that given by trade unions to their members, was afforded them. An ever-increasing number of women toiled on under the burden of a life which was not life, but a hungry, hopeless existence, with nothing but 'work, work, work, from morning till night.' In the summer of 1874, however, some 20 ladies and gentlemen met on the invitation of Miss Paterson and determined to endeavour to introduce trade associations among women, and by them was formed the Women's Protective and Provident League,

> for the purpose of encouraging and assisting women earning their livelihood to combine for the protection of their industrial interests, for the provision of benefit funds to assist them in illness or in times of slack trade, and for the interchange of trade information.

This was a reversal of the usual masculine method. Men organise unions in different trades and then form a federation or central league. In the case of the women it was determined to begin by forming a central league which should encourage women in different trades to form unions among themselves. These unions were organised by the League, which assisted in preparing their rules and arranging their business affairs, and was always willing to advise or to procure legal advice if necessary; but, aiming at the development of self-reliance among women, it was determined to give no pecuniary help to a union after it was once started. Each of the unions, to prosper, must be self-supporting, but the League, although not subsidising, does much which perhaps is even more valuable than pecuniary assistance. The rooms in Great Queen-Street are open every morning for members as well as for any other women without employment to register their names and to examine the advertisements in the various trade papers. There is a circulating library, where at a small charge books are lent out to members, a women's halfpenny bank and a co-operative society for wholesale purchase and retail sale of tea and sugar. Among other institutions of the League may be mentioned a sea-side house subscription, where at a small cost the summer holidays may be spent, a swimming club, which is at present in a flourishing condition, and last, but not least, the monthly social evening meetings, a kind of musical conversazione, much appreciated by the women.

The rules of the Women's Trade Union are few and simple. Any person wishing to become a member has to be recommended by two members who can vouch that she is a competent workwoman. An entrance fee of 1s, which may be paid by instalments of not less than 3d per week, a weekly subscription of 2d or 3d towards the benefit fund, 3d per quarter to the management fund (these latter contributions paid for one year), entitle a member to receive benefits. She is then called a free member, and as such, when out of work or disabled by sickness (excepting in confinements), receives 5s per week if paying a contribution of 2d per week, or 7s a week if paying 3d. No member receives more than eight weeks' benefit during one year or benefits for less than one week. At the death of a free member a levy of 6d per member is made and paid to the nominee of the deceased member of other person legally entitled; not more than £5 is paid in any one case. An experience of ten years has shown that the women are in no way inferior to men in managing their affairs. The great mass of women engaged in trades carried on at home cannot be persuaded to enter an association. They receive their work from the shops, but take it home, and, living apart from each other, find it more difficult to combine than those who day by day are gathered together in the same workshop. Shop girls also are prevented from forming a union, as the great majority of them sleep in the house of their employer and are not allowed to absent themselves at those hours when unionists meet. Women employed in the Post Office have their own friendly societies, which makes another union unnecessary. In 1874, the female bookbinders formed the first union, and women engaged in several different trades have followed their example. At present, the upholsteresses, the shirt and collar makers, the sewing machinists, the London tailoresses and the dressmakers, milliners and mantlemakers all have their societies; and though the movement spreads but slowly, women as well as employers begin to see that, far from being troublesome, unionism is favourable to all: to the women, because it assures assistance in case of ill-health and when out of employment; to the employers, because they can rely on the efficiency of a workwoman belonging to a union.

Mrs Paterson is somewhat weighed down by a sense of the difficulties with which her sex has to contend, for with respect to employment there is very little of that chivalrous regard for women of which so much is heard when questions of women's rights are discussed. Women have to struggle for themselves as best they can in the fact of grave disadvantages, and the chief privilege which is accorded to them is that by which the weaker are thrust to the wall. Like Miss King, who is concerned with women in a higher social position, Mrs Paterson is much exercised by the refusal of equal wages to women when their work is equal to that of men. One-third of men's wages is too often considered good enough for a woman who does exactly the same work. This difference between the wages of women and men is the great obstacle in the way of admission of women to ordinary trade unions. Women undersell men, and the latter resent it bitterly, as the riots at Kidderminster prove. Not only this, but also many employments for which women are peculiarly qualified are invaded by men, and as the result the very narrow field of woman's labour is still further circumscribed.

Mrs Paterson looks with scant sympathy upon men employed in domestic service, and, if she had her way, would make short work of all men employed in drapers' shops and other places where women can be served by women. Concerning domestic servants, Mrs Paterson entertains very pronounced opinions. At present, if the servant is far from ideal, the great lack is the lack of liberty. If women could feel that, when in service, some time of the day was their own, there would be much less reluctance to go to places, and consequently much less pressure upon other industries. As the case is, women will work far harder at almost any kind of business that will give them their evenings than take much more comfortable situations in houses where they would but once a fortnight have an hour to call their own. The result of this overcrowding upon those industries now open to women is that wages are cut down to starvation point, and any attempt on the part of women to organise for self-defence is swamped by the rush of non-unionists, who, in the struggle for existence, are willing to take whatever is offered and submit to whatever hardships may be imposed. Take, for instance, the case of truck. Women are constantly compelled to submit, even in London, to what is little better than truck system, which no working man would stand for a moment. As for wages, women are often reduced to work for a mere pittance, insufficient for decent maintenance.

Although there are three and a half millions of women earning wages in this country, the members of the union already formed can be numbered only by hundreds. A large field, therefore, remains for the labours of the

League. As has been explained, the unions when formed pay their own way; the subscriptions and donations of outsiders by which the league is supported are consequently devoted to propagandist purposes. Notwithstanding the small amount of support that has yet been accorded to this excellent movement – the income of the League last year was under £200 – Mrs Paterson refuses to despair. She believes that the public will in time understand that by thus helping women to help themselves they can best give effect to that sympathy which they undoubtedly feel with those who, at all costs, prefer honest industry to the fearful alternative of 'gilded vice.'

'Ferny Hollow,' *Women's Union Journal*, June 1884, pp. 51–52

More than two years ago we gave an account of the purpose and working of the House of Rest for Women in Business, opened at Babbacombe, Devonshire, in 1877, and now called Ferny Hollow. From the sixth yearly Report of the Committee lately issued we are glad to learn that the usefulness of the house increases, as many as 300 visitors having been received last year. Among the visitors there have been, every year, a few members of London Women's Unions who, without exception, speak in the highest terms of the admirable arrangements and of the constant, whilst not over fussy, attention of the Misses Skinner, the two members of the Committee who were the founders.

We give some extracts from the Report, and the statement of accounts. The plan for the purchase of a house will, we hope, be soon carried out, as it seems probably that the saving effected in rent, with at the same time the advantage of increased accommodation, would do much towards placing the institution on a self-supporting basis.

"The Vistors" – Shop Assistants, Employees in large Houses of Business, Milliners, Dressmakers, Post Office Clerks, Book-keepers, &c. – have come from all parts of England, through the greatest number are still drawn from London. Their own payments have amounted to £416 18s 6d (many of them paying 12/– per week) thus forming a considerable part of the income of the House. The House is now much used in winter as well as summer and has been fuller all the year round than at any period of its existence; those requiring a warm climate for restoration to health having been received for longer visits during the winter. The usual term of visits is from a fortnight to three weeks during the summer holidays; at other seasons – for rest or health – if practicable, until recovery. About 300 Visitors were received last year.

'The House of Rest is distinctively for Business Women (servants are not eligible); it is a House of Rest for the prevention of illness, not a Convalescent Home; it is also a Holiday House, to afford the means of taking a holiday, by the seaside, to workers who could not procure it without help. It is managed rather on the principle of visits to a Country House than as an Institution – this domestic, and personal method of management having been a large element in its success."

'It is open all the year round. Visitors are received irrespective of religious distinctions and attend their respective places of worship."

'In order to put the work on a permanent basis, we appeal for further contributions towards the purchase of a house, having, hitherto, only rented one. The sum of £198 12s 7d, being the balance of the Revenue Account for 1882, was laid aside as a nucleus of a Purchase Fund, there being then added to it the sum of £100, at that time standing to the Reserve Fund, upon the understanding that the deficit in Revenue in any future year should, to that extent, be made up out of the Purchase Fund. This, which, by the last account rendered, amounted to £298 12s 7d, is now increased to £522 9s 8d, by the addition of the sum of £87 5s 6d subscribed during the year for purchasing a house, and the sum of £136 11s 7d, the saving on the Revenue Account during the year. It is probable that £3,000 would be required to purchase a house."

'The League and Its Work,' *Women's Union Journal*, August 1884, p. 68

One of the most cheering events in the history of the League has to be recorded in this month's Journal.

The Rev. Stephen Brooke, who at the foundation of the League, showed his sympathy by giving his name for the Council list, and in other ways, selected for the subject of his morning Sermon at Bedford Chapel, Bloomsbury, on Sunday, July 20th, the 'distress and oppression' which overwhelm large masses of working women, through the greed of the tradesman, on the one hand, and of the buyer, on the other. A most powerful and impressive description of these evils, was followed by an appeal for help for the League, in its attempt to apply the remedy of Union among workwomen. It is very difficult, to select passages from such a discourse, when every sentence seems to be of equal value, but we cannot refrain from making a few extracts.

"Only imagine it for a moment, you who have leisure and comfort, and who think eight hours a day a good day's work, on good food and in a comfortable home! Most labour has some joy, some relaxation, some out of door work, but this is unrelaxed, and always without excitement. Women rise to it weary, and go to sleep from it weary, and it goes on all the year round without a break of peace or a breath of summer air."

"There is but one dreadful chance of escape for the young, and many find it in shame. But thousands would rather die, and do die. The better the woman, the more faithful to womanhood; the more proud of her purity, the more honest in doing her work; the worse off she is outwardly, the nearer starvation and death, the more she is preyed upon by the greedy. This is the position we have found for upright poor women in the midst of our civilisation!

They have reward, no doubt, and God gives it to them. They have the wealth that is within, and the glory of righteousness, and the hope that makes not ashamed. And it appears that we think that enough for them, and are quite content with our share in the matter. But if God gives them their spiritual reward for spiritual work, and their moral reward for faithfulness to morality, as He will, we, one and all as citizens of a State in which these iniquities are possible, shall also have our reward, and it will not be one we shall like at all. I am told that we are not responsible for these things. I say that we are; I have said it for 20 years and shall not cease saying it as long as I preach. One and all, you are your brothers' and sisters' keepers, and that is the view the Most High will take of it when the day of proof arrives. You will be judged not only as persons, but also as members of a State, and it will be asked – 'What have you done for your fellow-citizens?' It will not do then to fall back on the theories you have made into laws to suit your greed and laziness, and to talk of supply and demand, of over population and competition."

"Still, the old phrase will be used – It cannot be helped. These things, it is said, must be. Women's labour is there to be sold, and men will buy it as cheaply as they can. They can get it cheap. There is an almost unlimited quantity of it. 'The supply is greater than the demand.' Women have no protection against employers without a conscience, or without a heart. Women have no means of protecting themselves, such as the working men have created in the trade unions. They are fair game, and their labour is bought at starvation wages. There is no remedy. And this, we are told, is law!"

"The working men found a remedy. They made themselves into unions, and the result, after years of struggle, obloquy, and of some mistakes on their part, has been such that even the employers recognise the use of the unions; and the unions have learnt toleration of the masters who are open and just with them. Both classes have been drawn together. Arbitration and co-operation have both grown out of the unions."

"Well, since we cannot hope, as yet, that tradesmen or buyer, as a whole, will become as thoughtful as we wish, since they appeal to their so-called laws – let women adopt the same remedy which the men did of old, and fight competition and over-mastering capital with the weapons of the Unions."

"And this is what the Women's Protective and Provident League is doing in a quiet and practical fashion, without violence, without abuse, and on steady business principles; keeping always also in mind the mental and social improvement of the women who belong to it. I spoke of it some years ago, I recommend it again to your investigation and help. The league has just issued its tenth annual report. Its protective section has organised, both in London and the country towns, unions in several trades. Their combination has given these small societies the power to do something of the same work which the trade unions among men have done on a larger scale. The women who join them are good workers, and the employers have already, in many cases, found it for their benefit to employ them. The women have discovered the benefit of helping themselves, altogether one of the last discoveries they seem to make. They have learned courage, have gained faith in effort, new hope and strength. Instead of roving all over London and losing days in seeking work, they find it easily at the union centre, where information is given, and where the employers send for workers. Instead of isolation and competition with one another, they have learnt some solidarity, some duty to their own class, and self-sacrifice for one another. The moral effect has been as great as the economical."

The Sermon has been published, and a number of copies have been generously placed at our disposal; most of these will be distributed to the Trades Councils and Unions of workmen, whose duty in the matter of helping their sisters to form trade organisations was forcibly urged. We have a few copies to spare and they shall be sent to any of our readers who apply for them at once.

In 1879, when Mr Brooke preached in aid of the League, £53 was collected. Now, without any collection at the Chapel, and without indeed a direct appeal for money, the still larger sum of £70 has been poured into the League treasury. Another and equally satisfactory result is the receipt of numerous letters of sympathy and enquiry. Some of these will almost certainly lead to the establishment of new Unions of women in provincial towns. It is well known that the congregation at Bedford Chapel is not a merely local one, but that visitors from far distant places are always present. Communications about the Sermon have come from residents of Birmingham, Belfast, Chatham, Huddersfield, Londonderry, Manchester and New York, besides many from London. One of the latter, from a lady who had not before heard of the League, contains some telling facts, and, with her permission, we quote these:

> I have known women who made, that is, curled and wired, feather aigrettes for 6d the gross, that is ½ per dozen. The contractors for the government orders, policemen's dresses and for the army, grind down their workpeople to starvation wages; 1s each for completely finishing a policeman's coat, sometimes 50 inches in the waits, which is given out just cut out and machined up the seams. They had to press, line

with black linen, make 24 or more buttonholes, and put on buttons and braid and turn it out fit to put on for 1s. After a severe struggle one poor woman had to go to the workhouse, and there is a really good and industrious workwoman lost, and the ratepayers have to maintain her.

Sometimes Mrs ___ got long flannel waistcoats, with long sleeves, to make for the same government contractor, in St Martin's Lane, near Charing Cross, for which she was paid 2d each. I know the work there was in these, for I machined six for her, and it took me quite two hours, and after that there were the button-holes and felling down to do. I wish when the estimates for Army and Navy services are voted, some MP would enquire *how* these contracts for clothing are managed. They seem to be given to the man who has sent in the lowest tender, and that means the one who grinds down his workpeople to the very lowest starvation prices.

We hope our readers will not think that they may fold their hands and do nothing because many new friends have come forward, but that they will be encouraged by this good news, to make every effort in their power to help the Committee of the League, both by suggestion and by active co-operation, to use to the greatest advantage the aid already received. The Committee will be ready, early in October, to get up Meetings for forming new societies in any part of London, or of the provinces. Advice and suggestions as to where and in what trades such meetings might usefully be held, will be heartily welcomed. Let our gratitude to Mr Stopford Brooke, take a form he is sure to appreciate, that of new courage and vigour in the crusade we have commenced.

'Working Women's Meeting in Aberdeen,' *Women's Union Journal*, September 1884, pp. 76–77

Last night a public meeting of working women was held in the UP Hall, St Paul Street, Aberdeen, for the purpose of taking steps to form a protective and benefit society. There was a large attendance.

Mr JC Thompson, president of the Trades Union Congress, presided. The chairman expressed his sympathy with the movement and said it would be well for the working women in Aberdeen to unite for mutual help and sympathy (applause). There was just this thought that had occurred to him – what had brought the present company together? Was it curiosity? He sincerely hoped it was not; but that the working women of Aberdeen felt a want and that was that they had no medium whereby they could express their feelings one to the other. He sincerely hoped there was a desire on the part of working women to raise themselves to a higher and better social status. Unity had helped the male portion of the community to rise to a higher social status, and if the working women would only unite, they would in a very short time be as much benefitted.

Mrs Paterson, Women's Trades Council, London, who next spoke, said that in Aberdeen there was such a large and well-organised Trades Council – representing about 4,000 members – that she had no doubt many present, who were the sisters, wives and daughters of working men, knew pretty well what the objects of such societies were. In looking over the list of trades represented in the Aberdeen Trades Council, she found that there was no representative of one of the most important trades in the city and that was weaving and spinning. The reason was that most of the workers were women, who had not united to form a society by which they could be directly represented in the Trades Council. If the working women in Aberdeen did unite, they might quite hope that if a society were formed the Trades Council would not refuse to admit delegates (hear, hear). A greater number of women were employed here that she had had any idea of. She was told that the number was close upon 5,000 in all the different works. She saw the Broadford workers come out the other night, and she must say she regarded it as one of the sights of the city to see such a large body coming out in such an orderly manner – all self-supporting, independent women. At the Trades Union Congress most of the trades in the city were represented, excepting the weavers – the women who formed such a large proportion of the working population. She thought the present meeting was very encouraging, as showing that this state of affairs would not be long continued, but that they would make an effort to unite, help and support each other, and in doing that they would not merely be helping themselves, but would encourage the women all over the country, because it would go over all the country that the women of Aberdeen had decided to form themselves into a Union.

It was only by union that women could help each other. In this country there were three millions of working women, and if a 35th part of these were to become united and only pay 2d per week there would be a fund of £40,000. What an advance that would be; how much more people would respect the working women of England if they had all that money at their back (laughter). They must not think that she was a worshipper of money, but after all money did make people respected (hear, hear). So long as women had nothing whatever to fall back upon there was no doubt they would be very little thought of, and that reductions in their wages would be frequently attempted. When she read a short notice in the London newspapers of the dispute at the Jute Works, she thought that as the Trades Congress was to be held in Aberdeen it would be useful so to get up a meeting there. She did not know when she read that report how sensibly the women had gone to work about the dispute. They drew up a very business-like letter to the Trades Council and put the facts of the case before them and asked advice. She had read that letter very carefully, and the very fact that six of the women could draw up such a letter showed they were quite able to form and conduct a good society (applause). She was very glad to find that the Trades Council had kindly entertained the memorial and had appointed a committee to meet with the women-worker and that the result of their deliberations had been that the dispute had been referred to arbitration. Wherever it was at all possible arbitration was the best way of settling such disputes.

Whether the result of the arbitration were to be in favour of the workers or not, the formation of a union could not fail to do good and be beneficial. They would then have some kind of defence against further attempts at reduction. They would also get information about rates of wages in other towns, such as the fact which had been brought out through the dispute referred to, that in Dundee the wages for the same kind of work were about 15 per cent higher than in Aberdeen. It would be a long time before women could get their unions into such a position as the men had got theirs but if they wrought patiently and earnestly together, there was no doubt that they would do a great deal in the same direction. They need not be afraid that employers would oppose such a movement among women. Employers were sensible of the position that men's unions had attained and knew that the Trades Council of the city would help the women (applause). She did not think there was a want of public spirit among women, although they had not yet votes for members of Parliament. That, however, she believed, would come in time (applause). She had been reading how the shore labourers improved their position. She dared say they were not very much better paid than some women were, and yet they all at once developed a very large and powerful Society. That should encourage the women of Aberdeen, and there were a great many other things to encourage them. She hoped the result of the meeting would be the formation of a really good and strong society, and that by the time the next Trades Union Congress met here there would be some representatives of the Aberdeen Working Women's Union present.

Report of the Trades Union Congress, 1884, p. 41

Employment of Young Girls as Ironworkers
   Mr Juggins (Darlaston) moved –

> That it be an instruction to the Parliamentary Committee to use their best exertions to reintroduce the Factory and Workshops' Amendment Bill of [?] that applies to the employment of female children under fourteen years of age at forging nails, chains, bolts, or any such articles that are made from iron or steel.

He said it had not been an uncommon thing for years past in South Staffordshire and East Worcestershire for girls of seven, eight and nine years of age to be engaged in the manufacturing of nails, chains, rivets, bolts and so on, a calling which was a disgrace to their sex. This had been allowed to go on, and without some extraordinary exertion on the part of the Parliamentary Committee or the bringing to bear on it the influence of the Congress, it must continue to go on unless it was stopped by legislation. It would no doubt be remembered that Mr Broadhurst, acting under the instruction of the Parliamentary Committee, paid a visit to the district in order to ascertain its particular requirements, as regarded the Factory Act, and how far it was necessary to legislate in the interests of young female children in the district.

After making that visit Mr Broadhurst was convinced, as were also the Parliamentary Committee, that an alteration in the law was required. They at once set to and brought a Bill into the House of Commons for the purposes of preventing children working at forges or in shops making nails, rivets, and bolts, after the manner of blacksmiths. In submitting the resolution, he did not wish to interfere in the slightest degree directly with female labour. He considered that the trades best adapted to female labour were those that should be encouraged for females, and not those that were adapted only to males, such as those of blacksmiths and of working in shops. He had spoken several times in his own district on the immorality of the system against which his resolution was aimed – (hear, hear) – and he repeated that where boys and women worked in one shop in an almost nude state, each being exposed alike, it was a disgrace to civilisation and a disgrace to this country. (Applause.)

Mr Joseph Arch said he would second the resolution with very great pleasure. He could confirm every word that Mr Juggins had spoken. He had travelled through the nail- and chain-making districts of the country, and his heart had ached to see you girls of nine, ten and eleven years of age as black as soot and smoke could make them, and thought they would be doing a great act of justice if they called the attention of Parliament to this most disgraceful procedure. (Applause.)

Mr Holmes (Barnsley) though their friends were hardly taking the best course to obtain redress. He knew there were districts in the cotton trade in which, before asking Parliament to interfere, they took care to establish their case themselves. (Applause.) It would be much better if they instructed the Parliamentary Committee to obtain a Royal Commission to inquire into the cause of the complaints, and if the case was made out he was sure the Committee would have little difficulty in getting complete redress. He would propose the following amendment –

That instruction to the Parliamentary Committee to obtain a commission to inquire into the cause of complaints made in reference to the employment of females and young persons in the trades named in the proposition.

Miss Wilkinson seconded. She thought in taking up this question they should remember that the boys wanted protection quite as much as the girls, and if there was a Commission of Inquiry that would be brought out. Mr Juggins had said he had no intention of directly levelling this motion against female labour, but indirectly he had, because he would keep them from work under fourteen, knowing that would be as keeping them from work after fourteen. She had always understood that the majority of these children worked at home with their fathers and mothers, and, if so, what she wanted to know was, how their surroundings were to be altered by simply preventing them from working at home.

Mr Wilson (Durham) said if measures had to be passed to prohibit female labour in their mines and factories to a large extent, and if it were right to prohibit females from working in the mines, it must be right to prohibit them from the arduous work of forging.

Mrs Ellis (Derby) thought the word 'female' should be struck out, and that the resolution apply to all young children, and moved accordingly. If as was said, the resolution was not directed at woman's labour, there could be no objection to that course.

Mrs Paterson seconded the amendment. The argument that all working men ought to support their wives would strike against women's employment altogether. That would be a very desirable thing, but she was afraid that it was very far from attainment.

Mr Threlfall supported the resolution.

Mr King (London) thought Mr Juggins should accept Mrs Ellis's amendment.

After some remarks from Mr Brickland,

Mr Rowland [?] (London) hoped Mr Juggins would accept the amendment that the word 'female' should be struck out. If there was one occupation that should be closed to children under fourteen years of age, he thought it was forging.

Mr Broadhurst, MP, said that the amendment of Mrs Ellis was representative of that class of the community opposed to any legislation whatever for the restriction of female labour; therefore an amendment of this sort must be looked upon with the greatest suspicion. If the object of the mover of this amendment was to make the proposal contained in the resolution ridiculous, that would be obtained by the acceptance of the amendment. However desirable it was to prevent boys working under fourteen years of age, they knew perfectly well that it was utterly impossible that such a proposal could be carried. With regard to the suggestion that there should be a Commission appointed to inquire into the matter, the gentleman who made that suggestion would, if he turned back a few years, find that there had been a Commission, and that every possible tittle of evidence necessary for legislation on the question was fresh in print, or very nearly fresh, and had not been carried into law. He was at a loss to know how it was possible that Mrs Ellis – the mother of a daughter – and other ladies, could for a moment stand there, or anywhere else, and oppose any proposal that had for its object the elevation of their own sex. He would ask Mrs Ellis, and he would ask Mrs Paterson, to go into those blacksmiths' shops and look at the women of mature years, and he would appeal to them whether it was not a disgrace to this boasted civilisation of ours that women should be found in the degraded position in which they there were – whether they were not ashamed to see the mothers of families having to work for 2s 6d, 5s and 7s, a week.

Mrs Paterson said she had seen women employed at the class of work referred to and found them merrily singing hymns. She saw nothing objectionable.

Mr Snow (Cleveland) did not think they had any right to drive women out of the different classes of labour.

Mrs Exxes said if there was work for the women at these forges, and if there was no work for them anywhere else, what she would ask, were they to do?

Mr M'Kay (Edinburgh) said that although Mrs Paterson had found the children singing hymns, if she had gone a little farther she might have found them saying prayers to their Maker to be delivered from such a state of bondage.

'Women as Nail Makers,' *Women's Union Journal*, November 1884, pp. 99–100

In moving his resolution at the Trades' Union Congress against the employment of girls under 14 in nail-making, Mr Juggins, of Darlaston, Staffordshire, was careful to disclaim any desire to interfere with the work of adult women in that trade. From the Quarterly Journal of the Nut and Bolt Makers Association, of which Mr Juggins in the General Secretary, we find that, in making a report to his Society, at a meeting held at Smethwick on October 3rd, when we presume no 'female delegates' were present, Mr Juggins was less guarded in his remarks. This is what he then said:

> The next question to which he proposed to make reference was one which had caused them considerable anxiety, viz: that of Female Labour in factories. (Applause) It was one of the subjects discussed at the Congress at its last sitting, and which he (the speaker) had the honour and pleasure of introducing. (Hear, hear). It gained much more sympathy this time than it had ever done before, and a number of the delegates

said that in their judgement this question ought to take precedence over some of the others which were discussed, and that it deserved the best attention the Congress could give it. (Hear, hear). He was pleased to say that Mr Broadhurst, MP, Secretary of the Parliamentary Committee, and Mr Joseph Arch, in supporting his (the speaker's) statements upon the question, appealed to the Congress to use its influence to stamp out this iniquitous system of female labour in the workshops, which was a disgrace to civilization. (Hear, hear, and applause.) They pointed out that if it was necessary to pass an Act of Parliament to keep women out of the mines, which everybody admitted to be a disgrace to civilization, then an Act was as equally necessary to keep these young girls from working in the factories side by side with men, and thus turning themselves into female blacksmiths, which was altogether contrary to their delicate sex and their calling. (Hear, hear) The Mail had taken exception to some remarks he had made upon this point, as had also the Post, and the question was naturally, he admitted, asked, supposing they did away with female labour, what would the women do? Why he would tell them, but first let him say this, that the very fact that the women in some districts, particularly Old Hill, Rowley, and Black Heath, had been for so many years engaged in this calling at such low remuneration had been the means of driving their brothers, as soon as they arrived at years of maturity, into other districts to seek better wages. But even they had left their sisters there, still to perform the same amount of work at a miserably low remuneration. ("Shame.") A contributor on Saturday last to the Post, under the heading of *Leasowes*, gave a review of the whole district, in the course of which, after commenting upon the low wages paid, and the small children employed in the shops, the writer proceeded to assert that their calling was a disgrace to civilization. (Applause) In an Edinburgh evening paper on the following Saturday, was a further article, in which it was stated that there were about 30,000 women throughout Great Britain employed in these callings. The question very naturally arose, what was to be done with the surplus female labour, if all these were prevented from working in the workshops? Wherever they found a predominance of female labour, there they were certain to find wages miserably low, simply because no master would pay a man more than a women while she was able to do the same amount of work. Wages ought not, however, to be based upon the labour of the female, because she had only to support herself, and it she managed to get sufficient for that, she seemed to think that she was earning a comfortable wage. Was it possible, he asked, for any man to keep a wife and family with the same amount as was earned by a women under circumstances he had described? ("No.") He would ask a still further question; was it fair that a women should be toiling from morning till night, and from

Monday morning till Saturday night for such a paltry pittance as 4s or 5s per week? It was, he said, a disgrace to the age (hear, hear) and all this was going on the midst of a christian country with open Bibles and gospel privileges! It was high time that they had missionaries of mercy in the districts, opening the eyes of the people.

He might tell them that at the Congress this subject was not allowed to pass without opposition, and what surprised him most was the fact that some males opposed it. ("Shame.") He knew there would be opposition from the females, but he was proud to say that he had a larger majority this year than ever he had had before on his resolution. (Hear, hear, and applause.) One of the Female Delegates said she contended that the women had a perfect right to compete with the men in any work of calling which they might be engaged. (Laughter, "Shame," and "I wish my wife would do it.") He asked them as sensible men, if this was right? ("No, it's wrong.") If their own wives were to become competitors, what chance was there for them to live? As to the question of what was to be done with the surplus labour, he advised that the females should look over the long list of advertisements for servants, which were constantly appearing in the papers, remarking that they would be much better employed in domestic pursuits, and would get far better remuneration. (hear, hear.) It was argued, he said, that the trade (the Nail and Chain Trade) was over-stocked; then rid it of its female element – (hear, hear) – and let men do the work that belonged to them, and so rid the country of this lasting disgrace. (Applause) He was very pleased, he said, to be able to mention that the resolution he had the honour to propose on the subject at the Congress was carried by a very large majority. (Applause) They were all sent into the world, he said, to help one another, and if they could do anything to ameliorate the condition of their follow workman they would have accomplished a noble work. (Hear, hear) Some advocated that children under 14 years of age should not be allowed to work, but they did not interfere with the general question. If, however, they could succeed in preventing female children from working it would be one step towards this object.

Mr Juggins leaves out of sight one main cause of the low prices, which can we believe, be remedied only by union of the workers, both men and women: it is the keen competition among the small masters. When three members of the League Committee, Miss Heather-Bigg, Miss Brown and Miss Simcox visited the district and held a meeting of the women, they found ample evidence of this. The evil appears to be one of long standing, if we may judge from the quaint old song that we now reprint. The song is well known in the district, but printed copies are exceedingly scarce, and it was only with great difficult that Miss Brown succeeded in securing the much worn specimen she has not lent us for the Journal; it is supposed to be at least seventy years old. No women are mentioned as workers; only one as an employer, 'as bad,' unhappily, 'as all the rest.'

We advise Mr Juggins to invite the women to join his trade union, instead of trying to 'ameliorate their condition' by the harsh and undeviating operation of a law forbidding them to work.

> The Nailer's Song
> Nail Masters are hard-hearted
> They on the Nailers frown
> They always take delight
> To keep our wages down.
> The time is quickly coming
> When our Maker will descend,
> These Masters will cry out,
> For they will want a Friend.
> Our Maker He will judge them
> And many a million more;
> He will say "depart ye cursed"
> For you have oppressed the poor.
> There is a Lady in the trade
> For a time she seemed the best;
> But now, alas! We have to say
> She's as bad as all the rest.
> There is a few more Masters
> That have given us the PRICE
> It's made our children for to smile
> They have had an extra slice.
> There is some more bad masters
> The PRICE they will not give;
> I'm sure they are not fit to die
> They are not fit to live
> The poor men when they go to weigh
> It makes them for to pant
> The Masters harshly say to them
> These nails we do not want.
> Now if you wish to weigh these nails,
> We'll tell you what we'll do
> Full ten per cent we will take off,
> Whether there by many or few.
> The other men that do stand by,
> They say that is not right,
> It's worse than robbing on the highway,

When it is dark at night.
There is a God above them
That still forebears the blow
Some day they will be called away
And their bodies cold as snow
The time is fast approaching
When strikes will have an end
Those people that do serve the Lord
They then will find a FRIEND
My friends that stand around
I hope they'll think this right;
I made these lines my own self
When it was dark at night.

– JOHN COLEY

Note

1 The Daughters of St Crispin was the first national women's union in the United States, originally formed in 1869, and modelled on the union of male shoemakers, the Knights of St Crispin.

3 Final Years
1885–1886

We now come to the last two years of Emma Paterson's life. It begins with her own historical reproduction of an earlier working-class movement which brought women into the fold, the Grand National Consolidated Trades Union of the 1830s. It ends with a prelude to her own death: a memorial service for one of Emma's oldest comrades, Ellen Wilkinson, who died in August 1886, only two months before Emma and at the untimely age of 44. In between, as she pushed on through fatigue and untreated diabetes, she continued many of the struggles described in earlier chapters. The dispute at the Royal Army Clothing Depot in Pimlico rolled on, the cause of women factory inspectors remained another constant, and there are reports with Emma continuing to address meetings of working women all over the country.

Despite her deepening illness, she continued to write weighty articles and addresses. This chapter includes her introduction to Thomas Paterson's unfinished work on political economy, which she took the time to edit on top of all her other duties. That introduction was part-ode to her departed husband, and part description of their unusual and active social and intellectual life – nights spent conversing and debating with strangers met at open-air discussion meetings along Euston Road and Chelsea Bridge.

In this difficult period, she also brought together nearly 20 years of experience and research into two related questions, both of which are again as relevant in the twenty-first century as they were in the nineteenth: women's wages and short-term work. 'Continuity of Employment and Rates of Wages,' a paper presented at the Industrial Remuneration Conference in 1885, is the longest and most comprehensive statement of Emma's work on the gender pay gap, and how what we would now call 'casualisation' hit women and their standard of living especially hard.

Other articles testify to the moral dimension of Emma's work. In 1885 the Pall Mall Gazette published a series of articles, collectively titled 'The Maiden Tribute of Modern Babylon,' on what we would now call the trafficking of young English women and girls for prostitution. They sparked a moral panic, debates in Parliament, and the raising of the age of consent from thirteen to sixteen. The League met in August to consider the articles and to resolve that unions alone could protect young women from the fate of those described in the Gazette:

> Higher wages, a higher object in life, a wide circle of sympathising and worthy friends, some pleasures, a possibility of pleasant relaxation, these, we maintain, are the most effective antidotes against vice, and these can only be obtained by the moral and material force of combination and association.

This is not the default position of most feminists today, especially the connection made between sex work and vice. Yet one can't understand Emma Paterson's insistence on women's unions without recognising the fear that many working women felt at being forced onto the street – literally and metaphorically – by low wages and unemployment.

As Emma approached her own death, the list of obituary notices for friends and sympathisers piled up. Ellen Wilkinson, whose connection to the Women's Protective and Provident League went back to its second year, was not the only one. Hannah Ellis, a weaver from Huddersfield and a leading member of the League, died in September 1885. As you will see, she died as many other Victorian working women did, in poverty, trying to provide for her children and with a husband in poor health who had tried and failed to start a new life for them in the United States. Emma also used the pages of the Journal to lament the death of Henry Fawcett, the husband of the famous women's suffrage advocate Milicent Fawcett. Twice she called on her readers to subscribe to a Women's Fawcett Memorial Fund.

While she mourned her departed colleagues, she also confronted doubts about the future of her League. In January 1886 she published a long appeal to readers for money and volunteers to keep the League going. 'Hitherto,' she wrote,

> the benefits of the existing Unions have been felt only by the few hundred women who have actually joined them [...] but it is impossible for small Unions numbering scores or at most hundreds of members to influence the conditions of work in trades counting tens of thousands of workers.

This downbeat stocktake of over a decade of tireless work led to a conference held by the League, in July and October, 'to invite and discuss suggestions for extending the work of the League.' It may as well have been convened to debate whether it should continue to exist at all.

Emma put the issue in stark terms. 'I think it is a question for serious consideration,' *she told the conference,* 'whether the League should continue to exist, or whether we should dissolve it and trust that the example of those few Unions which seem firmly established may gradually lead to the organisation of similar Societies in other trades.' *As you will see when reading the report of the conferences, the delegates rejected that proposal. But the fact that Emma Paterson could make it, having sacrificed a decades' time, and her own health, suggests that at the very end of her life she had severe doubts as to whether it had all been worth it. On that depressing note, we begin the chapter that ends with Emma Paterson's life ended.*

'Straw Bonnet Work Fifty Years Ago,' *Women's Union Journal,* January 1885, pp. 1–2

We take the following from the Pioneer, or 'Grand National Consolidated Trades Union Magazine,' of May 24th, 1834. The Magazine, like most of the early Trade Associations mentioned in it, has long disappeared, but it is both interesting and instructive to look back at some of the labour struggles and grievances of fifty years ago; and to see where progress has been made. Many of our readers will learn with surprise that the heroes who returned from the war of 1815 invaded the straw bonnet trade and lowered the prices paid for the women's work. However that dispute may have been settled, the suitability of the straw industry for women seems to have clearly asserted itself, for the Census Returns of 1881 show 27,983 women and girls thus employed, chiefly in Luton and Dunstable, and only 3,001 men. The trade is in full activity for about half the year, and the earnings are then from 9/– to 22/– per week. The blocking is now done by machinery.

> To the Straw-Bonnet Makers
> Fellow Workwomen,
> I am happy to inform you we are on a straight road towards our emancipation; but it is necessary that we take a right position, and most resolutely keep it. Let no man laugh you out of your claims to liberty; nor let flattery deter you from the hope you have now of gaining your freedom. At the same time, let the woman of the Union be known by her modesty, virtue, sobriety, and cleanliness, not usurping the man's power, but wisely defending her own.
> I have seen in the Pioneer, a notice from the Blockers and others, calling a meeting of the trade. As we hope for support and protection from our brothers in union, and their wives, (for we do not mean to let our money lie idle), it is but just they should know what right we have to demand the whole management of our own affairs. A titled

lady in Essex, nearly a century since, wishing to employ her own sex, ingeniously invented the platting and sewing of straw bonnets. In the reign of George the Third, his queen, Charlotte, seeing the number of industrious women supported by that one article, and most likely being wise enough to know the capital it would raise for the British realm, patronized it: seldom the queen or her daughters were seen in public without a straw bonnet. Under these circumstances, the business was brought to the highest perfection; and there are those, whose fathers were mere beggars, now in the city, who keep carriages from the produce of women's labour. When the war ceased, many useful men were thrown out of employment, their wives having to support them. The men, not wishing to be idle, were taught by the women to block; and in a very short time, these men went round to all the principal houses in London, and offered to take home the work, and finish it for less money than the masters gave in-doors, the latter finding everything for the girls' use. It was soon discovered by the women that these men were more tyrannical than their former masters; and, to get the business out of their hands, they offered to take it for less still. This mad competition has sunk the business from one of the best to one of the worst a woman can have. The men will, perhaps, attempt to deny the charge; but was it not against the principles I hold sacred to throw public odium on any individual, I would give the names of the first men, and those who have been actively engaged this spring in lowering the prices of our labour. Yet these men we will forgive, if they are willing to take their proper place; and we will be proud to own them as our brothers, and to promote their interests we will go hand in hand together with them to attain the full reward for our labour, without contention or fear.

My next letter will inform you where to find our Grand Lodge, to give you publicly our intentions and laws, and to show you the advantage of being a member – P.A.S.

'The Women's Trades Council: Report,' *Women's Union Journal*, January 1885, pp. 1–2

The Women's Trades Council was formed in August 1882, with the object of affording the Trade Societies of women in London and the Country, a centre for friendly co-operation and union, without in the slightest degree interfering with the independence of each Society either as to funds or management. It was considered, and this view was strongly urged by the Committee of the Women's Protective and Provident League, that the League could not conveniently serve as such a centre. The League, in order to continue its propagandistic work of encouraging and promoting the establishment of new unions, is obliged to look to outside subscriptions for support. The unions, however, when once started, are self-supporting and it seemed fitting that any form of association among them should also be self-supporting.

A low rate of contribution was agreed upon, so that the smallest of the Societies need not be excluded. At first the rate of one penny per quarter for each member of a Society joining the Council was fixed; this was reduced in October 1883, to one halfpenny per year for London Societies and a penny a year for country unions. Five of the London Societies have joined, but at present none in the country have applied for membership. It is expected that some of these will join during the present year; the new Society of Working Women in Aberdeen has been admitted to the Aberdeen Trades' Council, a body having about 4,000 workmen as its constituents. This step the Women's Trades Council regard with great satisfaction and they hope that other local Trades' Councils of workmen will follow the excellent example of their Aberdeen brethren, and of the Leicester Trades' Council, who have for some years admitted a delegate from the Hosiery Seamers and Stitchers Union.

Rule 3 of the Women's Trades' Council provides that 'each Secretary of a Union shall be a member of the Council and there shall be an additional delegate for each Society having less than 50 members, and one for every 50 members over the first 50.' Under this rule the Council now numbers twelve representative members. The Committee of the Women's Protective and Provident League have lent their office for the meetings, and two members of the Committee have, at the unanimous request of the Council, acted as Hon. Treasurer (Miss Simcox), and Hon. Secretary (Mrs Paterson). The Council was represented at the Trades Union Congress of 1883 and 1884; also at the Congress of Trades' Unionists held in Paris, November 1883 and upon the large deputation to Mr Gladstone organised by the Trades' Union Congress Parliamentary Committee in January 1884, on the question of the extension of Household Suffrage. It will be represented at the Conference on 'Industrial Remuneration,' to be held in London, January 28th, 29th and 30th. [Then provides a balance sheet.]

'The Women's Fawcett Memorial Fund,' *Women's Union Journal*, February 1885, pp. 9–10

A number of women have expressed their desire to recognise in some special way the valuable services rendered by the late Mr Fawcett to the advancement of the questions chiefly affecting the social and political interests of women. Among these questions may be mentioned the extension of university education to women, the claim of women to be admitted to the parliamentary franchise, the introduction of women into the civil service, their election as members of school boards, and as poor law guardians, and their employment as medical practitioners. These various movements received, each in turn, Mr Fawcett's active and cordial support. For more than twenty years he was one of the wisest and most trusted friends the women's cause possessed. It is therefore desired to place on record, in some abiding form, the gratitude felt by the women of the United Kingdom for Mr Fawcett's services, and their own deep sense of the loss they have sustained by his death.

A Committee of nearly one hundred women has been formed under the presidency of Lady Goldsmid, for the purpose of carrying out the object above indicated. At a meeting of the Committee on February 9th, it was decided unanimously that the Memorial Fund should be devoted to the erection of a Drinking Fountain, of artistic design, to be placed in some much frequented thoroughfare.

It is particularly desired that the Women's Memorial should in no way interfere with the larger or general Memorial which has been started by the Duke of Westminster. Many women will probably take part in both. The special Memorial will for the most part be raised by small contributions from women of all classes of society, the object being not so much to collect a large amount of money as to represent the gratitude of a considerable number of women, many of whom have been helped in the hard struggle of their lives by Mr Fawcett's active and courageous sympathy. The Committee hope, that as the object of the fund becomes more widely known, a sufficient number of ladies will be found willing to collect small sums from those interested in the work of the late Mr Fawcett and thus enable this record to be made in some degree worthy of his memory.

The Hon. Secretary will be glad to receive the names of friends each of whom will undertake to collect £10 in small sums from women in aid of the Women's Fawcett Memorial Fund. Subscriptions may be sent either to the Bankers or the Hon. Secretary.

(Collecting cards can be obtained from the Hon. Sec.)

Hon. Treasurer – Louisa, Lady Goldsmid
Hon. Sec. – Emily Tomlinson, MB, Lond. 30 Devonshire Street, Portland Place, W.
Bankers – The London and Westminster Bank, Limited, 4, Stratford Place, W.

'The "Pall Mall Gazette" Revelations,' *Women's Union Journal*, August 1885, pp. 61–62

At a Special General Meeting of the Committee of the Women's Protective and Provident League held at their Office, 36, Great Queen Street, Long Acre, London, on Friday, July 24th, when in addition to give ordinary members of the Committee, five representatives of the London Women's

Unions were present and expressed on behalf of their Societies earnest approval, the following appeal was proposed by Mr Adolphe Smith and adopted by the Committee –

The startling revelations which have caused so deep an emotion, clearly show that women of the industrial and poorer classes are greatly in need of instruction, protection and organisation.

If women and girls were paid higher wages for their work the allurements of vice would no longer prove so fatal.

In successfully seeking to form trades unions among workwomen, the Protective and Provident League, has helped to raise the material and moral tone of the classes who are most exposed to the dangers denounced by the Pall Mall Gazette. By continuing this work on a larger and more extensive scale we shall surely restrict the recruiting ground of vice. Whatever view may be taken as to the causes of both ordinary and criminal vice, associations for self-protection and education, in order words trades unions, naturally suggest themselves as the most effective remedy.

The impossibility, in many trades, of earning sufficient to live respectably, undoubtedly forces many young women on to the street. Again, even where the wages earned just cover the cost of a little good and scant clothing, the life of uninteresting unceasing toil is so appallingly dull that it is no wonder if many women rebel against such an existence. But how can we hope to raise wages unless to be by combinations, by associations among the workpeople?

In other cases, it is not so much the prevailing poverty as the ignorant vanity, the love of show, of dress, that bring about thus ruin of young girls. For this, education of the higher social order is the self-evident remedy; and how better is this social and semi-political education attained than by Trades Unionism? The sense of self-reliance, of personal dignity, of pride in honest work and collective responsibility are all strongly developed within trades unions. Women who join unions soon find something worthier of their ambition than the tawdry finery which is so attractive to those whose social surroundings supply nothing better to think about.

Finally, the solitude and dullness of existence is often the cause of ruin. On leaving business, many young women have no other diversions, no other associates, than those they may find in the streets. But a union provides a large circle of friends bound together by the same common interest. Concerts, social evenings, excursions to the country, facilities for spending a holiday at the sea-side, a swimming club, co-operative stores, reading room, library, etc., all these forms of relaxation are organised and enjoyed by the women trades unionists.

Higher wages, a higher object in life, a wide circle of sympathising and worthy friends, some pleasures, a possibility of pleasant relaxation, these, we maintain, are the most effective antidotes against vice, and these can only be obtained by the moral and material force of combination and association.

We therefore invite all those whose feelings have been stirred by the knowledge of the degradation and suffering endured, especially by the women of the industrial classes, to help us to organise protective and provident trades unions.

In this task, we have already achieved some small measure of success. The receipts of the three most prosperous Women's Trades' Unions of London have exceeded £1,500, and the members have been consequently able to tide over long periods of illness or slack work. But the propaganda necessary to create these institutions naturally costs a considerable sum. Women have to be educated to a true understanding of their interests, and therefore the League must appeal for help in money and in personal devotion. The Women's Unions are self-supporting once they are constituted, but considerable sums must be expended in getting the women together and teaching them how organisations are managed.

It may be objected that the *Pall Mall Gazette* dealt principally with criminal vice, that is to say with very young children who are too young to be members of Trades Unions. Yet many of the actual cases described by the *Pall Mall Gazette*, related to girls who were working in business or in service and who might therefore have belonged to a trade society. Also it is difficult to draw the line at any particular age. If our arguments do not apply to any one particular child in consequence of her extreme youth, they still apply to the older women by whom the child was surrounded and influenced.

Broadly speaking, and whatever ameliorations may be effected in extreme cases of criminal vice by the Criminal Law Amendment Bill, the general prevalence of vice is due, not so much to vicious tendencies, as to poverty and ignorance. We submit that these two causes can only be removed by associated effort, by combinations among the workers, and by the elevating educational and moral influences that result from such organisations.

Subscriptions and donations may be forwarded to the Hon. Sec. Mrs Paterson at the Office, 36, Great Queen St, Long Acre, or to the Hon. Treasurer Mrs Sims, 48, Hamilton Terrace, N.W.

'The Labour Parliament,' *Women's Union Journal*, September 1885, p. 69

The Trades' Union Congress which met this year at Southport, Lancashire, from the 5th to the 12th inst., was remarkable for the advance of opinion shown in the direction of recognising the claims of women to wider social and political power. 156 men and five women were present as delegates.

At Tuesday's sitting the resolution recommending the appointment of practical working men and women as sub-inspectors of Factories, so often a bone of contention at previous Congresses, was unanimously carried, and one delegate Mr Drummond of Glasgow, who was formerly very much opposed to the appointment of women as inspectors, spoke strongly in its favour. We regret that the local newspapers, upon which we depended for our report, gave but very meagre notices of the debate and omitted altogether the excellent speeches made by Miss Wilkinson, who congratulated Mr Drummond on her conversion, and by Mr Coote (London). We are informed that one of the workmen recently appointed as an inspector, is led by his official experience to favour the appointment of women in that capacity. When the new Parliament has been elected, efforts will be made by our League to press forward this reform.

Another important gain was in connexion with a Political Programme, submitted by the Parliamentary Committee for adoption as the Congress Manifesto to constituencies in the approaching election. After four additions to it had been carried Miss Wilkinson proposed, as a fifth amendment, the extension of the suffrage to women, and the motion was carried by 70 votes to six. We give as full a report as possible of this debate. Mr Battersby, a most thoughtful and highly respected member of the Congress, who was its President at Glasgow in 1875, made a telling speech in favour of the amendment, although we believe he has not until recently approved of the proposal.

On Saturday morning, Mr Juggins proposed a resolution similar to that which he moved and carried last year by a considerable majority, in favour of the exclusion of girls under 14 from chainmaking, nailmaking, etc., but the Congress after hearing the statements of Mr Bailey and Mr Sedgwick, would not even debate the question. Mr Juggins' speech showed that his resolution was really aimed at the work of *women*. We therefore regard his decisive defeat with much satisfaction.

'Women's Fawcett Memorial,' *Women's Union Journal*, June 1885, p. 41

The Meeting unavoidably postponed from the 3rd of June is now fixed for Monday, the 29th inst. The amount at present subscribed being still quite insufficient for the proposed Drinking Fountain with portrait medallion, further donations are earnestly requested and will be thankfully received and acknowledged by the Hon. Treasurer, Louisa, Lady Goldsmid, St John's Lodge, Regent's Park.

'The Women's Union Journal: An Encouraging Letter,' *Women's Union Journal*, June 1885, p. 41

Office of the Women's Journal, No 5, Park Street, Boston, Mass, USA, June 2, 1885.

To Mrs Paterson
Dear Madam,
Please email to me at this office the nine volumes of the Women's Union Journal, copies of which are advertised for sale. I enclose PO order (12s 4d) for the same. I shall be very glad to have them It is only lately that I have begun to read the Women's Union Journal and found out how interesting it was. It is at a certain disadvantage because of its small size, which makes it likely to be overlooked in the pile of exchanges. But it is one of the cases, very frequent in nature, where much is stowed away in little bulk.
Yours very truly,
Alice Stone Blackwell.
Any surplus over postage, please accept as a contribution to the League.

'Women's Work in Aberdeen,' *Women's Union Journal,*
September 1885, p. 72

(The following letter was not sent for publication, but we feel sure it will prove interesting – Ed.)

Dear Mrs Paterson
I take great pleasure in writing to you once more, hoping you have been successful in Southport this year. Twelve months ago there was nothing in the daily papers, but the Trades' Congress; this year there is nothing but the British Association: since last Wednesday it has caused quite a sensation, they visited most of the public works in the City at the end of last week and there are lectures in the evening; on Thursday, there was a grand Conversazione held in Gray's Art School, and the Autumn Flower Show in Gordon College Grounds, which is at the back of the Art School, and then the Artists' Exhibition in the Art Gallery all of which were open for members of the Association only. Surely Aberdeen must have a good turnover of money this summer: since the end of July there has been the large Cattle Show which only comes once in the nine years, then came what is called the Timmer Market where the last fruits of the season are sold, then the horse racing, also the Druggists' Conference last week.
I will now tell you about our Society which is now a year old; it has met with a fair success, we have 56 Members on the Roll; we have not given benefit, our first two got four days' benefit for being out of work. Then came Mrs S – who has received eight weeks' sick benefit, the whole time being in the Infirmary, but she being a widow had to pay for her children; her benefit ran out a fortnight ago when two others dropped in, one for sickness, the other for want of work. I left the Jute Works after the nag was settled, as every movement I made was watched, so thinking it better to take it than to get it I then went to ___ Mills but got my leave

from there for fighting against fines; it did not matter what part of your machine wore down or broke you had to pay for it and keep them in needles, so I thought it was rather too bad; a fortnight before I had the last quarrel I was fined a sixpence for talking to my companion, so you can judge that there is great need for reform amongst working women. I was glad to see you had taken up the Pall Mall Gazette question; I quite agree about low wages being one of the great causes of vice, I have known girls in ___ Mills go out with 5/- wages and some less, for a full week's work, 56 hours, and suppose you made more there were always a few fines to make it less. If you were late at work in the morning then you would be fined twopence and you a piece worker. I believe there is not a city like Aberdeen for fines in the Factories.

We have our meeting on the first Thursday of October when there will be new office-bearers to elect: would you kindly write before that time and give us any advice as to how we could push on. I remain yours, etc.,

Jemima Moir

I forgot to tell you I am working at Morton's Provision Factory, Rosemount, they have a branch in London, they are a very respectable firm, no fines there, very honest, Christian employers.

'Hannah Ellis,' *Women's Union Journal*, September 1885, p. 72

We deeply regret to announce this great loss that has fallen upon our much respected friend Mrs Ellis, a member of the Huddersfield Woollen Weavers' Union Committee. Her eldest daughter, whose death from decline has now occurred, after six months' illness, was possessed of much amiability and gentleness, although some people assert that such qualities must inevitably be crushed out by work in mills and factories. She had considerable musical knowledge and a good, well-trained voice, so that she was always welcome as a singer at the Weavers' Union entertainments. Naturally she was her mother's loved and trusted companion and helper in family cares, arising from the charge of two younger children, and anxieties concerning a husband in delicate health, who has for some months been trying his fortunes in the United States but with so little success that he has now return to England. Mrs Ellis left her factory work some months ago, to nurse her daughter, and it can be well understood that her pecuniary resources must have been severely taxed.

The Testimonial fund already referred to in this Journal, which was commenced early in the year, when Mrs Ellis was discharged by her late employers, for attending the Industrial Remuneration Conference, has we understand reached only about £20. It has been decided that the fund shall remain open a little longer, and contributions may therefore still be sent to Mr EB Fleming, Storths, Mold Green, Huddersfield.

Final Years: 1885–1886

Report of the Trades Union Congress, 1885

Miss Wilkinson (London) moved, as an addition to the address, that the franchise be given to women upon the same conditions as it was or might be given to men. She asserted that the men had not fairly represented the women in parliament, and the consequence was that questions deeply affecting the well-being of her sex had been neglected. Had women been given the political power to which they were entitled, many reforms of the most beneficial nature would have been made before this. She was surprised that the members of that Congress who had brought forward and supported motions for restricting the employment of married women had not brought forward some motion by which wives could compel their husbands to maintain them, which a wife could not do now without making herself a pauper. (Applause.)

Mr Toine (Cleveland) said rates and taxes were paid by women. They were quite capable of exercising political power, and on these grounds, he thought women ought to be recognised as well as men. He seconded the motion.

The discussion was continued by Mr William Pickard (Wigan), Mr Battersby (Glasgow), Mr Coote (London) and Mr Maddison (Hull).

Mr B Pickard (Barnsley) said he objected to the amendment, unless the power was given to married women equally with those who were not seeking the franchise.

Mrs Paterson (London) argued that single women and widows were entitled to have a vote as compensation for not having a husband. (Laughter and applause.) She quite agreed that married women who had husbands like Mr Pickard would not require a vote. (Renewed laughter). Mrs Paterson explained that before her husband died she held the opinion that it was a hardship that single women and widows should be denied the power of voting at the elections of Parliamentary representatives.

Miss Wilkinson's amendment was carried, the voting being 70 for and 10 against.

'Room to Let for Meetings,' *Women's Union Journal*, December 1885, p. 107

One of the rooms of the Women's Protective and Provident League, at 36, Great Queen Street, WC, may be hired by Societies, for three hours during the day for 4s (including fire) and for the same time in the evening for 5s (including gas and firing). A reduction for a series of engagements. The room has seats for 80 and a platform accommodating 10 persons. Applications to be addressed to the Hon. Sec., Mrs Paterson.

'The Work of the League,' *Women's Union Journal*, January 1886

About Christmas and the New Year, little can be done in the way of public meetings, and the Annual Reports of existing societies, for the same reason, do not come in at this time.

We may therefore take advantage of the space usually reserved for these items of intelligence to recapitulate some of the objects of the League and point out some of the various ways in which friends and well-wishers in all parts of the country may help to promote them.

There are few to whom the objects of the League have been explained who fail to approve and sympathise with them. Everyone knows that the wages of many women in all trades are deplorably low; their hours of work so long as to be fatal to their own health and to all domestic comfort and order, and the competition of the unemployed so keen that it seems almost vain to hope that any influence can be brought to bear upon the labour market powerful enough to at once raise wages and shorten the hours of work. Everyone knows the evils that arise from this state of things; no one better than the district visitors, mission women, clergy of all demonstrations and the other agents of the many forms of charity which have tried so long, and we must add so unavailingly, to remedy them. Cases of hardship arising from overwork, low wages and want of work are constantly described in the reports of societies which base their prayer for subscriptions on the existence of this distress. But both subscribers and almoners seem to us too ready to assume that the alternation of overwork and want of work, which the one stable accompaniment of low wages, is inevitable and unalterable, a dispensation of Providence or political economy against which it would be impious or unscientific to rebel.

Now we should like, first and foremost, to lead all those who, as they saying is, 'work amongst the poor,' to see that these things are not necessary evils and that the remedy lies to a considerable extent in the hands of the suffering workers themselves. We do not ask them to withhold the gifts that may alleviate distress for a moment, while recommending that we believe to be a more permanent remedy. But while giving the help which, at the moment, it might be cruel to refuse, they should seize the opportunity of showing how the need for it may be avoided in future.

All that is true now of the position of working women might have been said with equal truth fifty years ago of working men. The wages of working women, except as domestic servants, have not we believe on the whole risen appreciably during this half century; poor seamstresses still starve upon 3s 6d a week as they did in the days of Hood, while even then a skilled, fine stitching shirtmaker in good work could earn 3s a day, or 18s a week, which still passes for good wages. Engineers used to work sixteen hours a day instead of nine, and their wages have increased. Dressmakers and Tailoresses still, in spite of the Factory Acts, work for fourteen hours or more and their average earnings are practically stationary. Men as well as women are suffering throughout the country from depression of trade, but the existing distress is not to be compared for severity to that which was frequent, if not chronic, during the 'thirty years peace' before 1848. We should now be on the verge – or in the midst – of a revolution if there had been as little improvement in the industrial position of men as there has been in that of women. The demand for the industrial services of women has meanwhile increased more than in proportion to their numbers, yet as compared with men workers they have lost rather than gained.

The 'reason why' is to be found in the simple fact that the Trade Unions of men are many, rich and powerful, and the Trade Unions of women few and feeble, and poor in comparison to the vast field of work which lies before them.

What it is exactly that the existing Women's Unions propose may be seen on the outside page of this Journal, by any of our readers to whom the subject is new. Hitherto the benefits of the existing Unions have been felt only by the few hundred women who have actually joined them, and who in many cases have been saved from pressing want and suffering by the sick and out-of-work allowances due to members. But it is impossible for small Unions numbering scores or at most hundreds of members to influence the conditions of work in trades counting tens of thousands of workers; and in the majority of women's trades there is not even so much as a small society yet formed.

What is needed then is the formation of new local branches in the trades where organisation has already begun; branches, to begin with, in the different districts of London, branches in the large provincial towns and at least one branch in every centre of population where there are as many as fifty women working at the same trade. Every friend of the cause who counts among her neighbours that small number of Bookfolders and Sewers, Upholsteresses, Dress and Mantlemakers, Machinists, Shirtmakers and plain Needlewomen or Tailoresses, has the wherewithal to organise an independent, self-supporting branch of what, by the multiplication of such branches would become powerful, national organisations, for the purpose of securing to every competent and industrious woman 'a fair day's wage, for a fair day's work.' In all these trades London has led the way, but in the remainder where it is still behindhand, if other towns will let us hear that they have made a beginning, London will doubtless endeavour to follow the good example.

It will be observed that this is a very large programme, but we venture to think the larger it is the more chance there is obtaining the help necessary to its completion; nothing succeeds like success, for people do not like to subsidise a losing cause, and we have explained that complete success cannot be obtained until our organisations include at least a working majority of the three millions of women now industrially employed. This movement is little more than 12 years old, and it may be doubted whether there were more than 1,000 workmen belonging to Trade Societies in the eighteenth century, a dozen years after the first attempt at combination had been made. But there can be no doubt also that the faster our work proceeds, the more help and sympathy it will meet with. Already, the announcement of projected meetings made in the last number of this Journal has brought in a variety of special contributions; and we may take this opportunity of mentioning that donations to meet the additional expense of an active Unionist propaganda will be gratefully received and should be sent by all those who have no fault to find with the work of the League, except that it does not progress rapidly enough. The money so bestowed will be spent in the hire of suitable rooms for public meetings, in printing handbills to announce the same, and also when necessary in defraying the first expenses for printing or room rent, incurred at the foundation of new Societies, though the latter are of course self-supporting, as soon as they are once fairly established.

All this of course costs money; even to work all London thoroughly – to say nothing of the rest of England – would cost a great deal of money, and those who are able to do nothing else for the cause may send their subscriptions with an easy conscience, knowing that no one will be pauperised or demoralised by such gifts; but only put into the way of becoming truly independent, taught how to live on their own earnings without the need of charity and at the same time to help others without depriving them of the same just instinct of self-respect.

But, though money is indispensable, there are other forms of help which are still more so. Public meetings may be held, and, if the speakers are well known and popular, may be well attended, and yet no practical result attained. A mixed audience may come, and listen, and say, 'Oh, yes: how sad! Very true!' and agree to what they hear, as people do to sermons in church, which have very little effect upon their conduct on the following Monday morning. It would be rash to say that no good result follows from such meetings: people may become familiarised with the idea of Unionism for women, and a train of thought may be begun in the minds of a few, which in the course of time may ripen into action. But there is no direct practical result in the way of trade organisation to be secured by this sort of general speech making.

Working women are cautious, timid and naturally suspicious when a number of strangers come to them with a new doctrine, including a demand on them to pay some of their few and hard earned twopences to secure a distant result, which many of them, with the unconscious cynicism of despair, look upon as 'too good to be true.' Many again of the best and most sensible and intelligent workers are shy, unaccustomed to any kind of publicity; and while able and willing to speak sensibly and to the point in a small conference of friends and acquaintances, yet would not care to be the first to come forward at a public meeting to express the agreement they might feel. In all cases where a successful and durable society has been formed, the first step has been to make acquaintance privately, with a few intelligent and thoughtful members of the trade, to discuss with them the principles and objects of Trade Unions, and as these brought their friends to successive conferences, the nucleus of the future society was prepared, before the Public Meeting was held at which its formation was formally resolved upon. This most necessary and valuable preliminary work may be undertaken by ladies who, like the workers just described, are 'unaccustomed to public speaking' and perhaps disinclined for it. The best qualification for this branch of the League's work, is, of course, a personal knowledge of the regions where the women workers at any particular trade are congregated; in this case the first step is no doubt the most difficult, and there are two drawbacks for which all who wish to take a practical part in the League's work must be prepared; namely, that it must all be done at night and mostly in unfashionable parts of the town. Anyone who is prepared to face these two obstacles will surely be able, through some friend or acquaintance who has been brought in contact with the working classes in any other way, to obtain an introduction to one or two women working at the trade in which the visitor in anxious to promote organisation.

There are ways and means by which women who are desirous of 'getting into society' of any particular class can accomplish their aim, and it is not more difficult to acquaint with seamstresses than with singers, with machinists than with marchionesses. No meetings of a 'mutual improvement society' could be compared, as regards pleasure and profit, with evenings that we remember, with talk lasting even into the small hours of morning, while members of the League explained over and over again how and why they believed women could benefit themselves by Union and learnt in return a thousand facts, strange, interesting and hitherto undreamt of, concerning the scenery and circumstances of modern industrial life. Such intercourse teaches other not less valuable lessons. Many quiet, hardworking women, who have always 'kept themselves respectable' and never come in contact with the charitable agencies that hover round the less capable and less deserving, are discovered to nurse a secret grudge against society, and without consciously professing any kind of political discontent, are yet prepared by the whole experience of their hard life, to welcome any new doctrine which shall give hopes of setting things upon a juster base. The district visitor never sees these women; they are out at work till after the time when even charitable ladies go home and dress for dinner; and if such a woman is for a time laid up by illness, the chances are that while help goes to chronic paupers, perhaps on the floor above and below, moments when she would not be too proud to take it. Women like this are the first to join a society for their trade; and from them these visitors may learn what a command of language, what an amount of practical sagacity, ready wit and delicate good feeling are possessed by the 'intelligent working woman.'

It is evident that if the League is to do all the work that is waiting for it, more working members must be enlisted as well as more money subscribed; but those who are unable, from health, family ties or other reasons, to engage in this direct personal canvass may yet do useful work by converting those of their friends who already visit the poor by day into a sort of supplementary agency for the distribution of Unionist literature, notice of meetings and reports of the existing societies.

We would an appeal to those who are interested in clubs, friendly societies and social amusements or homes for young women, not to be too ready to encourage their desire to 'sink the shop' and play at being young ladies who do not like to talk about anything so vulgar as working for their living. In this way good women who really wish to be of use to the girls go on knowing little or nothing of the realities of their everyday life; and instead of helping them to improve their own position, tacitly encourage the 'shabby genteel' sort of false pride which is one of the most ruinous follies of the sex – ruinous, because it is incompatible with the proper professional pride which every worker ought to feel in his or her calling, and without which there is little to encourage the cultivation of technical skill, without which again no class of workers can command either due respect or adequate remuneration.

It is well known that the women's unions serve as a centre for social intercourse and amusement as well as for serious business. One of the ways in which friends from outside can be of use is in arranging for entertainments which are enjoyed in common by the members of different societies; hitherto there has been no dearth of such help, but the entertainments, which are undoubtedly useful in bringing doubtful or wavering workers within reach of unionist influences, have hitherto been given only at the offices of the League in Great Queen Street. It is evident that as soon as societies or branches are established in less central parts of London there will be a large increase in the demand for volunteer help, unless these branches are to find themselves less fortunate than their parent stem. Indeed, if the work of the League increases as much as we all wish and desire, it might be expedient to hand over all arrangements of this kind to an 'Amusements' Committee,' which might find work for many who wish well to the Unions without being able to contribute directly to the work of their formation. There is already a large and valuable Library at the League Office, from which books might possibly be obtained on loan by local branches; though there are difficulties in the way of the full utilisation of books by women unionists that will hardly be removed till the unions themselves have gained much in numbers and strength. A trifling payment is at present required from those who use the library, and when we enquire why it is not more used the answer is, when women are busy they work too late to have any time for reading, and when they are slack they are too poor to afford the most trifling subscription.

'The Late Parliamentary Elections,' *Women's Union Journal*, January 1886

If the enfranchisement of women were not likely to be effected in a good deal less than twenty-one years we should advise all friends of the cause to christen their daughters Frances. It is one of the peculiar features of the British constitution that a woman is at present only allowed to vote at Parliamentary elections if a man has made a mistake about her name. Two ladies, at Hanley and Manchester, duly qualified as occupiers, gave their votes the other day, owing to their names having been placed on the register as Francis. Another woman at Hull was enfranchised by the accident that the officer compiling the register did not read his Bible and thought that Keziah was a man's name; the worthy namesake of Job's daughter claimed her rights, and the name being on the register the vote was accepted. An Irish girl named Jesse Russell voted by an opposite chance, Jesse being naturally taken for a man's name, while a real Jessie got registered by mistake. In all ten women voted, and one or two others said to have been qualified in the same way, might have done so if they pleased.

It cannot however be owing to these ten valuable votes that 314 members of the new House of Commons are known and pledged supporters of Women's Suffrage, while of the remainder only 104 are known opponents. We hay hope therefore, that it will not be necessary for women to adopt nondescript names as a roundabout way of getting from masculine ignorance, what masculine enlightenment will now probably hasten to bestow.

Emma Paterson, 'Preface,' in Thomas Paterson, *A New Method of Mental Science, with Applications to Political Economy*, London, 1886

Had the writer of this book lived to compete it, he would probably have published it anonymously; such was his frequently expressed intention, notwithstanding the advice of friends to the contrary. Under the circumstances about to be explained, however, anonymous publication appears especially inadvisable. The posthumous work of any but a well-known writer, if produced under the most favourable auspices, is less likely than the work of a living author to arouse attention and interest, but such a work by a new writer, not having been completed, even in M.S. form, stands in a still more unfortunate position. I have therefore determined to give the author's name and to offer a brief explanation concerning the objects of the book and its unfinished condition.

For quite fifteen years the desire to write the results of his studies of mental and social science had been foremost in my husband's mind. The delay in writing was caused by many and heavy cares, both public and private. His death occurred more than three years ago, but everyone to whom he was personally known will remember how ungrudgingly he devoted much of his time to practical works of social reform. He had also in hand private interests, involving intricate legal questions. At his death some of these cares necessarily fell upon me, and, to my great vexation, still further delayed the publication of the book.

When the movement for establishing Workmen's Clubs and Institute, now widely spread over the country, was commenced, about the year 1863, Thomas Paterson entered into it with energy, devoting most of his leisure time to the duties of Honorary Secretary to the Club first established in Clerkenwell, and to one of the earliest distributive Co-operative Societies, connected with it. In 1866, a series of discussion upon social questions was held by the Working Men's Club and Institute Union, in Exeter Hall, and one of these, when he opened the subject of 'The Dwellings of the Working Classes,' excited considerable attention, and led to his being invited to join the Council of the Union. Afterwards, he acted for some time as one of the Honorary Secretaries of the Union, and, for two or three years before his death, as a Vice-Chairman of the Council. He was thus brought into contact with Mr Hodgson Pratt, the late Lord Lyttleton, Mr Stephen Seward Taylor, Dr WH Hodgson and many others well known for their untiring efforts in public work. One of these, Mr CE Maurice, thus wrote of him in the Spectator, shortly after his death:

> It was in the year 1866 that I first saw Thomas Paterson. He was then reading a paper on the question of the way in which working men could best save money, and if I remember right, could buy their own houses. I remember that my father who was with me, was much impressed with Paterson's clearness of statement and with his power of passing from somewhat dry statistics to eloquent appeal. He also said that there was something in Paterson, I think both in his face and way of putting things, that reminded him of John Stuart Mill.

Arrangements for Workmen's Excursions, upon a large scale, to the Paris Exhibition of 1867, absorbed, in that year, much of his time. Then, and again in 1878, he was deputed by the Society of Arts to write a Report of Cabinet work and wood carving shown in the Paris Exhibition. Soon afterwards he became associated with the Hon. Auberon Herbert and Mr JW Probyn in organising the Workmen's International Exhibition of 1870, at the Agricultural Hall, under the presidency of the Right Hon. WE Gladstone, the complete success of which was marred only by the outbreak of the Franco-German war. The Echo, in October 1882, remarked that this undertaking led to the opening of similar Exhibitions all over the country. Two important points about it were introduced by husband; one was the publication, as far as possible, of the names of all workmen employed in producing the articles exhibited, and the awarding of prizes to them, instead of to the firms by which they were employed; another was the passing of a short Act of Parliament for the provisional protection of inventions exhibited. Patent-Law Reform was a subject to which he had long given careful thought, and his speeches both upon deputations and at public meetings, as a member of the Council of the Inventors' Institute, helped to pave the way for the Act lately passed, whereby the heavy fees which formerly practically repressed the talents of non-wealthy inventors were considerably reduced.

The formation and encouragement of discussion classes engaged a large share of his attention. He was an intense lover of debate, and it was chiefly his remarkable skill in such contests that first brought him into active public life. His speech at a Conference held in 1864, to consider 'Why Working People do not attend Church,' deeply interested the Chairman, Dean Stanley, who shortly afterwards invited him and a few of his friends to the Deanery to further discuss the question. One suggestion made by my husband was that visits of working people to Westminster Abbey on Saturday afternoons should be organised. The Dean readily assented and added that he and Lady Augusta Stanley would themselves guide the parties and give historical accounts of the Abbey and its monuments. How popular these visits have become is well known, and the Dean, Dr Bradley, continues them.

My husband's evenings were frequently engrossed by meetings of the Council of the Workmen's Peace Association, the Labour Representation League, the Free Libraries' Association, and the Land Tenure Reform Association. In the organisation and business of these societies, in conjunction with Mr WR Cremer, Mr Henry Broadhurst, Mr GF Savage, Mr JT Dexter, Mr Howard Evans and other leading workmen, he took an active part. I should needed be ungrateful if I did not also record here his readiness at all times to assist in any projects for the benefit of women. Not only did he afford me invaluable advice and aid in the formation of the

Women's Protective and Provident League in 1874, and in its subsequent work, but he also most generously sanctioned the absorption of much of my own time in the movement. Indeed his views upon the necessity of raising the political and social position of women were so liberal and unprejudiced that they frequently drew down upon him the displeasure, and even sometimes the contempt, of some of the men with whom he was publicly associated.

Allowing for all these numerous and engrossing pursuits, besides his occupation as a cabinet maker and wood carver, in which he attained great excellence; also taking into consideration his extreme dread of making the effort, imperfect as he felt it would be, of expressing his views in writing, it is not surprising that the attempt to commence this book should have been long deferred. He found that in order to gain time for it he must give up some of his more active work, but the determination was not very strictly adhered to, except so far as regarded his personal interests. The M.S. was somewhat hastily written at last, and in 1881 the printing was commenced and was continued until the summer of 1882 when there came the illness – rapid decline – which resulted in his death on October 15th of that year. Up to page 204 the proofs were corrected by his own hand, but all the succeeding pages, with the exception of the Appendix, are put together from rough, unfinished notes, and it is for the imperfect condition of those pages that I now ask the indulgence of every reader. I have preferred to leave incomplete, disjointed sentences, of his own words, in however rough and simply a form, rather than to attempt to finish or connect them, at the risk of misinterpreting his meaning.

The title he finally decided upon was 'A New Method of Mental Science, with applications to Education and Political Economy,' but the notes relating to education it has been impossible to use, as they were little more than mere headings; the title is therefore now slightly contracted.

As I have already said, the book is the result of mature thought. Whenever he could snatch a few hours' leisure he went to the Reading Room of the British Museum; each time the books consulted were noted, and as proof of his wide research I have a long list of them, too long to give here, but I may mention that with the works of Berkeley, Kant, Spinoza, and among modern scientific writers, Carpenter, Darwin and Lewes, he had long been familiar, and 'possessed' most of them in fully his own meaning of mental possession.

One strong motive impelling him to write the book was a desire to refute the materialistic views of the day by what he ventured, with some boldness, to term a 'New Method of Mental Science.' He knew that those views were rapidly spreading and that it was futile to cry 'Believe, and do not think' when the reason had once become dissatisfied. Some years ago, open-air discussion meetings, consisting chiefly of workmen, were held in certain parts of London, on Sunday evenings. The railways arches near the Euston Road, and the open space at the north end of Chelsea Bridge, were favourite spots for these gatherings. Groups were formed around lecturers of many shades of belief; Secularists, Methodists, Humanitarians, Unitarians, Vegetarians and Teetotallers were all represented. When some ardent exponent of Secularism had apparently silenced, if not convinced, all his hearers, my husband, who usually joined the first named group, would by means of a few well-put scientific questions, completely rivet the attention of all, and evidently lead many of the listeners to reconsider their hasty conclusions. He would show them, for instance, how impossible it was for students of science to follow the lecturer's advice to believe only what they could actually see. Frequently, upon breaking up a discussion prolonged until nearly midnight, two or three of the more eager enquirers walked with us, far on our way home, still debating, with intense interest the views put forward by my husband. As I listened, it seemed to me that work of this kind was at least equal in usefulness to much of the preaching in church or chapel. The rigorous Calvinism of his early training, and indeed, for the most part, all formal creeds, he was obliged to relinquish, but for that hope within, which never left him, he wished to give a reason, for the help of others in a similar position. Strangely enough, his father, a citizen of Elgin, although belonging to Scotland's most rigid religious school, and strict in observance of the Sabbath, and in family discipline, yet allowed his children complete liberty in discussion, and would join them in the freest speculation upon subjects that in many families are forbidden subjects of argument. No books were kept from them, excepting on Sundays, and provided the Shorter catechism was not forgotten. This freedom must have surprised many persons at that time, over forty years ago. When little more than a youth, Thomas Paterson was turned out of a debating Society connected with a popular Dissenting Chapel in London, for reading a totally unorthodox paper upon the creation of man in the image of God. It is scarcely necessary to add that he had a passion for books, sometimes neglecting his work for them, and so incurring the displeasure of his father, to whom, as a cabinet maker in London, was apprenticed for the usually tedious period of seven years. The Birkbeck Institution, then recently opened, he joined at the earliest age allowed by the rules, and afterwards attended the Science Lectures at the School of Mines, given by Professors Huxley, Tyndall, Geikie and others. He often regretted that his younger days were passed in England instead of Scotland, where poor men are not shut out from a high-class education.

The second motive that impelled him to write this book was a strong conviction that the laws of Political Economy, as they are called, could be shown to have serious errors, and to be an unsafe guide for dealing with human commodities. He lived to see some of the fallacies overthrown, and, in the three years since his death, further enquiry has been aroused about others. With the late Dr WB Hogdson he frequently had tough arguments upon Political Economy; one of these took place at the Club in Clerkenwell, already mentioned, when Dr Hodgson accepted an invitation to a supper prepared by bachelor cookery, and afterwards listened, with unfailing good humour, to attacks, with blackboard illustrations, upon the science he had adopted as a profession.

One of the last books my husband read during his illness was 'Progress and Poverty,' by Henry George, then and since very widely discussed; he agreed in the main with the views put forward in that book respecting property in land, but said he regretted that the author had not examined the equally important question of interest, as a cause of poverty. He also spoke often of that which he firmly believed, about the future of labour; of the time not far distant, when to work, even with the hands, and to successfully lead work of any kind, would be an honour, a mark of social distinction. Great social changes were, he believed, much nearer than was generally supposed, and recent events have to some extent proved this to be true.

In conclusion, I must once more earnestly ask those who read the book to forgive all the shortcomings of its attempted completion, and to accept this very imperfect apology from one who for nine years shared, with the keenest interest, the writer's hopes and fears about it. Fears were predominant, for he felt most acutely the deficiencies of even the four completed chapters, and he never anticipated ready acceptance of his views. The subject of the chapter upon which he was last engaged is 'Omniscience.' If there truly be, as he fully believed, an after-existence, when 'we shall know even as we are known,' how intense must be the delight of the 'all-knowledge,' to that teeming, active brain and broadly sympathetic heart.

EA Paterson, March 1886.

'The Case of the Women Employed in the Royal Army Clothing Factory in Pimlico,' *Women's Union Journal*, March 1886, pp. 25–29

The interest felt in this subject continues unabated. In another place we give a report of the Meeting held last month and attended by as many of the Factory workers as the Hall would hold. It is impossible to suppose that the wide and deep feeling of discontent which evidently exists among the women can have arisen without cause or provocation. One point however is curious and significant. The authorities of the Factory do not justify the reduction of wages, of which the operatives complained, by a reference to the competition of Contractors, or the supreme exigencies of economy. They flatly deny the existence of any recent reductions at all.

If any reductions then have recently been made, they are practically given up as indefensible.

Meanwhile a question asked by Mr Albert Grey in the House of Commons elicited a reply from Mr Woodall, which was calculated to produce an illusory feeling of satisfaction in the minds of those who do not know how easily official statistics can always be made to wear a pleasant countenance. Mr Grey asked if it was true, as stated in an evening newspaper, that the wages of the workwomen in the Pimlico Factory had been reduced 25 per cent in the last year.

Mr Woodall's answer was:

> No sir. The average wages of the women employed in the Army Clothing Factory during 1884 amounted to 15/8 a week of actual earnings. The average for 1885 was 15/8½. The corresponding average for the four weeks ending February 17th last was 17/1½. Perhaps the numbers at different rates of wages will make the comparison more intelligible. In 1884 and 1885 respectively there were employed in all 1,259 and 1,399 women. Of these 231 and 262 received respectively less than 10/- a wee; 752 and 805 from 10/- to £1 a week; 254 and 291 from 20/- to 30/- a week; and 22 and 41 respectively over 30/- a week. I may add that certain memorials and representations have been addressed to the Secretary of State concerning the general administration of the clothing factory, to which I am giving my own very careful attention.

A moment's consideration will show that Mr Woodall's figures are not in the least inconsistent with the worker's facts. We are that in 1885, when the factory was exceptionally hard at work, was on one occasion open on Sunday, when overtime was common and taking work home allowed and encouraged, and when extra payment was temporarily allowed for certain garments that were needed in great haste, under all these special conditions which might have been expected to make 1885 a fat year for the operatives, the average wages of those employed was only 1/2d a week more than in the year before. If prices had not been lowered the average earnings were virtually stationary, and more than the average amount of work done in the factory, the complaints of the women are well founded, for they have had to do more work to earn the same money as before, and when this is the case it is absurd to say there is no reduction of wages.

But this is not the whole of the workpeople's case. In 1879, as now, the workers declared, in general terms, when they could do so without incriminating themselves, that they did habitually increase their earnings by taking work home, in defiance of the rule by which a woman caught in the act is suspended or locked out for a month. The more their prices are reduced, the more resolute they are in breaking the rule against home work, just as smuggling increases, the more the duty on imported goods is raised. At the same time, it is scarcely to be wondered at that the officials of the factory decline to believe in the existence of the practice which all the women combine to conceal from their official knowledge. So far as the wages of the workers are reduced by their own habitual resort to overtime, they must be told frankly that the remedy is in their own hands and that their best friends can only advise them to apply it for themselves. Let public opinion in the factory declare that, at the present crisis, every woman who takes work home, to increase her own earnings for the current week, is helping to reduce the prices for all work done in the factory, perhaps for years to come, and there will surely be none so short sighted as to refuse to obey, say for one calendar month, a self-denying ordinance, by which all the workers should resolve to content themselves with what they can earn during the lawful factory hours, so that it may be practically proved how much of the average earnings in past years has been gained by the illicit use of overtime. The higher officers of the Factory declare that the present earnings are what they consider fair under all the circumstances of the case, and if it were proved that the women cannot earn as much as they have been receiving in the recognised hours of work, we are given to understand that an appeal for increased prices would be entertained. Many of the women, on the other hand, declare that they would be satisfied with their present earnings if they represented a fair day's work, instead of, as in many cases, a day of 16 or 18 hours, and that if prices were modified to this extent, home work should be really and truly given up, a result which would be satisfactory to all parties.

One more comment must be made on the high average earnings which, according to Mr Woodall's statement, ruled in the Factory during February, at the very time when the discontent of the workers had begun, so to speak, to boil over and become manifest in the press and platform. Averages are the half way house between extremes, and after the low earnings of broken holiday weeks no doubt more work than usual is taken home, but apart from this there are special causes which make the earnings of one week or month higher than another: last week for example, the number of garments turned out by the factory was lower than usual, while the earnings were above the average; the two facts taken together explain each other: 'Frocks' and 'tunics' which are more elaborate and comparatively well paid garments were in the majority and ten-penny and eleven-penny trousers few in proportion; in other words more women were engaged on the better class of work and therefore more were earning satisfactory wages. But such variations as this are as far as the annual average earnings from proving that prices have in no cases been reduced.

In some cases what the workers complain of as reductions are declared by the authorities to be only a reasonable adjustment of pay consequent upon alterations in the work. Of course this is a point as to which there will always be room for difference of opinion, and fair play can only be secured by full and free discussion. Perhaps none of the women's grievances have received more universal sympathy than the complaint that they were liable to find their wages altered or reduced without warning or discussion. Apparently the theory in the factory has been that when any change was projected, it should be discussed with the practical tailors of the establishment, the 'foreman cutter,' the 'foreman viewer,' &c., and also with some representatives of the women. In practice, however, the men alone are consulted by the manager and it rests with them to take counsel or not, as they please, with the women, and in any case the views of the latter are not directly represented. The change is made, and the Manager's view seems to be that if the women don't complain it is because they are satisfied that it is all right. This little circumstance goes a good way to explain the unsatisfactory relations which exist between this manager and his 'regiment of women.' Everyone knows that women (to say nothing of the free Briton irrespective of sex) will grumble loud and long before they will adopt practical measures to redress a grievance; workwomen especially are slow and shy to complain, fearing always to get a black mark against themselves as troublesome characters or perhaps to be put as a penalty from 'best work' to commoner and less profitable tasks. Supposing after all the women do complain and have their complaints favourably received, it is certain that the memory of the wrong complained of will remain and be resented while little gratitude will be felt for the redress consequent on their complaints. It is evidently much better to guard against dissatisfaction by consulting the workers before hand, than to say: they can appeal to the manager if they have anything to complain of.

We believe that this is now understood by the authorities at the factory and if the whole body of workers would resolve themselves into a Trade Protection and Arbitration Society, electing representatives from each division, authorised to speak on behalf of the workers of every class, we are given to understand that such a standing Committee would be recognised and consulted about the various re-adjustments of price which become necessary when the patterns of work are changed. Many women who would not like to put themselves forward in the way of complaints or appeals would be ready and willing to speak on behalf of their fellow workers when they were authorised and invited to do so, in order to arrive beforehand at an amicable settlement of what was fair and reasonable in apportioning work and prices.

One point which may be noticed in regard to Mr Woodall's figures is that there is an increase in the number of women – of course all machinists – earning the highest rate of wages, while there is corresponding increase in the number of those earning the lowest, i.e. under 10/– a week. This fact is not impossibly connected with some of the complaints made by the workers about the way some work has been re-distributed between sewers and machinists. Details of this kind can only be satisfactorily settled by a Committee or jury of experts, all interested in seeing fair play on all sides.

It is alleged that in some cases the machinists are overworked, not overpaid for the work they do, but forced to do more than a fair day's work during the factory hours in order to keep the hand sewers in their group fully employed; then if the machinist is unable or unwilling to keep on incessantly at the hardest pace, the hand-workers lost time, and consequently money which they can hardly spare, while waiting for her. This is only one illustration among many of the minor inconveniences and injustices which might be obviated if there were a standing committee of the operatives, authorised to discuss these matters with the managers.

It is perhaps too much to expect that the existing Trade Union should receive the adhesion of the 12,000 women of the factory, as the rate of subscription and the rules for sick benefit, &c., may not exactly suit every individual in so large a number, but the society supplies a ready-made machinery which might be adapted to the wants of the factory. Many trade societies have no provident fund or sick benefits, and the factory workers have constant employment so that there is not the same need of an out-of-work fund as in other cases. A very small subscription would therefore suffice to keep together a purely trade association, including all the workers and having for its main object the election of a Standing Committee by which the views of the operatives upon all questions of work and wages might be represented in amicable discussion with the chief officials.

One part of the legend respecting the present manager which has obtained currency among the workers must be pronounced baseless. Mr Safe was not appointed in the first instance for seven years, or any other fixed period; his salary was raised, from £400 to £500 a year after five years' service, mainly in recognition of economies he had effected in the management of the factory, partly in the cutting and partly in the 'trimming' department, where in 1879 the labour of girls was largely substituted for that of men and youths; there seems to have been room for reasonable saving as regards the cutting, but it need hardly be said that this Journal can never approve of the substitution of women for men to do the same work at a lower price. And we may add that it is still thought by the respectable matrons of the factory both unseemly and undesirable for a parcel of girls to be working in a separate department, under men. Mr Sage's reputation as an economist however rests upon the saving made in this way rather than upon any decreased outlay on the women's wages. As the women contend that they cannot live upon less than their present wages and make up therefore by additional home work for any reductions of price, it is evident that the only room for economy here would be if the factory got more garments made in a year for the same wages, and this is a very difficult comparison to make, as the cost of the different garments and the number of each sort made in the year necessarily varies much.

As regards the particular grievance of the greatcoats given to be made at the Carteret Street workroom at a price below that paid in the factory, there is no disagreement as the main facts. The greatcoats, when made in the factory are paid for at the rate of 2/2, while 1/10 was given to the managers of Carteret Street, out of which 4d or about 18 per cent was deducted for management and working expenses. Of the 1/6 left for the workers 3½d we understand went to the machinist and 1/0½ to the hand sewer, the pressing being done by time-work; we were not able to ascertain the average earnings of the workers respectively it follows that the wages of the machinists would vary from 14/- to 24/- a week, and those of the hand sewers from 3/1½ to 12/6. These wages are entirely inadequate, and the low price which necessitated the low wages was quite insistent with the sound opinion expressed by Mr Sage in his evidence in 1879 that more, rather than less, should be paid for work done out of doors, because the wear and tear of machinery has to be considered. The explanation offered at the factory is as follows: the great coats in question are plain, common work, of the sort that is usually done by contractors at contractors' (i.e. very low) prices; if they were made in numbers in the factory, the skilled operatives there would get used to the work and turn them out in greater quantities so as to be able to earn their usual wages even at reduced price. But the work being of a common sort can be done by contractors, and therefore it is argued more than a contractors' price need not and should not be paid for it. This is what the benevolent ladies of Carteret Street were told, and all unconsciously, with the best of motives, they were tempted to re-enter a market which had actually been deserted by private enterprise, as unprofitable at the market rate of wages.

It appears that since 1881 the government has made it a condition that contractors undertaking work for the army should do it in their own factories; this excellent rule has not been in force long, and it still does not apply to all branches of the government service, policemen's clothes and some others being still abandoned to the enterprise of sweaters. The application of the rule has, however, had one remarkable result, serving, on the one hand, to show that the women of Pimlico are not over-paid, but contributing, on the other, to increase the general depression of trade in London. As was pointed out in our last number, London contractors subject to the Factory Acts cannot undersell the Pimlico establishment. The prohibition of 'sweating' and the continued demand for cheap contracts has had the effect of sending almost all the army contract work out of London. It goes to Ipswich, Derby, Newcastle, Crewe, Swindon, Leeds and Limerick, to regions where a single woman can perhaps live upon six shillings a week instead of having to pay that sum in rent for a single room.

The hard realities of life have an educational effect, and the Pimlico workers feel no anger at this result; they only wish the standard of life in Ireland to rise so that 6/– a week may no longer be thought 'fair wages' for the factory workers of Limerick. They are as clearly right in this as the philanthropic ladies were clearly wrong in their attempt to set the unemployed of Westminster to compete with the – to some extent legitimately – cheaper labour of the provinces and Ireland. Room rent and the price of potatoes must fall in London to the Limerick level before it can be any kindness to London workers to secure them contracts at rates governed by Limerick competition.

Some of our friends warn us, at this point, of the danger of proving too much. Will not some economists urge that if provincial contracts are cheap all the army work should be done through them? To this objection the officers of the factory have a conclusive reply. The cheapness of the present contract work is partly conditional on its limited amount. No contractor depends entirely upon the government work alone; that is of a plain and easy sort, which they are allowed to do at leisure and which it pays them to take cheap so as to have something to go on with in the intervals of more profitable private orders. If other work had to be put on one side for it, or if it were of a sort requiring more highly skilled labour, the contract prices would rise enormously; and there can be no doubt that large sums were saved to the tax-payers last year by the existence of the factory, which met nearly all the extraordinary demand for clothing without any advancement of price. The fact that it is the plainer and commoner sort of work which is usually done by contract makes it possible for the contractors to economise in another way, by the division of labour which enables a larger proportion of unskilled workers to be employed, of course at proportionately low wages. One of the failures of the present Manager was the attempt to introduce the same system at the Pimlico factory. It failed, even as an economy, because, fortunately for the technique of the profession, the exigencies of the army are a little incalculable, and there is liable to be a sudden demand for one elaborate garment or another, which can only be met by turning the whole strength of the factory upon it for a time. The majority of the workers are thus expected to be able to turn their hands to anything from 'dress-jackets' to tweed trousers, while girls trained under the division of labour system can only do the one part of the one garment to which they are accustomed and never become 'tailoresses' at all. The versatility of the workers is evidently a marketable commodity, which has a money value to the State and ought therefore to be considered in the worker's wages, and as no contractor could offer corresponding advantages, it would be most short sighted to cripple the strength of the factory staff because single tenders are sent in for particular garments at rates with which the factory cannot and ought not to compete.

It is so much easier to do harm than good, and people are so much readier to seize an excuse for lowering than for raising wages that it was with great hesitation we allowed ourselves, in our last number, to reveal the fact that the soldiers flannel shirts were extravagantly made. Our compunction was increased when a gentleman connected with the factory pathetically remonstrated against attention being called to the 'one bit of sentiment' sanctioned by the department. The sentiment is no doubt most reasonable and creditable: by an old tradition, the soldiers' wives are considered entitled to make up the soldiers' shirts, and they are given out through 'Garrison Associations' to these women who are glad to earn a couple of shillings now and then in their spare time. This is all very well in the case of women who are unable to do anything but the coarsest plain needlework; nowadays however there must be soldiers wives, as well as other women, who can work a sewing machine, and though we would still have hand work accepted from the poor women who can do nothing else, the time has surely come when the neater and more substantial machine work may be accepted as well; and in fact nothing but the natural pedantry of routine could for a moment have suggested any other conclusion.

If we are not asked what practical measures the friends of the workpeople should set themselves to secure we should still put in the foreground the first point urged last month in this Journal and in the memorial to the War Office, viz.: the publication in the factory of the authorised price list, with a full opportunity for elected representatives of the women to explain their objections to such items in the list as they are prepared on mature deliberation seriously to contest. It would come within the scope of M Woodall's promised enquiry to ascertain exactly how far prices have or have not been reduced of late, but apart from its bearing upon the judgement or veracity of the manager, this historical investigation does not interest the workers unless they might hope to have a reconsideration of the reductions actually made. The second point is to clear up the question of home work, which as already pointed out, rests with the women themselves. Let them remember the universal experience of working men, and the universal conviction of Trade Unionists, that overtime means reduced wages. The third point is for the general public and the legislature to realise that there is no worse economy in relation to broad national interests than to be always scamping work and scamping wages. Paper is cheaper than leather, shoddy than cloth and pauper labour than that of skilled artisans, but an army clothed in the cheapest coats and boots dies of disease before the battlefield is reached, and a pauperised nation revenges itself expensively upon those who trade too long on its endurance.

Let us have economy, by all means, in the public service, but the time is past when we can tolerate the impoverishment of a thousand homes to effect a trifling saving that might be doubled by abolishing a single well paid post. The annual estimate for the wages of the Pimlico factory workers is £60,000 to be divided between some 1,500 hands; in the higher regions of the same establishment, and in the War Office itself, nearly four times that sum goes into a third of that number of pockets. The officials of the War Department and the Factory Establishment are no better paid than their colleagues in other branches of the public service, where, as we all know, salaries are ruled by custom, not competition. But the custom by which a gentleman who works six hours a day, receives on the average 12 times as much as a tailoress, who workers more than half as long again, is not so deeply rooted in the nature of things but what it can be revised if necessary – if, that is to say, we have to choose between that alternative and the adoption by the State of contractor's prices. Rather than see decent hardworking women reduced to serve their country for 6d a day (with 8½d to come out of it for rent) we would dispose of the great Departments of state by open tender and instead of paying decorative salaries to honourable gentlemen for managing affairs with which they are (by sacred custom) entirely unacquainted, we might save the revenue by employing gentlemen (not perhaps less qualified) who would be willing, like dressmakers to 'give six months' or even like the candidates for admission to a prosperous firm to pay a handsome premium for permission to learn their work.

In all seriousness, in this parliament, where the interests of the working classes are more strongly and creditably represented than has ever been the case before, we cannot believe that it will be accepted as a sufficient reason for giving or offering starvation wages either to tailoresses, postmen, policemen or any other civilians in the public service, that there are starving operatives about who will accept any wages rather than none. An inheritance of bad laws badly administered may account for this tragic fact without heaping any great burden of responsibility upon individual shoulders. But it is a maxim of law that no one may profit by his own default and we can give no credit for economy of administration to a government under which the very foundations of national well-being are undermined by the growing impoverishment of the industrial classes.

'Factory Inspection by Women,' *Women's Union Journal*, March 1886, p. 34

Not long since an article upon Factory and Workshop Inspection, written by a working woman, was published in a monthly review and excited so much interest that another contribution upon a kindred subject was invited from some equally well qualified writer of the same class. The invitation was forwarded to one of our contributors who happens to be a tailoress and while expressing her willingness to furnish the desired article she explained that, as she was employed 'from 6 in the morning till 8 at night,' she could not do so very promptly. Many of our readers, it is to be feared, will not find these hours of work exceptionally long; though it may be news to the denizens of factories and workshops that their present inspectors are supposed to work 13 hours a day. The 'long journeys in bad weather' commonly taken by working women are accomplished on foot and if they are to be counted as part of the day's work there are probably more women than not who work for hours which Lord Thurlow thinks too long except for a man. As a matter of fact we all know that women, disorganised and disunited as they are, work in spite of the poor protection of the factory acts for longer hours than men do. Of all the bad reasons that may be given against the employment of women as factory inspectors, Lord Thurlow has thus been so unfortunate as to hit upon the worst. However the subject is still 'under the consideration' of the Home Department, where we must not forget that our old friend Mr Broadhurst is Under Secretary. This is not against us; government nowadays 'follow before' the gale of public opinion, and Mr Broadhurst is used to being out-voted in the Trades Congress on this particular question. Did not Peel carry Free Trade, and Disraeli enfranchise the borough householder? We shall no doubt live to hear Mr Broadhurst murmur 'Auch-io son pittore' – 'I too am a Statesman' – and to see him introduce to the general satisfaction of Commons Lords and Ladies an adequate number of appointments of the kind advocated by Viscount Enfield.

'Continuity of Employment and Rates of Wages,' from *Industrial Remuneration Conference* **(London, 1885), pp. 199–214**

The continuity of industrial employment and the rates of wages are questions of deep interest, not only to men but also to women, for it appears from the latest census returns that, without including domestic servants, girls and women now constitute one-third of the industrial portion of the population. They are often ignored in investigations relating to wages, and truly the amount of their remuneration is in most cases so small, that one might suppose they worked for amusement rather than a livelihood. Mr Giffen, in his recent paper on the Progress of the Working Classes, makes no reference to working women. All through he speaks of the 'working man,' and in the list of thirteen industries which he gives as showing a great increase of wages during the last fifty years, trades in which women are employed, with the exception of weaving, do not appear. I can only suppose that he consigns working women to the 'residuum still unimproved' mentioned in page 20 of his paper. 'Where all are getting on,' he says on the same page, 'it does not seem very practical in those who are getting on slowly to grudge the quicker advance of others.' Women often doubt whether they are getting on, even slowly, in this matter of remuneration for their work, but I think they cannot be accused of impatience about it, and I believe that until they become more impatient, very little improvement will take place in their position.

I have found, however, during my ten years' experience in helping to establish Women's Trade Societies, that many women feel a deep sense of injury and wrong in the fact that their wages reach only one-third or one-fourth of the amount paid to men for any kind of skilled work, though they are not sure upon whose shoulders the blame should be laid. I am taking, and I shall deal especially with, that which should be considered the skilled industry of women, leaving out the comparatively rough work, such as sack making and paper-bag making, ranging from 4s to 7s per week. Considering the high prices paid by fashionable ladies for their dresses, there seems to be no good reason why West-end dressmakers should not be as well paid as West-end tailors and tailoresses; yet, in some of the largest West-end houses, time workers receive only 12s and 14s per week, and against those amounts must be placed serious deductions at slack seasons, varying from two to three months' loss of work in the year. The West-end upholsteresses succeeded by means of a general petition to the employers, about fourteen years ago, in getting their wages raised to 15s a week – the only case of that kind I have heard of – but they are liable to be out of work for three months of the year. We often hear it said that the workers take no share of the risk of a business, that this is borne wholly by the employer, yet the loss of work from dullness of trade is surely a considerable share in the risk, and it is one not felt by the more highly paid workers – the foremen and overlookers. Holidays also have to be deducted, for, unlike the salaried class, workpeople are required to pay for these. In many workshops even Christmas Day and the Bank holidays are deducted from the weekly wages. Enforced holidays, such as a week required for removing machinery and material to new premises, are also deducted. Where both men and women are employed it is not an unknown event for the day of the men's shop-dinner or 'beanfeast' to be possibly the day of no dinner for the women; it is not the custom for them to join in these festivities, but as their work cannot go on while the men are absent, the workshop is closed and the women lose a day's pay.

a The continuity of industrial employment – The case which most prejudicially influences this, with regard to women, I consider to be the length of their hours of work. If not all working women, surely a far larger number than are at present in regular employment might gain it if there were a general reduction of working hours. This has been the experience of men, who have often strived harder for shorter hours than for higher wages. It is supposed to be a peculiar advantage to women that their hours of work are fixed by law, but what is the boon thus afforded? Twelve hours, with a deduction of two hours for meals – two hours more than the limit men have, in many trades, gained through combination. The Factory Act also provides that in season-trades women may work for fourteen hours, on forty-eight days in the year; it also legalises employment in workshops until four oclock on Saturday afternoons, and the fullest advantage of this is taken in most dressmaking, millinery and tailoring establishments, so that the Saturday half-holiday, supposed to be now general in trades, is still unknown to many workwomen, and no money compensation for the loss of it is given. I have heard one restriction much complained of; it is that the dinner hour must be taken before 2 pm on Saturdays, as on other days, so that although the women would prefer to work on until three o'clock and then leave, and have their dinner at home, they are obliged to stay until four and waste an hour wandering about the streets. This is only a small instance, but it is a striking one, of the harassing effort of legislation in matters which could be much better arranged by agreement with the employers. I have but little hope of the reduction of women's hours of work by legislation; for children such protection may be necessary, but women, in this, as in other matters, must work out their own salvation.

I know how strong a pressure is put upon employers by the public with regard to speed, as I have for some years had to do with the management of a women's printing office. The public is a monster of unreasonable impatience. In counting the days since an order was given, it includes Saturdays, Sundays and general holidays. It also appears surprised that a dinner hour is necessary. 'You should get more hands,' it calmly says – for that barbarous term is applied, even in these enlightened days, to the men and women who toil for the good of the community. It professes, in the abstract, to wish every worker to have constant employment, yet it desires that a small army of unemployed 'hands' should be hanging about, ready to be drawn upon when it wants a piece of work done that in nine cases out of ten might have been ordered at a week's, instead of a day's, notice, and this usually in the busiest seasons, immediately before holiday times, when, fortunately for the 'hands,' it is no easy matter to find them. A Member of Parliament, a prominent advocate of factory legislation, once ordered an Ulster coat so hurriedly, before going on his summer tour, that the Factory Act had to be broken to get it done in time. Employers are naturally afraid of offending a good customer and of losing work, but if they could say that the 'hands' generally all through a trade absolutely refused to work beyond certain hours, they would have a strong protection against unreasonable demands. The reform must come from the determination of the 'hands' to assert that they possess also heads, nerves and digestive organs, all requiring consideration and attention. It is useless to plead legal restrictions; everyone knows how easily these are evaded.

The extensive employment of young girls as 'improvers' or 'learners,' often without any formal apprenticeship, is a serious evil in women's trades, and it is one which, so far as I know, can be touched by nothing but combination. The principal causes prejudicially influencing.

b Wages, are, I believe, so far as women are concerned:

1. The want of any common agreement with employers upon rates of payment, especially for piece work, and, in connexion with this, the ignorance of the workwomen as to prices offered for similar work in different localities, or even in the same town; and the want of a fund to fall back upon to enable them to refuse work offered at starvation wages.
2. The absence of any provision such as trades unions afford for the registration of trade requirements, and for the payment of travelling expenses from a town where an industry may be temporarily overcrowded to another where workers are wanted.
3. The absence in certain trades of any apprenticeship. This is especially complained of in East London tailoring.
4. The competition of married women, who work at home at the lowest rates, and without restriction of hours.
5. The cause assigned by John Stuart Mill, viz. 'prejudice.'
6. The demand for cheapness and low estimates.
7. The cost of overlooking.
8. The prevalence of the sweating system.
9. The diminution in agricultural employment, by which men and women are driven into town trades.

The first three of these causes I need not enlarge upon. They have been met with by workmen who have succeeded in bringing about marked improvements through trade organisation, such as I recommend for women. The remedy is, I think, obvious, but here is just one instance with reference to prices. I have heard of an East-end tailoress going to a West-end house, and offering to make waistcoats at 2 shillings less than the price usually paid there; she did this in ignorance arising from the want of communication with other tailoresses.

It may be urged that the crowded state of needlework trades and the competition of home workers will be an effectual barrier to organisation. But we must remember that only a portion of working men are unionists; these being, however, the steadiest and most skilful workers, they are able to influence the wages and other conditions of employment, so that if some common standard of prices were agreed upon for women's work, varying, of course, with fluctuations of trade, similar results might be expected. Women who were not sufficiently skilful to earn these prices would probably fall off into other occupations, such as domestic work, here or in the colonies.

Cause 5 would, I am convinced, by beneficially influenced by combination, through which women would gain a higher standing in industry; also by the removal of electoral disabilities, now, I hope, rapidly approaching. Within the last ten years the Home Secretaries of both great political parties (Sir RA Cross and Sir William Vernon Harbourt) have refused to receive deputations of working women upon questions directly affecting their work, and indirectly affecting their wages – the Factory Act and the appointment of Factory Inspectors – although several deputations of working men on those questions have been received. 'Prejudice' and the want of political power may explain this strange fact.

Causes 6, 7, 8 and 9 would, I believe, be to a great extent remedied by trades unions, but still more by small experiments in co-operation, such as that described by Mr H Broadhurst, MP, in a most interesting article of recent date, and the Working Tailors' Association in Whitechapel. These would be possible in many, though not in all, women's trades, and trades unions would afford the organisation necessary for initiating them. I am glad that the workmen Mr Broadhurst speaks of 'will not undertake low-price work.' Protests against the nastiness of cheap work are much needed in these days, when many people are taking to bargain hunting and low estimate seeking, as a new form of excitement. I quote in an Appendix some excellent remarks on this subject, from a technical journal which is in itself a specimen of high-class workmanship.

The stimulus given to the work by co-operation in workshops might diminish the cost of overlooking and 'driving,' now so serious an item; by bringing the workers and customers into more direct communication it would also powerfully tend to diminish he sweating, or 'middleman' system. I think this directness of contact partly accounts for the fact that the wages of domestic servants and charwomen keep up to a certain level. No sweating is adopted in those industries.

One objection that I wish to refer to before closing is frequent urged against the higher payment of women and the organisation of their trades. It is that men are the breadwinners for a family, and that women work only for their own support. I answer that women also, when their husbands die, become the breadwinners for families; but both men and women who are in this position have at least the comforting thought that in old age their children will help them, and will not, except at the last extremity, suffer them 'to go on the parish.' The large and increasing number of women who reach middle age and old age unmarried have no help of this kind; therefore it is of especial importance to them that their wages should enable them to make provision for the time when they are past work. Another singular disadvantage of women is that, as statistics prove, they live longer than men; consequently, if they want to but a Government annuity, they are required to pay a rate of premium higher than the men's rate. Notwithstanding their greater tenacity of life, workwomen as they get into years are often weakly and ailing and are called upon to pay for medical advice or to resort to dispensaries and hospitals, thus burdening the rates, or depending upon private charities kept up by philanthropic people, perhaps by those very employers who have underpaid them for their work. Their ailments, it is said, may be chiefly traced to poor living, close lodging and overwork. How much, I wonder, of the meat, bacon, ham, eggs, butter, cocoa, coffee, wine and other articles that Mr Giffen finds the 'masses' now obtain more abundantly than they could fifty years ago, can be purchased out of 12s a week, when there are also rent, coals, light and clothing to be provided, and perhaps an invalid or aged relative to be helped!

A movement in the direction of spreading trade organisation among women has been commenced. It is only in its early stages; no radical change in the rates of remuneration has yet been attempted, but many cases of small improvements might be cited, and there have been successful temporary combinations in the mill districts against reductions of wages, such as that at Dewsbury, entirely conducted by women. One important result has been the admission of women as delegates of their trade societies to the Annual Trades Union Congress and a marked decrease of the hostility formerly shown by workmen towards the work of women – a natural hostility so long as that work assumed the form of totally disorganised competition.

A centre of agitation and encouragement has been established at 26 Great Queen Street, Long Acre, where an increasing number of inquiries are received from all parts of the country, showing that a feeling in favour of union among workwomen is steadily developing. General information about the movement will be found in the Women's Union Journal and other papers published by the Central League.

[...]

Mrs Paterson, in reply [to comments from male trade unionists], said that no one had disputed the lowness of women's wages, and, indeed, as a fact it was generally admitted. She hoped that the workmen would do all they could to help women to form societies. The working out of figures in regard to men's wages was helping trade unions greatly, by showing that trades unions had been able to raise wages, in spite of the declarations of professors years ago that they never could do it. As they had done it for men, there was hope that women's unions would do it for women. It was not necessary to quarrel with statisticians about their figures; let them enjoy their statistics. Working people knew that trade societies rested on something far deeper than figures – on sympathy, and fellowship, and experience. If workers had listened to those who said that unions would not stand unless based upon strict actuarial calculations, much good would have been left undone, for so high a rate would have been fixed as to deter many from joining; but workers had learned that figures did not rule everything in these matters. (Hear, hear.)

'Army Clothing Work,' *Women's Union Journal*, April 1886, pp. 37–38

In another column will be found a report of the second Public Meeting held by the women employed in the Army Clothing Factory, which has resulted in a very satisfactory addition to the number of the Westminster Tailoresses' Union. The enquiry into the workers' grievances, promised by Mr Woodall, is not yet concluded, but one important advantage has already accrued to the women. Though the complete price list for all work has not yet been produced, the prices of fresh jobs are now posted up, in somewhat obscure language it is true, but still in a manner intelligible to the most experienced workers, through whom the needful information can spread through the factory; and what is even more satisfactory, the new prices now posted up show in several cases a considerable advance upon those recently paid and complained of. Sea-kit frocks, of which a good deal was heard at all the women's meetings, are among the garments for which an increased price is given.

The Second Report of the Workroom 2, Carteret Street, Westminster, issued last month, contains the following passages:

In the daily press, at public meetings we have been attacked without mercy and alas! By some of the very class we would help and protect, or rather, I should say, by those who style themselves their friends and champions. The subject is an intricate one and can only be explained by going into the while history of our connection with the War Department.

It is alleged by the Secretary of the Women's Protective League, that

1st – Owing to the establishment of our workrooms, numbers of hands have been discharged from the Government Factory at Pimlico.

2nd – That the same work is paid for at a lower rate in Carteret Street, than in Pimlico, and that we are in collusion with the Government to bring down the rate of wages in the Government Factory.

The 'Secretary of the Women's Protective League' has not made these allegations, nor have they been made in any publication of the League, or in any document published by Miss Simcox while carrying on the work of its Honorary Secretary and Editor of the Journal, during the seven weeks' absence of that official, necessitated by ill-health.

It has been stated in the Women's Union Journal and elsewhere – unfortunately with truth – that 'the same work is paid for at a lower rate in Carteret Street, than in Pimlico,' and this is admitted in the Report referred to.

As to the discharge of workers from the factory, in the February number of the Journal these words appeared:

They (the workwomen) say that women are discharged from the factory for no fault at all, and told, if they lament, that they may apply for work at Carteret Street.

The state here prefaced by the words 'they say' has since been investigated and fully established by the League Committee, who are now in possession of the names of the women so discharged after being employed for many years in the factory.

As to the second clause of the second 'allegation,' so far as anyone was 'attacked' in the organ of the League, it was the Government for paying, rather than the Carteret Street workroom for accepting, a reduced price for the great coats in question. In the March number, therefore, the defence of the officials was quoted:

The explanation offered at the factory is as follows: the great coats in question are plain, common work, of the sort that is usually done by contractors at contractors' (ie very low) prices; if they were made in numbers in the factory, the skilled operatives there would get used to the work and turn them out in greater quantities so as to be able to earn their usual wages even at a reduced price. But the work being of a common sort can be done by contractors, and therefore, it is argued more than a contractor's price need not and should not be paid for it. This is what the benevolent ladies of Carteret Street were told, and all unconsciously, with the best of motives, they were tempted to re-enter a market which had actually been deserted by private enterprise, as unprofitable at the market rate of wages.

We fail to see that these can fairly be styled 'attacks without mercy.'

After this protest against the inaccuracy of the Workroom Committee's statements, and also after mentioning that it was only by a side wind that we first heard of this attack upon the League – although the Women's Union Journal is presented every month to the Workroom – we will refer our readers to the Report we have quoted, so that they may determine how far the Workroom gives promise of helping to raise the industrial position of needlewomen. Copies can, we believe, be obtained at 2, Carteret Street.

'Leeds Tailoresses,' *Women's Union Journal*, May 1886, p. 50

A Special Meeting of the above Union was held on Friday, March 26th, at Stephens' Cocoa House, to consider a resolution moved at the last meeting, for dissolving the Union. Mr S Marks was in the chair. After some discussion, and seeing that the contributions now being received will not pay for rent of Meeting Room, it was unanimously resolved 'To dissolve the said Union, and to make a grant of 10s to the Women's Protective League for the great assistance received from them.' 10s was voted to the Secretary, Miss Stobbs, and the balance was divided amongst the few members remaining. Much sympathy was expressed for Miss IO Ford in her sad bereavement. A vote of thanks to Mr J Bune and to the Chairman closed the proceedings.

'Women's Protective and Provident League: Report of Conference,' *Women's Union Journal,* **July 1886, pp. 67–72**

A Conference was held at the new Office of the League, Industrial Hall, Clark's Buildings, Broad Street, Bloomsbury, on the afternoon of Tuesday, July 20th, 'To invite and discuss suggestions as to extending the work of the League.' There were present Miss AE Bell, Miss A Heather Bigg, Miss ML Bruce, Miss AL Browne, Mrs Brooksbank, Miss Carey, Miss Crossman, lady Goldsmid, Miss E Guest, Mrs Hamer, Miss G Hill, Mrs Hallock, Rev. SD Headlam, Miss Johnson, Miss Kilgour, Mr Sydney Lee, Mr CF Nash, Mr S Prout Newcombe, Mr T Pagliardini, Hon. Maude Stanley, Mr and Mrs DF Schloss, Miss Simcox, Miss AC Symons, Miss Thornton, Mr Stephen Seward Tayler, Miss Caroline Williams, Miss JE Williams, Miss Wilkinson, Mrs and Miss Wade and others.

Miss Simcox was elected to the chair, and called upon the Honorary Secretary of the League, Mrs Paterson, to read letters expressing regret for absence which had been received from Miss Brassey, Mrs NL Cohen, Miss Cust (sending £1 1s donation), Mrs Fawcett, Miss IO Ford (of Leeds), Professor Lindsay (of Glasgow), Mr CE Maurice, Mr FD Mocatta, Mrs Pennington, Miss Soames (Brighton), Mrs Arnold Toynbee, Mrs Winkworth enclosing £5, and others including the two following which we publish in the hope that they may give rise to some discussion in the Journal.

The first is from Mr Mawdesley, Secretary of the Amalgamated Association of Operative Cotton Spinners, etc., Manchester, the second from Mrs AH Johnson, of Oxford.

> Thanks for your invitation to attend your Conference on the 20th inst., of which, however, I shall not be able to avail myself. I trust you will have a successful meeting, as the more I see of industrial life the more it becomes clear that all sections of workers are hampered for want of organization, and this is especially the case with women. Enclosed you will find my annual subscription 5s. JA Mawdsley.

I am very grateful for your kind invitation to the Provident and Protective League Conference on Monday, and exceedingly sorry that I am not able to avail myself of it.

My wish would have been to suggest to the League the cause of Women's Benefit Societies. There is, it seems to me, a large field there to be worked, and I am most anxious it should be worked on the principles of the League, that is, for the encouragement of real independence. I feel quite convinced that women are not quite ready to enter into the spirit of mutual help and will catch at anything offered to them in the way of attractive Benefit Societies. That they are able to produce the necessary subscriptions is proved by the large sums of money paid by them into Burial Clubs.

The other day, when in the Black Country, I heard of a Club of the kind entirely set on foot by women and subscribed to by them alone, and they mostly the wives of working men lately very short of work. This Club had accumulated in a very few years over £1,000. Some of these women will take out their £10 on the death of a relative and spend every penny of it on the funeral. It seems a pity that all this saving power cannot be turned into a better channel.

Many will, I have no doubt, be anxious to set on foot Societies for women, but the League could do the work in a thorough, systematic way, establishing some connection between the Societies and securing to them the management by the women themselves rather than by any Committee, however gifted with wisdom, of men. Each Society, no doubt, would need at first one or wo persons of education and leisure to give it the help of advice but they should only be in the position of the invited and have no legal right, with the exception, of course, of the Secretary, Trustees and Treasurer.

Our Oxford Benefit Society so far is a great success. BJ Johnson.

Mrs Paterson then read the following paper:

The Committee of the League have thought it desirable at the close of twelve years' labours to call this Conference, for the purpose of reviewing the work, of obtaining suggestions as to how it can best be extended, and above all of enlisting new helpers.

I have been asked to make an introductory statement of our experiences – both successes and failures – and this I will do as briefly as possible, so as to allow ample time for discussion.

Some of those present may not be fully acquainted with our objects, and it may therefore be well to state, first, that the League was established and has continued to exist chiefly as a propagandist Association for encouraging and aiding women who work for weekly wages to form Trade and Benefit Societies upon a self-supporting, self-governing basis; the chief objects of which Societies should be to watch the trade interests of the members, to seek, by united appeals, redress for any serious trade grievances and provide the members from the funds raised by their own subscriptions of twopence or threepence per week, with 5s or 7s weekly when out of work from sickness or slackness of trade. It is for the expenses of forming such Societies in London, and, whenever opportunities have arisen in the provinces also, that we have asked subscriptions from sympathisers, and to that object we have devoted most of our modest income, which has averaged only £107 a year, except in 1879 and 1884 when it was considerably increased by sermons given on behalf of the League by the Rev. Stopford Brooke. The official service has from the first been gratuitous. We have held each year a General Meeting of subscribers and have then given an account of our stewardship, but at those meetings, publicly called, there is no opportunity for the exchange of views and opinions such as we hope for this afternoon. The history of the foundation of the League is given in the first Annual Report and is also well and concisely stated in the slips from the 'Pall Mall Gazette,' both of which are at hand for distribution, so that I do not think it necessary to repeat it in this paper. The few of our oldest friends who are present will remember with what misgivings we called our first meetings of working women, and how greatly encouraged we were to meet with a ready response from a much larger number of women than we expected, and to hear from many of them that they had long wished to form trade and benefit societies but had not known how to set about it, and that the League was offering them exactly the kind of help they needed. The London Unions now in existence have at this time from 600 to 700 paying members, and, although when we think of the great mass of workwomen in this big city, we may well say 'what are they among so many,' we must try to realise the immense difficulties such women have to contend with in any attempts to improve their position.

We have formed in London ten societies – among women employed in Bookbinding, Dressmaking, Upholstery work, Hat-sewing, Shirtmaking, Sewing machine work, Tailoring, Laundry work (at Hampstead) and one of women engaged as Clerks and Bookkeepers; four of these ten Societies have failed and been dissolved, two of the Tailoresses' branches are still very small, but the five other societies are thriving, and have funds in hand amounting to £475, after paying away over £750 for out-of-work and sick allowances, besides all working expenses: in those expenses one saving is effected by their using the League office for their business, and thus incurring a smaller rent than they would have to pay for separate offices. Since the first year of their establishment the League has given them no other help, and they are entirely managed by the Committees and the Quarterly meetings of their members.

In the Provinces, the League has formed, or helped to form, twenty-one Societies, viz., in Bristol, Dewsbury, Leicester, Manchester (2), Glasgow (2), Brighton, Dublin (2), Liverpool (3), Birkenhead, Oxford (2), Portsmouth,

Nottingham, Aberdeen, Leeds, Dundee; of these I regret to say that only nine are still in existence. Women were also admitted last year to the National Union of Operative Boot Rivetters and Finishers in Leicester, and more than 300 have joined. This I think we may fairly claim as a result of the Women's Union movement; and, wherever it is practicable, and the men will agree to it, we are strongly in favour of mixed Societies, consisting of men and women working in the same trade.

The first question that will naturally arise is, why have some of the Unions formed by the League continued to exist, while others, the larger number, have failed. Special reasons for some of the failures have been given in the League reports from year to year, and copies of those Reports may be had by anyone wishing to study them, but I may say that in nearly every case failure has been caused by want of outside encouragement and advice.

To the London Societies the League has been able to give this help, also to make its office a centre for them, and only a small proportion have failed. Out of London the percentage of failures has been much larger. With one exception, no Committees of sympathisers outside the trades have been at hand to offer assistance at the time when most difficulties arise – in the first year of a society's formation. The one exception is Oxford, where the branch League Committee has been very active and helpful, and the two Societies formed are consequently flourishing.

It has often been said in the League Reports that working women cannot be expected to form, and at first, manage their Societies, entirely without aid. Their want of leisure arising from long hours of work – three hours per day longer under the protection of what is considered benevolent legislation than the hours of most skilled workmen – the depression and hopelessness arising from all 'work and no play' and from low wages, as well as their scanty education, are serious drawbacks. If the objects of this League are to be attained to any general extent, it appears to me that a considerable increase of active voluntary helpers in all parts of London and in other large towns will be necessary; as has been said in connexion with other work, 'Those who wish to help must give not only their money but themselves.' The League may help to form Working Women's Societies anywhere, by holding preliminary meetings and distributing papers, but it is impossible, from a distance, to follow up the work so commenced. This must be done by persons in the locality, and perhaps can best be done by local Committees. Continuous aid would not be required, one evening a week devoted to the new Society for a year would usually be quite sufficient to set it in good working order and to train a Secretary from among the members. This aid was given to all the London Societies that have succeeded. There are many ladies who have freely devoted much more time than this for some years in other movements, such as the Metropolitan

Association for Befriending Young Servants, the Girl's Friendly Society, the Young Women's Help Society, and Working Girl's Homes and Clubs, all of which excellent movements have, I may point out, been set on foot since our League was established, so that it does not seem improbable that we may have indirectly given an impetus to these efforts for aiding working women in other ways than by trade organisation. Indeed to find that numbers of ladies and gentlemen are really anxious to help working women, in what they consider to be safe ways, only they continue to hold aloof from the league because they have an impression that we want to attack the employers, many of whom are their personal friends and are believed by them to be kind-hearted, just men who could not possibly oppress their workwomen.

This may be quite a correct estimate of the character of most of the employers, but even the best of them – who by the way are usually inclined to approve of the Women's Unions – cannot know half the oppression to which workwomen are subjected by foremen and forewomen, who even sometimes lower the rates of wages at their own caprice, inflict harassing fines, distribute the work unfairly or give it out to middlemen. It has frequently been said to me 'If your League sought to form only Benefit Societies for women, we would gladly help; it is the trad aspect of the Unions that we object to,' and many letters come addressed 'Women's Provident League' or 'Provident and Protective' – Protective being considered a secondary matter. Everyone is anxious that women who work should be provident, but are not always equally anxious that they should have the means of being provident, in the shape of better wages and shorter hours of work, which would mean increased opportunities for thought of the future, and for study.

The help such timid people would offer seems to me to be of no more value, perhaps of less value, than that of the Army Clothing Factory authorities who in the pressure of war orders in the spring of last year required the women to work all Sundays, but at the same time provided missionaries to read aloud to them the Bible and other good books, to which, I fear, in the driving atmosphere of piece work not much attention was paid.

I have not time to speak fully about other directions in which the League has taken action for the benefit of working women; such as holding meetings and giving evidence before the Royal Commission on the Factory Acts, the admission of women as delegates to the Annual Trades union Congress, the agitation for women as Factory Inspectors – an object not yet attained, but one that the League Committee intend to still strive for – the Circulating Library formed, though unfortunately but little used at present because of the length of women's working hours; the monthly Social Meetings which have given great pleasure to hundreds of London workwomen, and above all the institution of a centre of information such as this office is becoming for women out of work, who find it of immense comfort in winter to have a warm room where they can rest when on their search for employment and can sometimes find applications from employers which save them any further weary journeys to the shops.

Such is the work we wish to extend. We are anxious to have not only one League Office with its group of Women's Trade Societies, but 50 or 100, one at least in each large centre of industry, so that women may no longer be mere blind, ignorant tools in the hands of those who 'grind the face of the poor,' but may have a voice, a status in the industrial world. Unless we can arouse sufficient enthusiasm for this, it is I think a question for serious consideration whether the League should continue to exist, or whether we should dissolve it and trust that the example of those few Unions which seem firmly established may gradually lead to the organisation of similar Societies in other trades. We invite your advice and freest expression of opinion upon these matters.

Miss Simcox, before inviting discussion, made a speech in which she said that one difference between the League and other societies was that it did not attempt to get other people to do anything for working women, but put in them in the way of helping themselves. Yet propagandism must be carried on by persons of leisure. Miss Simcox referred to Mrs Barnett's article in The National Review of last month, which showed how some three-fourths of the working classes did not earn wages enough to supply their families with a sufficiency of the plainest nutriment. Mrs Barnett's figures proved that even £1 1s 0d a week was too little in London, to provide adequately for their wants. All who knew anything of the improvements that Trades Unions had effected in the position of working men were naturally anxious that working women should have similar societies. The first societies formed by the League went on well, but the Committee soon came to an end of the districts that could be worked from a centre, and, as Mrs Paterson had pointed out, a wider area of active help was now urgently needed. As long as people insisted on buying articles of clothing at very low prices all were more or less to blame for the starvation wages, though a remedy, doubtless, involved some sacrifice somewhere. We should so open our minds as to look at the matter as if we were working women ourselves, and we should ask, if there any other way than Trade Unions by which workwomen can help themselves and is there any better way in which those outside the trades can help them, than by encouraging them to form such unions?

Mr Adolphe Smith said that he feared the League was in bad repute among working men, who spoke of it as a goody-goody society and declined to help its work because of the air of patronage which the names and subscriptions of rich people gave it. Possibly the same objection might

Association for Befriending Young Servants, the Girl's Friendly Society, the Young Women's Help Society, and Working Girl's Homes and Clubs, all of which excellent movements have, I may point out, been set on foot since our League was established, so that it does not seem improbable that we may have indirectly given an impetus to these efforts for aiding working women in other ways than by trade organisation. Indeed to find that numbers of ladies and gentlemen are really anxious to help working women, in what they consider to be safe ways, only they continue to hold aloof from the league because they have an impression that we want to attack the employers, many of whom are their personal friends and are believed by them to be kind-hearted, just men who could not possibly oppress their workwomen.

This may be quite a correct estimate of the character of most of the employers, but even the best of them – who by the way are usually inclined to approve of the Women's Unions – cannot know half the oppression to which workwomen are subjected by foremen and forewomen, who even sometimes lower the rates of wages at their own caprice, inflict harassing fines, distribute the work unfairly or give it out to middlemen. It has frequently been said to me 'If your League sought to form only Benefit Societies for women, we would gladly help; it is the trad aspect of the Unions that we object to,' and many letters come addressed 'Women's Provident League' or 'Provident and Protective' – Protective being considered a secondary matter. Everyone is anxious that women who work should be provident, but are not always equally anxious that they should have the means of being provident, in the shape of better wages and shorter hours of work, which would mean increased opportunities for thought of the future, and for study.

The help such timid people would offer seems to me to be of no more value, perhaps of less value, than that of the Army Clothing Factory authorities who in the pressure of war orders in the spring of last year required the women to work all Sundays, but at the same time provided missionaries to read aloud to them the Bible and other good books, to which, I fear, in the driving atmosphere of piece work not much attention was paid.

I have not time to speak fully about other directions in which the League has taken action for the benefit of working women; such as holding meetings and giving evidence before the Royal Commission on the Factory Acts, the admission of women as delegates to the Annual Trades union Congress, the agitation for women as Factory Inspectors – an object not yet attained, but one that the League Committee intend to still strive for – the Circulating Library formed, though unfortunately but little used at present because of the length of women's working hours; the monthly Social Meetings which have given great pleasure to hundreds of London workwomen, there were among those who supported the league many who think that Trade Unionism is dangerous, it became a question whether the League, as at present constituted, should continue to exist. He believed that good as Trade Unionism was, it would never by itself get rid of poverty. Therefore we should urge the women to take part in political movements. With the view of bringing this question to a point, he would move the following Resolution:

> That the best way to extend the work of the League is to lay stress on its Protective – Trades Union – element as distinct from the Provident element, and further, for the League to use its influence to support such Political action of an economic description as will tend to bring about a better distribution of wealth.

Mr Adolphe Smith seconded the Resolution.

Mr SS Tayler thought that the resume of work given at the opening of the Conference was very satisfactory considering the small amount of the annual income – a little over £100. He did not agree with what had been said about patronage. Sympathy between the different classes was needed before much progress could be made in work of social reform. Neither could he concur in what had been said about the impossibility of a working-class family living upon £1 1s 0d a week, but he was in favour of doing anything that could be done fairly to increase the rates of wages. One suggestion he had to make about extending the work of the League was that the ladies on School Board Committees should be asked to try and influence the younger generation in favour of trade organisation. He did not believe that much could be done with the older people, whose habits and ideas were fixed.

Miss Simcox here said, in reply to a question which had been put by Miss Wade, that the Men's Trade Unions did not require all workmen to be paid alike but that they merely fixed a minimum wage below which they considered that no one who had even an average amount of skill should work.

Miss Wilkinson said she believed the League had done a great deal of good, not only in actually forming Societies among workwomen, but also in leading people to give thought to the important question of the industrial position of women. The greatest difficulty in the way of the rapid growth of the Societies was the depressed condition of women employed in trades. If the League could spread its work in the Midland and Northern countries, where working women are more massed together than in the South, she thought greater results might follow. She had never heard workmen speak of the League as a middle class, patronised affair; some few might regard it in that light, but many of those whom she had met at the Trades' Congress expressed the deepest sympathy with the League. Working women were now beginning to take an interest in politics; union was an educative force in more ways than one, but she did not agree that it would be advisable to mix up political agitation with the promotion of the Women's Union movement.

Mr S Prout Newcombe said that he should be glad to devote a large portion of time to the extension of the League work if any good opportunity presented itself. He feared, however, that little could be done by combination unless we had international combination, and as evidence of this he mentioned that many articles were sold in Paris at about one-sixth of their cost in England, and at a still lower rate in Italy.

Miss E Guest spoke of the desire that many rich people showed to get their work done cheaply. She had heard of a lady who said of a Co-operative Work Society that she had supposed the work would have been done more cheaply than it was, 'as the Society was a charity.'

Mr DF Schloss said that if Mr Headlam's resolution were carried, many of the present supporters of the League would leave it. The League might go on but it would have no money. He hoped the work would be continued on the old lines with, of course, as much new energy as could be found available.

Mrs Paterson thought that the absent subscribers might fairly complain if a Resolution so radically changing the basis of the League were to be passed without printed notice having been given.

Miss AL Browne proposed and Miss Wilkinson seconded, 'that the Conference be adjourned until the autumn, and that Mr Headlam's Resolution and any other resolutions previously sent in to the Committee, be printed on the notices.'

Mr Headlam having agreed to the postponement of his proposition, the Resolution moved by Miss Browne was unanimously carried and the proceedings were brought to a close.

'Our Loss,' *Women's Union Journal*, September 1886, pp. 83–84

'Life struck sharp on death makes awful lightning.' These words most truly illustrate our sudden loss. We can scarcely believe that our friend, Miss Wilkinson, who spoke at the League Conference on July 20th, with all her wonted vigour and practical good sense, has gone so soon from our midst. Twice after the Conference she was with us – on July 26th at a Meeting of the Women's Trades Council, and on July 30th at the League Committee. Early in August she was taken ill, and on the 22nd of that month she died from a severe attack of asthmatic bronchitis. Asthma was her old enemy, and twice we have seen her almost at death's door from its tortures.

She was surrounded in her last illness by loving care and attention, in her brother's house at Walworth, her sister-in-law, Mrs Wilkinson, proving a most devoted nurse.

Jeanette Gaury Wilkinson was born in London, in 1842; her father held for 40 years the position of foreman at a large warehouse: he lived to see the talent of his daughter publicly recognised, and was very proud of her. We are informed that after her mother's death, which occurred early in her career, she did much to make home bright for her brothers, one of whom is blind. From the age of seventeen she earned her own living as an upholsteress, working often at the heaviest branch, carpet sewing and devoted her evenings to study, with the brilliant results recorded in the notice kindly written for this Journal by Mr JH Levy. A member of the Birkbeck Institution who helped to improve her arithmetic and handwriting, when she determined to become an elementary teaching, says 'I could not but admire the patience with which she fought against the stiffness her former occupation had induced in the joints of her fingers.' He also says 'she was well known in the Debating Society, where she was ever ready to support radical opinion and to defend the rights of her sex.'

Miss Wilkinson connexion with the League, upon an introduction by Mrs Heatherley, commenced about a year after its formation, and a few months after the Upholsteress' Trade Society had been started by its aid. She was persuaded to become the Secretary of that Society, and nine times she attended the Annual Trades Union Congress as its representative. At the Congress she always received a most hearty welcome, even from those who took an opposite side in the debates. Her speeches there and at the League and Union meetings, her graphic descriptions of the ordinary workwoman's lonely life, of trials and privations endured in sickness and in failure of work, never failed to rivet the attention and draw forth the sympathy of the listeners.

Appreciative notices have appeared in the *Pall Mall Gazette*, *Dispatch*, *Liverpool Mercury*, *Women's Suffrage Journal*, *Englishwoman's Review* and other papers. All these have praised her wonderful power and eloquence as a speaker. It will, we fear, be long before her place, in this respect, can be filled, and we believe that had her opportunities of leisure been greater she would have become an equally effective writer. Many readers of this Journal may remember the animated correspondence kept up for some time upon the work and position of women, between our valued contributor 'JWO' (Mr Overton) and 'One of those who cannot be taught,' a signature afterwards abbreviated to 'OT.' It was a drawn battle at least, but the ability shown by 'OT' (Miss Wilkinson) in the inky warfare was undisputed. More recently she wrote an excellent article in the Charity Organization Review upon 'The Inspection of Workshops in London.' We were glad to recommend her to the Editor of the Review for this piece of literary work.

The portrait we present to our readers is copied from a photograph; it is not so good as we could have wished, but the brightness and vivacity of her expression when speaking could scarcely be found in any portrait.

It is proposed to raise a fund for erecting a small stone over the grave in Forest Hill Cemetery, and for some assistance towards the education of a niece – a work Miss Wilkinson was anxious to help in: also to have an enlarged photograph taken, to be placed, with a suitable inscription and frame, in the League Office. Contributions of any amount for either of these objects will be gladly received by the Editor of this Journal and will be duly acknowledged in the Journal.

'The League Conference,' *Women's Union Journal*, October 1886

The Conference on 'the best means of extending the work of the League,' adjourned from July 20, was held on the evening of Tuesday, October 19, at the Portland British Schools, Little Titchfield Street. Mr Hodgson Pratt presided, and about 40 subscribers and friends of the League were present.

The first question considered was the following Resolution, moved by the Rev. Stewart D Headlam:

> That the best way to extend the work of the League is to lay stress on its Protective – Trades Union – element, as distinct from the Provident element; and further for the League to use its influence to support such political action of an economic description, as will tend to bring about a better distribution of wealth.

Mr Headlam in explaining the scope of his proposition said he thought it cruelty to go on telling women that by merely joining Trade Societies, paying twopence per week and drawing a certain amount in sickness or want of work, they could ameliorate their industrial lot. While the present land system existed he considered it impossible for the League to do much to bring about an improvement in the condition of working women. Mr Headlam was going on to explain how the taxation of ground rents would benefit working women but was ruled out of order by the Chairman.

Mr Adolphe Smith seconded the Resolution and said that he became a member of the League Committee ten years ago, about two years after its formation. At that time to advocate trades' unionism for women was an advanced step; but what was then progressive had now, in the changed views upon social questions, become antiquated; yet the League had not added one plank to its platform. The Women's Trade Unions already formed grew very slowly, and he believed that women were deterred from joining them by the feeling that they did not go far enough. Men's Unions, even, were in danger of breaking up, under the altered conditions of society. He thought that, if the members did not promote such political action as, without respect to parties, would help to better the economical position of the producing classes – Trades Unions whether of men or of women, would not in themselves suffice to solve the social question and deliver the willing work from the danger of starvation, or the community from the increasing frequency and duration of periodical commercial depression.

Mrs Paterson, (Hon. Secretary of the League) read the following letter from Mr JH Levy, one of the earliest members of the Council:

> With reference to your circular of the 8th inst informing me of the resolutions to be moved at the Adjourned Conference on the 19th inst, I feel bound – as I shall be in Scotland at that time – to write to you a few words, as one of the matters to be decided is a crucial one.
>
> With Miss Browne's resolution and the first half of that to be moved by the Rev Stewart D Headlam I heartily agree; but the second half of Mr Headlam's resolution, if carried, would turn the League into a Socialistic association, and make it impossible for all persons who, like myself, are opposed to Socialism, to co-operate with the League in future. This I hope Mr Headlam will withdraw; or, if he finds himself unable to do so, I hope that an amendment will be moved and carried that all after the word "element" be left out of the resolution.

Mr DF Schloss said we must look facts in the face: the League carried on tis propagandist work by means of outside subscriptions, given by well-to-do people. If this resolution were carried many of these people would withdraw their support. Neither the mover nor seconder had denied that to organise Women's Trades' Unions might be one step towards bringing about better conditions of payment and hours of work. From his experience in East London, he knew that there was the greatest possible difficulty in forming Unions among unskilled workers, but he thought that the League should press forward its efforts among women of the more skilled trades and that the movement would then gradually spread to the poorer class of workwomen.

Miss Collett supported Mr Headlam's resolution and said that although she was not a subscriber to the League funds, she had been one of the earliest members of the Dressmakers' Society, which the League helped to form, and in that way had seen something of the work. The members had come in very slowly, and the bulk of the West-end dressmakers appeared to prefer joining such Societies as the Young Women's Christian Association. She thought that a Society which could get the women to consider social questions generally and lead them to think for themselves, would do more good than the League, though in trades where men and women were employed, such as Bookbinding and Upholstery, the Women's Unions appeared to have met with a certain amount of success.

Miss Mears, Secretary of the Upholsteresses' Society, did not think that the success of that Union in its early years was owing to the fact that men were employed in the Upholstery trade; the women had not met with much encouragement from them. Lately trade had been very bad, and her Society's funds had been severely strained by the payment of our work allowances, which last year amounted to £38. She considered that the high rents paid by working women had much to do with their poverty. When paying 6s a week for two small rooms at the top of a house – as she herself had to do in order to retain respectable lodgings – and having an aged mother or other relative to support, 15s or 17s per week left but a small margin for other necessaries; yet this was regarded as good payment, and £1 1s 0d per week as unusually high wages.

Miss Randell thought that with the first part of Mr Meadlam's resolution nearly every one present would agree, but that it was not within the province of the League to attempt political action. She wished therefore to move as an amendment

> That this Conference, while agreeing with the first clause in the Rev Stewart Headlam's resolution, resolves that the second clause – from the words 'provident element' to the end – be omitted: considering that political controversy is not within the province of the League and would not further its primary object, viz the organisation of Trades' Unions among women.

Miss Ada Heather Bigg seconded the amendment.

Mr Sidney Lee opposed Mr Headlam's resolution because of its extreme vagueness and said he was of opinion that much might be done towards extending the League work, on the lines already laid down, if the Committee would take more personal trouble about visiting workshops, and talking with the women employed; also, if they would get suburban Committees formed to educate workwomen upon the principles of Unionism, to show them that Trade Societies might bring about many beneficial, if not radical, changes.

Mr JW Overton expressed surprise to hear that Trade Unionism among workmen was on its last legs; he wished to deny this from personal knowledge of some of the largest Unions, but he admitted that at the present time it was being sorely tried. He considered that no misfortunate could happen to the Women's Union Movement greater than that of the intervention of Socialistic propaganda.

Miss Simcox said she could not support the resolution as it stood, but that in the event of Miss Randell's amendment being lost she would propose that the second clause should read as follows: 'And further for the League to use its influence to support all other modes of action of an economic description which may tend to bring about a better distribution of wealth.' Mr Headlam's speech this evening had shown that in using the word 'political' he really meant something likely to be distasteful to many of the supporters of the League; but these supporters might not be averse to all extension of the League's work. The advocates of the resolution weakened their case by denouncing Trades Unions as failures. If working women had joined these Unions by thousands, instead of by hundreds, they might have materially improved their position. Workmen had done this, and it was only about 20 years ago that Unionism was in the height of its power among them. She had found that working women were more often afraid that the Unions were go too far, than of their not being sufficiently progressive. The Young Women's Christian Association and Societies of a similar kind grew more rapidly than Trade Unions, because women had been used to being led and patronised, and could but slowly learn the advantages of self-government. She was sorry to hear Mr Schloss say that unionism could only help the skilled trades, because it was on that ground that the Socialists put forward their strongest arguments against it. They accused Trade Unionists of doing nothing to help unskilled labourers. If the accusation were just, if not help of this kind were possible through trade combination, then let us try other means. The practical question appeared to her to be this – are the supporters of the League ready to do more than they have done to actively help forward unions of workwomen, and in that way promote a better distribution of wealth. If not, it was impossible for the League to do much more on its old lines of work. If it should be decided to support, through the League, advanced political proposals, many of the subscribers might withdraw, but if, instead of this, it should be determined to promote only the formation of Women's Trade Societies, as in the past, what were our friends prepared to do to enable the resolution to be something more than a form of words? The amendment she proposed to move might, she thought, enlist new friends for the League, by holding out the hope of aid in co-operation and other improved forms of industrial organisation.

Mr Hodgson Pratt (the Chairman), said he could not admit that the Women's Union Movement had been a failure. Looking at the defective education of working women, their want of leisure, and of money, also considering the opinion which had until recently prevailed, that women were an inferior order of beings, it was a great step in advance that women who had never before attempted to help themselves by means of association, should have been brought into Unions, taught to pass rules and resolutions at their general meetings, and to manage entirely the business of their Societies. These efforts had given them new hope, new life and education of a most valuable kind, by teaching them that they can rely upon themselves and help to raise the condition of their class. The League having already done so much, he hoped the result of this Conference would be to provide increased machinery for developing the work and extending it throughout the country. To add its programme such questions as were indicated in Mr Headlam's resolution would not strengthen the hands of the Committee; working women could readily understand the advantages of Trade Societies when these were carefully explained to them, but they would simply be confused and bewildered by the introduction of totally different subjects. We must be content to advance step by step. There were several Societies formed for advocating reforms in the land laws; he could foresee no advantage, but positive harm, from burdening the League with such agitations.

The amendment moved by Miss Randell was then withdrawn by the seconder, Miss Heather Bigg, (Miss Randell having been obliged to leave early in the evening), in favour of the amendment moved by Miss Simcox.

Mr Headlam and Mr Adolphe Smith said they were willing to withdraw the last half of their Resolution in favour of Miss Simcox's amendment.

Mr Schloss hoped that the meeting would not agree to this. The words used by Miss Simcox were vague in the extreme, but it was evident that the mover and seconder of the original Resolution considered that those words had the same meaning as their own, or they would not so readily have accepted them.

The Rev. Vincent G Borradaile here moved that the second part of the Resolution, after the words 'Provident element,' be entirely omitted.

Mr Sidney Lee seconded. On being put to the meeting there were 7 votes for and 8 against this amendment.

The Resolution, worded as follows, was then carried by 9 votes to 5:

> That the best way to extend the work of the League is to lay stress on its Protective – Trades Union – element, as distinct from the Provident element; and further for the League to use its influence to support all other modes of action of an economic description, which may tend to bring about a better distribution of wealth.

The next Resolution considered was

> That the work of the League requires that the whole time of an organising agent shall be at the disposal of the Committee, who may employ such agent for secretarial duties if necessary, and that such agent shall be salaried.

Miss Browne in proposing the resolution wished first to acknowledge gratefully the services which Mrs Paterson had rendered to the League as Hon. Secretary. Mrs Paterson initiated the movement in 1874 and had given devoted work to the Society. To the work of Hon. Sec. she had added that of editor of the journal. In putting forward this new scheme she would have liked to propose that Mrs Paterson be requested to accept the position of paid secretary and organising agent, at a salary of £100 per annum, but she understood that such a proposition would be very distasteful to Mrs Paterson.

Miss Browne pointed out the varied nature of the work of the League, touching on the one side Parliamentary legislation, on the other, coming closely in contact with the women of the industrial classes and dealing with the details of their work. She therefore considered that the League required the whole time of an official, exclusive of the office clerk, whose services could not be made available for getting up meetings and new societies. She quoted a passage from the last Report of the League Committee, which referred to the necessity for forming Women's Unions in trades not yet organised and said, that in her opinion the movement could not be thus extended unless the whole time of a capable woman were to be devoted to organising work. At present, the League was known in a very small circle. She hoped that should the Resolution be passed, a suitable agent might be found, who could be sent about to assist struggling Unions in the provinces, and to spread a network of such Societies all over the country. The loss lately sustained by the death of Miss Wilkinson made this work all the more necessary.

Miss Amy Bell seconded the Resolution and expressed a hope that the agent would be a woman of the working class, who could sympathise with those among whom she would be sent.

Miss Ada Heather Bigg wished to propose that Mrs Paterson should at least be offered the new post contemplated.

Mrs Paterson said that under no circumstances could she consent to take money for any service she might render to the League: she had always regarded this service as a labour of love and preferred to earn her living by secretarial work of a different kind, whilst devoting as much of her spare time as possible, to the League. Whether, after the resolution just passed, committing the League to new modes of action, she should continue to act as Honorary Secretary she would not now say; if the words contained in Miss Browne's resolution as to the employment of the agent 'for Secretarial duties' were to be carried she would at once resign, as her assistance would no longer be necessary. She did not wish to oppose the appointment of a paid organising agent, although she had not much hope of the success of such a plan, the greatest requirement of the League work being, in her view, the personal enthusiasm of many of its friends, rather than the more mechanical services of one paid agent. She thought it a question for serious consideration whether the League should continue to exist, or whether it would not be the best plan to now hand over its work to the Women's Trades Council, a body consisting of delegates of the Women's Unions and supported by the Union funds. An independent Council of this kind would probably meet with more active co-operation from the leaders of men's Unions than had been offered to the League. She would now read a letter from Miss C Williams, one of the earliest supporters of the League.

> I regret that I am unable to be present at the adjourned Conference called to consider the position of the Women's Protective and Provident League. I took a great interest in the formation of this Society and I believe that such an organization has been quite necessary to promote the cause of union among women. It appears to me, however, that the time has now come when the further development of Unions may be safely left to working women themselves – and that the continuance of anything like Patronage will be injurious. A Women's Trade Council now exists, and the more independently working women can act in the protection of their own interests the better. I have therefore come to the conclusion that no good will come from keeping up the League, and I do not see my way to assisting the effort to collect the much larger sum which it is now proposed to apply to the payment of a more expensive staff of officers.

The Chairman agreed that some provision for more organising work was desirable but advised the withdrawal of the words 'who may employ such agent in Secretarial duties.' Miss Browne accepted the suggestion, but explained that the clause had been inserted with the view of enabling Mrs Paterson to delegate her duties if she herself were absent.

The resolution was carried, as follows, nem. con.:

> That the work of the League requires that the whole time of an organising agent shall be at the disposal of the Committee, and that such agent shall be salaried.

Miss Browne next proposed: 'That this Conference resolves that a special effort be made to raise funds for enabling the Committee to carry of this measure' – and said she had already received three conditional promises of subscriptions for the purpose indicated. An appeal might very properly be made to the League Council, for she found that only 5 of the 42 names on the list appeared also in the lists of subscribers to the League funds.

Miss Mears seconded and suggested that the fund might appropriately take the form of a memorial to Miss JG Wilkinson; also that entertainments should be got up on its behalf.

The Rev Stewart D Headlam pointed out that the Conference had no power to pledge the League to carry out this resolution and suggested that the word 'recommends' should therefore be substituted for the word 'resolves.' This having been agreed to, the resolution was carried.

The proceedings were then brought to a close.

4 Obituaries – 1886–1921

One way, but by no means the only way, to gauge the influence and achievements of an individual is to observe the quantity and quality of their obituaries. By that standard, Emma Paterson succeeded in leaving an imprint on Victorian Britain and its public life. This chapter repeats the long, mournful missive penned to her in her Journal by her colleagues from the Women's Protective and Provident League. It remains rich in biographical detail, as a guide to the depth and breadth of her work for the cause of women's unions, and as an indication of the depth of feeling women trade unionists had for her.

Another article from the Women's Union Journal from January 1887, and reproduced here, points to the great hole left by Emma Paterson in the work of the League. The way the article begins is itself an expression of her identification with, and indispensability to, the movement she started. 'It is probable,' ran the Journal, 'that after hearing the sad news of Mrs Paterson's death, the second or third thought of many of our readers has been: "what will become of the League?" "How will it go on without her?"'

And no one needs doubt Emma's public identification with the League. Read through her obituaries in the Times, The Pall Mall Gazette and other major papers. The Nottinghamshire Guardian described her as one of the 'most practised advocates' of the 'Women's rights movement.' The Pall Mall Gazette mused that 'it is more than doubtful if any of her successors will command all her personal popularity with the operative classes.' Her old friend Hodgson Pratt, writing in the journal of the Working Men's Club and Institute Union – the organisation that did so much to point her towards her life's work – rhapsodised over her 'wisdom, good judgement, good sense, and unceasing toil.'

Each obituary tends to repeat much of the same material as the others, but whether in the longer ones, those of the large-circulation newspapers, or taken together as a whole, you will be struck by the almost universal admiration and esteem in which she was held at the time of her death. That included those who never met her or saw her address a meeting organised by the League. This chapter also suggests how her memory continued for some time after her death. The League launched an Emma Paterson fund, and by 1893 it nearly reached £2,000. With that money, the League joined forces with the other institution that had done so much to shape Emma's life – the Working Men's Club and Institute Union – to open a new building in Clerkenwell in 1893.

The very first of Emma Paterson's articles in this book led to the Women's Protective and Provident League. The last source in this book commemorates the end of the League. In 1921, the Women's Trade Union League (as Emma's organisation had come to be called) became the Women's Section of the TUC. That move completed the integration of women's unions with their male counterparts, which had already begun over the previous two decades. Working women finally stood, it seemed, as equal partners in the British trade union movement with the men. Emma Paterson would probably not have been surprised to find that formal equality did not mean real equality, even down to the twenty-first century.

When Tess Gill wrote a review of Harold Goldman's book on Emma for the Morning Star in 1974, she issued a cautious note at the end. 'We need,' she wrote, 'more information on the role women have played in the labour movement as an encouragement to all of us, as the tasks ahead are still immense.'[1] More than forty years on, in our world of casual work, stagnant wages and a stubborn gender pay gap, those words remain apt. So do those of Emma herself, and the need to remember, reinterpret and continue what she worked for.

'The Funeral,' *Women's Union Journal*, November 1886, p. 104

The funeral of Mrs Paterson took place in Paddington Cemetery on the afternoon of Monday, Dec. 6th. The Service was read by the Rev. Stewart D Headlam, Mr Broadhurst, MP, Mr King, Mr Burnett (of the Board of Trade), several members of the Committee of the Women's Protective and Provident League, the Secretaries of the Women's Trade Unions and representatives of other societies were present.

Owing to the unavoidably short notice given, many ladies and gentlemen who wished to attend were unable to do so.

Several friends brought flowers, a beautiful wreath was sent by the Women's Trade Societies, and others by Lady Goldsmid, Mrs Sims, Miss Simcox, and by the staff of the Women's Printing Society.

'Mrs Paterson,' *Women's Union Journal*, December 1886, pp. 111–114

The readers of this journal have a right to expect from it some brief record of the life and work which have been cut short, to the deep grief of many and to the incalculable loss of many more. Brief and imperfect such a record must be in any case, and doubly so in this, for Mrs Paterson was valued and is regretted, as a personal friend, by all who worked with her, and it is not easy to write concerning the life of a friend so recently lost.

Emma Ann Smith was born on 5 April 1848; a record of the family history goes back to her grandfather, Stephen Smith, born 1781. Henry Smith, Emma's father, and son of the above, was born in 1808. In 1837 he became Head Master of a School at East Ham, and in 1843 Head Master of the School attached to St George's, Hanover Square, then situated in Belrave Street, Pimlico; a post which he filled with credit and success for 21 years till his death from typhoid fever, in 1864. During this interval Emma was born, and, as her exceptional ability showed itself, well and carefully educated under her father's eye. She was his constant companion; girl friends and cousins used to laugh at her devotion to study and call her 'the book-worm,' but though at that age she liked books best, she had other tastes as well, and her father's boasts of Emmie's progress in German or Italian were wont to end: 'and you should only hear her whistle, she can whistle as well as any boy!' Mr Smith's death in 1864 left his widow and daughter unprovided for; two unsuccessful attempts were made by the former to establish a school, in the second of which Emma took part for a short time, but she disliked teaching and after a short experience as governess to young children gave up the attempt. About 1866, she obtained more suitable employment as secretary or amanuensis to an elderly lady, who was employed as clerk by the then secretary of the Workmen's Club and Institute Union.

At this time she had leisure and opportunities for more reading, of which she eagerly availed herself, and she also became to some extent familiar with the work of the Union, so that, on the strength of her experience and the recommendation of her employer, she was appointed, in July, – when still only a girl of nineteen – assistant secretary to the Union itself. One who knew her well at that time writes a propos of the possible difficulties in the way of so young a woman doing the office work of a Society for men, in which men of all classes were calling constantly:

> there was a cheerful and equable presence of mind and self-respect, which made her relations with men perfectly easy, both for them and for herself. It would have been impossible for any man to make her a personal compliment, or to be rude.

Her memory for every name, fact or date that could be useful was noticed with admiration, as only to be accounted for by her genuine interest in what was going on, and her conscientious desire to do what she undertook with the utmost possible thoroughness. No better preparation for her future life could have been imagined than this work, which brought her naturally and pleasantly in contact with the elite of the London workmen, in a relation which caused her 'great capacity for business' to be first displayed in their service. Of the three honorary secretaries who held officer with her – Mr Thomas Paterson, Mr Hodgson Pratt and the Hon. Auberon Herbert – the first became her husband; the words of the second will be found on another page, and with the third also she formed a firm and lasting friendship.

In February 1872, after nearly five years services, she resigned her post in order to become secretary to the Women's Suffrage Association, and she was then presented with an illuminated address and a gold watch by the governing body of the Union, in token of the appreciation commanded by 'her practical ability and good judgement,' her eagerness to extend the sphere of the Society's usefulness, without regard to the consequent increase of her own duties, and other qualities equally familiar to those who know Mrs Paterson's later work. As secretary of the Suffrage Association, we are told that she 'fulfilled the duties of her office with great zeal and ability,' and it is at this date that we must begin her life as an 'agitator'; at least in a recent letter about the Staffordshire nail-making districts, she spoke of a visit to that county about 1871 as being made 'before I was an agitator.' She was married to Mr Paterson, July 24th, 1873, and at the same time resigned her secretaryship and accompanied him for a tour of some months in America, an experience upon which she always looked back with great enjoyment.

During this visit she was much interested by discovering that the experiment of Unionism had already been tried in the United States, and that the 'Female Umbrella Maker's Union of New York' had achieved some considerable measure of success. She had long wished for the establishment of Trade Unions for women in England, and on her return in April 1874, she contributed to the *Labour News* a paper, inviting the co-operation of all sympathisers, and sketching the constitution of a Central Association, to which local branches in different trades might be affiliated. In the following September she read a paper to the same effect at the Social Science Congress and attended a Conference at Bristol, which resulted in the formation of the 'National Union of Working Women,' which still exists in that town. Her connection with the Women's Suffrage Society was also resumed for a short time.

The formation of the Women's Protective and Provident League, with which Mrs Paterson was to be mainly associated for the rest of her life, dates from a meeting held on July 8th, 1874, at which an Executive Committee was appointed.

In September of the same year, after a preliminary conference with twelve women in the trade, a public meeting was held in the Harp-alley School-room, Farringdon Street, and attend by over 300 women employed in the various branches of the bookbinding trade, and a provisional committee of workers elected. At another large meeting in October the rules of the Society – which have formed the model for all subsequent unions of women – were adopted, and before the end of the year 240 members had been enrolled. In December, a meeting was held in Bethnal Green, under the presidency of the Rev. Septimus Hansard, at which two of the members of the Bookbinders Society were for the first time prevailed upon to make a speech in public, but unfortunately no practical result followed this, or later attempts at organisation in Hackney. The name by which the parent association is now known was adopted in the beginning of 1875, as some name was necessary, and the reminiscences of the Corn Law, and other militant and victorious agitations had lent a certain association of success to the word 'League,' which disposed Mrs Paterson to think favourably of the name. Henceforward it might almost be said, that to write her life would be to write the history of the League or conversely.

To give some idea of her activity at this time, we find in the first half of 1875 over twenty-five Meetings and Conferences of Bookbinders, Dressmakers, Upholsteresses, Hatmkaers and Shirtmakers at which she was present, in addition to her work as provisional secretary of most of the new societies, and adviser to the newly formed committees of workwomen. The formation of each new society involved repeated and prolonged conferences at the late hours alone possible to the workers, which, as their interest in the discussion of trade problems and grievances increased, often continued into the small hours of the morning. In August 1875, she enjoyed a short visit to Ilfracombe, but then, as always, grudged herself the rest necessary for health, and in writing to a member of one of the societies had apologised for her short absence, promising to come back stronger so as to be able to do the more work.

This was perhaps in some ways the happiest period of her life; though full of work, she was not oppressed by it, household affairs were looked after by her mother, who could also be depended on to keep an eye on the official correspondence, forwarding letters when her daughter was from home and in general saving the unworldly couple from the material inconveniences that arose from their common habit of paying more attention to 'Meetings' than meal-times. Mrs Smith, like her husband, took a genuine interest in her daughter's schemes and ideas and was lawfully proud of her growing reputation and influence. But this was not all. Mrs Paterson, like many men (and probably women also), whose time and thoughts are much taken up with public interests, was also extremely dependent upon the ready made affections of family life. Naturally reserved and undemonstrative, it would have been difficult for her in later years to find time to cultivate the degree of intimacy with any one of her many friends that could at all make up at the want of early memories in common. To know that the mother and the favourite puss were waiting with a welcome gave to the busy life of those days an element of repose, a satisfaction to the passive and emotional side of a fully developed nature for which no outside success or recognition could provide a substitute. Her mother's death was thus a greater blow to her than perhaps to most women who have also found complete sympathy in marriage; in one sense she never recovered from the loss, never ceased to feel the want of the something irreplaceable that was gone, and when her husband also died, in 1882, it was pathetic to see how little of personal interest or concern life seemed to have left for her.

Of course, in each case she only sought relief in silence and more work; but as no woman was ever more entirely free from what are called feminine weaknesses, it is perhaps worth while in these days, when we are told that the women who do masculine work must objure the distractions of womanly affection, to point out that the strongest woman, like the strongest men, require the help and consolation of the affections to enable them to do their best work with least effort and most success.

The year 1875 was important in another respect. In 1874 the Bristol National Union of working women already mentioned, had sent a representative to the Trades Congress of that year; he had been admitted after discussion, but not without opposition, one of the grounds of which was that if a man was allowed to come as a representative of women, the next thing would be that they would have women come wanting to represent themselves. This was exactly what occurred when Mrs Paterson and another member of the League were deputed to represent two of the London Women's Unions at the Trade Congress at Glasgow in 1875. Some little doubt was felt beforehand as to the action of the Congress, but in fact, not the slightest opposition was offered to the admission of the duly elected women representatives, who then and since met with all possible kindness and respect from their brother unionists. It is probably, however, that this satisfactory result was due, at least in part, to the fact that Mrs Paterson was already personally known to, and trust in by most of the working-class leaders, so that it was felt that any movement which she represented must be genuine and conceived in the true interests of labour. At the Congress she spoke, in connection with a proposal to extent the application of the Factory and Workshops Act, upon the injury to women from legislative restrictions on their labour, and dwelt upon the fact that men had got shorter hours for themselves by unionism than those which protective legislation had secured for women; but though she was in theory opposed to all restrictions on the labour of adult women, she never publicly attacked the existing system, as it was manifest that a majority, even of the most intelligent women unionists, were still in favour of the Acts.

When not attending the sittings of the Congress Mrs Paterson was busily engaged through the week in conference with employers, with working women, and in attending meetings organised by leading residents in sympathy with the work of the League. An unsuccessful attempt was made to reach the women bookbinders, but a Union was actually formed amongst the Tailoresses, and preliminary steps taken for the formation of a Society of Warehouse girls, i.e., those employed in making shorts, trimmings and various other articles of apparel for the large warehouses. A large employer, while admitting that it was impossible for women to live upon the prices which competition had fixed for their labour, added, 'What can I do? I would pay more if other people did, but we have to cut down prices to compete with the cheap London work.' It was mentioned at the same time that many women were still doing work by hand at the prices paid for the same work done by machines. The meeting of the Glasgow Tailoresses in the Trongate was very interesting, and the eloquence and volubility of the Glasgow girls much impressed the English delegates, who were not then aware that these qualities seem to be a peculiar property of the lady tailoresses throughout the country. Mrs Paterson was a little startled at the Scotch custom of beginning even Trade Unionist meetings with prayer, but the countenance of ministers of religion given to women's societies was thought to promise well for their peaceful progress. Unfortunately, however, the Tailoresses' Union gradually fell to pieces, no doubt mainly for want of such assistance as Mrs Paterson gave to all the London societies in their infancy, but such failures appeared less discouraging when compared with the statement of one of the friendly Glasgow tailors, a man still in middle life and member of a society containing tens of thousands of operatives, that at one time his own society, before amalgamation, had dropped to three members.

In this year the League was in correspondence with working women's associations in Dewsbury and Southampton as well as Glasgow, and the Committee of Woollen Weavers, who had successfully organised and conducted an important strike, were encouraged by the appreciation which their labours met with in London. A member of this Committee subsequently appeared at the Annual Meeting of the League, and like the delegate from Leicester on a future occasion, rather put the Londoners to shame by her story of difficulties overcome. This work of correspondence with the women of whatever district was suffering from industrial disturbance was always an important and favourite part of Mrs Paterson's task as secretary of the League, and its results are probably far from exhausted by any record of what is visible as yet.

Pall Mall Gazette, 6 December 1886

The death of Mrs Paterson, whose funeral takes place this afternoon, deprives working women of one of their most practical friends. For the past twelve years she devoted herself, to the sacrifice of her health and material welfare, to the difficult task of instilling women employed in trades with the independent spirit of trade unionism. Her labours were not crowned with the success they merited, but they have left a highly honourable record. To Mrs Paterson's initiative was mainly due the establishment, in 1874, of the Women's Protective and Provident League, for the formation of trade and benefit societies among women, and until her death she was honorary secretary and director of that organisation, which was fully described in our columns on April 10, 1884. The many women's trade and benefit societies which the League brought into being were the work of Mrs Paterson's own hands. As a representative of working women she claimed and gain admission to the Trades Union Congress of 1875, and her simply worded speeches delivered at that and subsequent congresses converted to her views many working men who from mistaken notions of self-interest were inclined at one time to offer her a bitter opposition. Mrs Paterson was also one of the first women to attempt the amelioration of her sex's political condition. She entered public life twenty years ago as secretary of the Women's Suffrage Society, and she lived long enough, although she died before she was forty, to see that movement, which owed much to her in its infancy, very nearly reach maturity. It is more than doubtful if any of her successors will command all her personal popularity with the operative classes, or in their endeavours to advance their cause will deny themselves, as Mrs Paterson did, almost all that is commonly assumed to make life worth living.

'Obituary,' *The Times*, **6 December 1886**

Mrs Paterson, the honorary secretary of the Women's Protective and Provident League, whose funeral takes place this afternoon at Paddington Cemetery, died very unexpectedly last Wednesday night. Born in April 1847, she was identified from her youth with almost all contemporary movements for the amelioration of the political and especially the industrial condition of women. As Miss Emma Smith, she was secretary, 20 years ago, of the Women's Suffrage Society, and subsequently held for many years the secretaryship of the Workmen's Club and Institute Union. She thus came into close contact with working men, studied their trade organisations and fully acquainted herself with the needs of the operative classes. Her marriage, at an early age, to Mr Thomas Paterson, a cabinet maker and an earnest practical student of all social and industrial questions, extended her knowledge and sympathies. In 1874 she induced working women for the first time to adopt trade unionist principles and established the Women's Protective and Provident League for the formation of trade and benefit societies among working women. The London Bookbinders' Union was the earliest women's trade society due to Mrs Paterson's exertions; the Upholsteresses,' the Shirtmakers,' the taileresses' and Dressmakers' Unions quickly followed. In 1875 Mrs Paterson was the first woman admitted to the Trade Union Congress, and she attended and spoke or read papers at all the subsequent congresses. As honorary secretary of the Women's League, Mrs Paterson worked indefatigably till almost her last hour; she organised and addressed public meetings in London and the provinces, she arranged social gatherings at the offices of the league, and she edited the Women's Union Journal, a monthly record of the league's work. Her husband died in 1882; and Mrs Paterson edited, with a memoir, a remarkable posthumous work by him entitled 'A New Method of Mental Science' which was published last spring. At the time of her death she was preparing for the press others of Mr Paterson's unpublished writings.

Nottinghamshire Guardian, 10 December 1886

The Women's Rights movement has lost one of its most practised advocates. Mrs Emma Paterson was an earnest partisan of woman suffrage, but it was to the commercial, rather than to the pollical, side of the woman's question that she directed her efforts. She was the chief promoter of the effort to organise female workers of all degrees into Trades Unions, and such success as has attended this attempt is mainly due to her indefatigable efforts. She was honorary secretary of the Women's Protective and Provident League, and in that capacity attended many Trades Union Congresses. Her husband was a zealous supporter of the Working Men's Club and Institute Union of which Mrs Paterson before her marriage was librarian. She was a persevering and disinterested worker and will be greatly missed in her particular sphere of action.

Reynolds Newspaper, 12 December 1886

The remains of Mrs Emma Ann Paterson, well known for years past as the energetic Hon. Sec. of the Women's Protective and Provident League, were interred on Monday in the consecrated portion of Paddington Cemetery, Willesden-lane. Shortly after two o'clock the cortege started from the residence of the deceased, 23, Grent College street, St Pancras, and the cemetery was reached at three o'clock, where a large assemblage of ladies had collected to pay a last tribute of respect to the memory of one who worked so long as laboriously in their cause. Amongst the many ladies' societies represented were those of the Bookfolders, the Upholsterers and the Shirt and Collar Makers. There were also present at the grave, in which already reposed the bodies of the husband and two members of Mrs Paterson's family, Mr Broadhurst MP and Mr Burnett, of the Board of Trade. In the chapel, as at the grave, the Burial Service was read by the Rev. Stewart D Headlam, of Upper Bedford place, who had been for years associated with the deceased lady in her work.

Hodgson Pratt, *Club and Institute Journal*, December 18, 1886

About 20 years ago, I think, Miss EA Smith became the Secretary of the Working Men's Club and Institute Union. I was then joint Hon. Secretary with Thos. Paterson, and, for a time, with Auberon Herbert. No society could have had a truer servant; conscientious, devoted, intelligent and practical. My friend and colleague, Thos. Paterson, a man of genius, and an honest, fearless man, or remarkable range of knowledge, yet belonging to the ranks of labour, by which he had secured a small independence, was indeed fortunate in finding such a companion and fellow-worker as our then Secretary. They were worthy of one another, incapable of any selfish or ignoble aim. They were full of a passionate desire to lessen the wrongs and sufferings of their brethren. She, without a thought of self, spent all her savings in many a wise effort to raise the position of working women; and he was equally full of sympathy for all true and noble efforts. He was ever ready to give time and strength, though at the cost of the hours necessary for his special occupation, that of a student of the social and metaphysical questions which he has discussed in the book which Mrs Paterson lately published. He gave at one period great and invaluable services to our Union and was an active member of the Council of the Workmen's Peace Association, of the Inventors' Institute, and others. He died, as you know four years ago; and she, through a crowd of anxieties and personal difficulties, and failing health, continued 'to fight her good fight' of faith.

Working women owe to her an eternal debt, for her wise, practical and incessant labours. She founded and conducted the 'Women's Protective and Provident League.' It has for its object to form in every trade where women are employed a society for help in sickness and absence of work, and protection of the rights of labour. She gave herself and her means with generous lavishness to spread this movement in London and the Provinces. It was no small task, indeed! It was not easy to teach ill-paid, over-worked women that by association among themselves they could raise their position, become independent of alms, find increased means of employment and combine for a demand for fair treatment by employers. Women accustomed to think themselves too weak and dependent, too 'inferior'; women isolated and struggling for bare life, poverty-stricken widows, with children perhaps, single women without friends – but how could they combine or do anything? Emma Paterson has taught hundreds of them – bookbinders, upholsteresses, dressmakers, machinists, tailoresses and others – that they can do all this. She has given them a new life – shown them the noble idea of mutual help and service, redeemed many of them from a crushing sense of loneliness and given them the power of organisation and self-government.

Her next great work was that of establishing the 'Women's Printing Society.' She saw how the field of female labour was over-crowded, and how wages were thus lowered by excess of competition, to the disadvantage both of men and women. Without any knowledge, of course, of the trade, but with much help from her able husband, she undertook this task of learning the printing art, and of teaching it to others. No one knows the wearing labour thus given to the instruction of poor working girls. For these two societies (including the editing of the Women's Journal, correspondence and accounts), she was always labouring, without rest or recreation of any kind; and she died worn out by over-work and anxiety.

To these tasks, she brought great wisdom, judgement, good sense, and unceasing toil and also remarkable quiet gentleness and unostentatious goodness. She hated praise; she shrank from all public acknowledgement. In an age which makes a god of 'popularity,' she only sought to do her self-imposed duty with as little fuss and notice as possible. All the women who have known her must deeply mourn her loss. It is only when such spirits depart that we feel their true worth, the true greatness of their souls. They should make us all better by their example; they give us new confidence in the future of humanity; we have less despair of success in our poor efforts to make this a better world for the people who live in it. The best honour we can pay to Emma Paterson's memory is to let her spirit dwell within us and inspire us for fresh efforts and for fresh courage in the service of our fellows. In a greater sphere of existence may her spirit find new and larger opportunities for good, inspired and guided by the Father of all spirits!

'The Work of the League,' *Women's Union Journal*, January 1887

It is probable that after heading the sad news of Mrs Paterson's death, the second or third thought of many of our readers has been: 'What will become of the League?' 'How will it go on without her?' Such doubt and anxiety is only reasonable – a just acknowledgment of the fact, that the greater part of the work hitherto accomplished by the Women's Protective and Provident League has been due to the personal exertions of the honorary secretary. But there are still upon the Executive Committee, some who have worked with Mrs Paterson from the first formation of the Society; many of the more recent members have been elected upon her suggestion and none without her concurrence, and there has never been the shadow of a difference of opinion amongst them, either in theory or practice, in relation to the main object of the association, as defined in the conference held on 8 July 1874. On this occasion, in addition to the appointment and nomination of a Committee, only two resolutions were adopted, viz. 'That one of the objects of the association shall be to enable women earning their own livelihood to combine to protect their interests'; and

> That it shall be one of the objects of the association to provide a benefit fund for assistance in sickness and other contingencies.

In other words, the association began, and has continued to exist, primarily for the sake of assisting and promoting the formation of self-supporting and self-governing Trade Unions of working women. The number of women as yet organised in such Unions, is still too small for us to flatter ourselves that the work of our association is accomplished, and yet too much has been done to allow us to despair of future success. It is therefore admitted upon all hands that the work of the League must go on.

Readers of our annual reports will remember that other useful undertakings have clustered round the Women's Unions: the Library for the use of members, Social Entertainments for members and their friends, a Co-operative Society, a Swimming Club, a Bank and Loan Society, a Seaside Holiday House, the publication of this Journal, etc.: and it is evident that, as the Women's Unions multiply and develop, the appreciation and use of these incidental advantages of association is also likely to increase. Even Mrs Paterson was hardly able to carry on all these little secondary societies or undertakings, in addition to the general Secretarial work of the League; and it would soon have been necessary to arrange for some division of labour, which would have left the honorary secretary free for missionary and organising work in connection with new societies and new trades.

The Committee has been able at once to find volunteers to undertake the responsibility for several of these subsidiary branches of the League's work. Miss Honor Brooke (1, Manchester Square) has kindly agreed to make all arrangements both for the Monthly Social Evenings held at the League Office, and for the occasional entertainments given in the interests of particular societies, as a means of bringing the members together and attracting outsiders in the trade. Secretaries of Societies who wish for such help, and amateur performers or other friends and members of the League, who may wish to contribute, in person or cash, to these amusements – which are the only things the economical principles of the League allow it to give away – are hereby requested to address themselves to Miss Brooke, as Hon. Sec. of the Entertainments Sub-Committee.

As regards the *Journal*, its management for the present has been placed in the hands of a small sub-committee, whose labours, it is hoped, members of Unions and other correspondents will endeavour to lighten, by sending it freely reports of meetings, and information about rates of wages and conditions of employment, as well as by notifying all attempts at trade organisation, which may be brought to their knowledge.

The future of the Bank and Loan Society will be settled at a General Meeting of the Bank Depositors, called for Monday evening, January 24th, when, if it is then decided that the Bank shall continue to exist, measures for increasing its sphere of usefulness will be duly discussed.

An attempt to revive the Co-operative Society is also in contemplation, and will, we hope, receive the energetic support of all those members of the League, who realise the advantages offered by Co-operation. We print elsewhere an extract from an article of Mr Geo R Sims, confirming in detail the well-known statement of Professor Walker, that 'The curse of the poor is their poverty... in quantity, quality, and price in whatever they purchase, they are unable to get even as much for their little, as the rich for their larger means.'

To give people the full value of their money, however, is not the chief nor the only function of a Co-operative Society, and it is for the more vital reason, that Co-operation helps people to save, does away with the grave evils of debt, especially in connection with small shops, rouses 'a desire for the well being of the community generally,' and develops intelligence, self-reliance and business knowledge, all qualities which are indispensable to Trade Unionists, that we wish to see the Women's Union Co-operative Society figuring once more as a 'going concern.' Volunteers are needed to assist in its carrying on and would be warmly welcomed. With regard to the Library, arrangements will shortly be made for the further utilisation of the books belonging to the League, and in the meantime, a lady on the Committee has kindly undertaken to act as Librarian.

So far, it has been easy to arrange for a division of labour, which the Committee hope and believe will result in increased, rather than diminished, efficiency.

But there yet remains the real work of the League – the work namely, of getting up meetings, and organising trade associations in all parts of the country. The appointment of a paid organising agent, which it will be remembered, formed the subject of a recommendation passed by the Conference of October 19th, is now being seriously considered, and before long, the Committee will be in a position to come forward with a definite announcement, as to the means they have taken to carry the recommendations into effect.

In the meanwhile, letters on general business may be addressed to Miss Simcox (1, Douro Place, Victoria Road, Kensington, W) who has been desired, for the present, to carry on the provincial and other correspondence which was conducted by our late honorary secretary.

Orders for Journals, requests for papers, etc., should be addressed to the Assist. Sec., 1a, Clark's Buildings, Broad Street, Bloomsbury, WC.

Pall Mall Gazette, 19 May 1892

The Women's Trade Union League still ask for funds to complete the memorial they are raising to Emma Paterson and her work. They have obtained nearly £1,800, and they have to make this £2,000 before the end of July in order to get certain premises in Holborn which are to be converted into a Paterson Memorial Hall. The trade union movement among women, although it has met with slow success, has been identified during its twenty years of existence with some of the most remarkable women of our time. George Eliot, Florence Nightingale, Mrs Fawcett and Frances Power Cobbe are a few among its many helpers, while among the men who have supported it none worked with more enthusiasm than the brilliant young Oxford scholar, Leonard Montefiore, whose brief and promising career will be well remembered by men who were at Oxford fourteen years ago. It has always been difficult work, but it has many fine traits that the men's unions lack. It is difficult, because most women hope to escape the workshop by marriage, and therefore never take up with unionism as men do. In some trades those who do not escape it by marriage escape it by an early death simply because they do not realise the necessity for uniting in self-defence. Emma Paterson and her co-worker Jeanette G Wilkinson, who should be remembered too, have been the only genuine Labour leaders that workwomen have had, and they did what no man could have done among women's trades. The Paterson memorial proposes to commemorate their work by extending its range and purpose. Those who think this worthy of support should write to Miss Monck, 76, Eaton-terrace, S.W.

Report of the Trades Union Congress, 1921, p. 226

Miss Tuckwell,[2] who was received with considerable cheering, said: Mr President and friends, old and new, I was absolutely taken by surprise when Miss Bonfield sent for me just now in this connection. I had no idea that you would so acknowledge our friendship and comradeship of many yours. This beautiful address speaks of the work of Sir Charles and Lady Dilke. I feel how deep their satisfaction would be, because of their devotion to the cause of labour, that the work always carried on under your aegis had at last passed fully into the new great development of your Trade Union Council. Most of the praise of which your President has spoken is not due to me, but to those earnest ones of the Women's Trade Union League who worked in the old days, and I trust that the wisdom and guidance that they brought to the work then will inspire it in the future. I would particularly mention that gallant little working woman who gave her life for the sake of working women, Emma Paterson, who founded our movement and who started the great tradition of helping women to help themselves, and to depend not on outside assistance except such as was given in comradeship. There are many of whom our minds are full because of their help to us. All along we have had great help from our good friend Margaret Bondfield. All this Congress I have been haunted with the thought of my dearest friend Mary Macarthur, whose too short life seemed burnt up in one great flame of love and service. We have still with us, I rejoice to say, not only Susan Lawrence but Madeline Symons, who, with Mary Mcarthur, did much latterly to shape our policy, and on whom her cloak has partly fallen. But it will be long before you will meet anyone who will do for you what our Mary did. It is perhaps because I am identified to you with all these people who were the leaders of the Women's Trade Union movement, some of whom, happily, are still young, that you have given me this proof of your great kindness.

Now I am going to ask you another kindness. I want you, now that the work of the Women's Trade Union League has passed from us absolutely into your hands, never to forget the weakest link in the chain of Labour – the women on whom all depend, the women who in many cases perform the double labour of home and outside work. These women have been championed ably, and still need it. I ask you to help them, not only because they are the weakest link in the chain of Labour, and because if that link snaps your own foundation, our own foundation, falls, but to help them because the greatest lesson of Trade Unionism is self-sacrifice and help to the weakest – that lesson which in the miners' magnificent struggle they showed so well and capably for the sake of others. Therefore I ask you never to forget the claims of the women, not only in their interests, and your interests, but in the interests of truth and justice and those great things for which the perfect Trade Union movement stands. I as you, above all, to remember that there is one thing to hold fast. You may in your statesmanship have to accept reductions of wages. You will accept as few and as little as you can, I know, but remember this: as you retire fighting – and you will retreat as little as you can – hold fast to the Trade Boards Act, the first instalment we have of the living wage. It is threatened. How threatened, you will hear later. For the sake of the women, the children and the home, we have to keep the prosecutions carried on on their behalf because they are paid at the rate of 7/8ths of a penny per hour; for the sake of all that was done in the past to build up a minimum wage, set your teeth tight to see that no harm comes to the Trade Boards Act. We have to build on the foundation laid by the struggles and the self-sacrifice of those who have passed. In the words of the motto of the Women's Trade Union League: 'Look to it that ye lose not the things that they have wrought.'

I thank you again. While my life remains you will know that the things dearest to me will be Labour and Trade Unionism.

Notes

1 Tess Gill, "She Helped Women Workers to Organise," *Morning Star*, 10 October 1974.
2 Gertrude Tuckwell (1861–1951) became President of the Women's Trade Union League in 1905 and of the National Federation of Women Workers in 1908. Her papers are available at the TUC Library, and for more information on her life see Cathy Hunt (2013), "Gertrude Tuckwell and the British Labour Movement, 1891–1921: A Study in Motives and Influences," *Women's History Review*, 22:3, 478–496.

Index

Amalgamated Society of Engineers 98–99
Arch, Joseph 77–78, 136, 139

Black, Clementina 14
Broadhurst, Henry 1–2, 9, 10, 12–13, 14, 51–52, 60, 75, 76, 82, 85, 89, 91, 95, 110, 114, 136, 137, 139, 162, 174, 178, 201, 208

child labour 4, 12, 21, 42, 50, 56, 60, 91, 104, 107, 135–140, 150, 176
Contagious Diseases Act 4

Daughters of St Crispin 95–96, 96–97
Dilke, Sir Charles 8
domestic workers 1, 4, 50, 61–63, 66–67, 128, 140, 155, 174, 178

Ellis, Hannah 9, 105, 121, 137–138, 153

Factory Acts 4, 34, 50–51, 55–56, 97–98; in France 56–57
factory inspectors 10–11, 41–43, 50–51, 60–61, 75–76, 89–92, 97–98, 106–110, 112–113, 150–151, 173–174; in France 56–57, 98, 107–108
Faithfull, Emily 9
Fawcett, Milicent 50, 122, 147–148, 151, 182, 213
Female Umbrella Makers Union of New York 6, 22, 23, 25, 32, 203

gender pay gap 7–8, 20–21, 26–33, 40, 62–63, 174–180
Grand National Consolidated Trades Union 145–146

International Workingmen's Association 3

Juggins, Richard 12, 135–142, 151

Knight, Robert 75, 76, 95

MacArthur, Mary 14, 214
Married Women's Property Acts 4, 110–111
Mill, JS 63, 161, 177
Morley, John 57

National Agricultural Labourers' Union 6–7, 22, 24, 37, 44, 46, 77–78
National Union of Working Women 10, 203, 205

Odger, George 8
O'Grady, Frances 2

Paterson, Emma: memorial to 213; obituaries 201–210; reports about 125–129; speeches in (Aberdeen 133–135; Dublin 88–89; Leicester 46–47; Manchester 38–40; Nottingham 120–122; Sheffield 37–38)
Paterson, Thomas 2, 5–6, 11–12, 160–165
Pattinson, Emilia (Lady Dilke) 8
Pickard, Benjamin 76, 94–95, 103–105, 154
Pratt, Hodgson 8, 52–54, 82, 88, 107, 161, 192, 195–196, 203, 209

Shipton, George 8, 34
Simcox, Edith 9, 10, 11, 34, 60, 113, 115, 140, 147, 180, 182, 187, 189, 194–196, 212

218 Index

strikes 29–34, 37, 61, 65, 77–78, 121, 137, 206; Carpet Weavers Kidderminster, 1884 124–125; Cotton works, Bristol, 1878 57–60; Royal Army Clothing Depot, 1879–1986 73–75, 82–88, 165–173, 180–181

Trades Union Congress 1, 2, 3, 49, 82, 98–99, 107, 113, 134, 135, 147, 179; Emma at 9–10, 34–35, 41–43, 50–52, 60–61, 75–76, 89–92, 135–138, 154, 191, 207

Tuckwell, Gertrude 14, 213–214

Whyte, Eleanor 9, 96, 122

Wilkinson, Jeanette 9, 122, 137, 151, 154, 189–190, 190–192, 197, 199, 213

women workers: casual work 3, 54, 64, 68, 115–116, 174–180; co-operation 113–114, 149, 178; domestic workers 61–62, 128; in nail and chain making 12, 51–52, 111–112, 114–116, 135–142; numbers 26, 62, 134; shop assistants 79–80, 81–82, 105–106; truck system 31, 128 wages 20, 27–28, 45, 46, 58, 62–63, 65, 73, 75, 166, 170, 174–180, 187; women's fashion 101–103; working conditions and hours 11, 20, 64, 73–74, 97, 132–133

women's unions 21–25, 30–35, 62–70, 98–99, 123–124; and the church 43–46, 68–69, 130–133; in France 47–49, 52–54; obstacles to 45, 98–99, 155–159; previous attempts at organisation 12, 145–146; in the United States 22, 25, 27–28, 32, 95–97

Women's Protective and Provident League 8–9, 34–36, 62–70, 99–101, 125–133, 146–147, 211–212; after Paterson's death 13–14, 210–214; bank 68–69; benefit societies 183; branches (bookbinders 36, 49, 59, 67, 126, 128, 204, 206, 207, 209; dressmakers 49, 67, 113, 118, 127, 129, 156, 193, 207, 209; taileresses 49, 67, 83, 89, 118, 121, 126, 127, 156, 180, 181–182, 184, 206; sewing machinists 37, 38–39, 67, 127, 184; shirt and collar makers 39, 49, 67, 127, 208; upholsteresses 9, 36, 38, 49, 67, 89, 118, 122, 126, 127, 156, 184, 191, 194, 204, 207, 208, 209); excursions 41, 117, 149; financial difficulties 99–101, 123, 193; geographical reach of 99–100, 152–153, 184; help with employment 132; holidays 1, 9, 15, 40–41, 54–55, 92–94, 116, 129–130, 149, 211; in Ireland 9, 88–89; membership difficulties 12, 68, 98–99, 124, 155–159, 181–182, 182–190, 192–199; parliamentary elections 77–78, 160; reading rooms and libraries 15, 68, 122–123, 127, 149, 160, 186, 211; sex work 148–150; social meetings 69, 117–119, 149, 154, 159; swimming club 9, 15, 118, 127, 149, 211; women's suffrage 15, 80, 66, 123, 147, 151, 160, 203, 208; Women's Trades Council 146–147

Women's Suffrage Association 1, 6

Women's Union Journal, operation of 3–5, 94–95, 10; letters from the United States 95–97, 151–152

Working Men's Club and Institute Union 4–5, 161, 208, 209

Printed in the United States
by Baker & Taylor Publisher Services